METAPHOR AND BELIEF IN *THE FAERIE QUEENE*

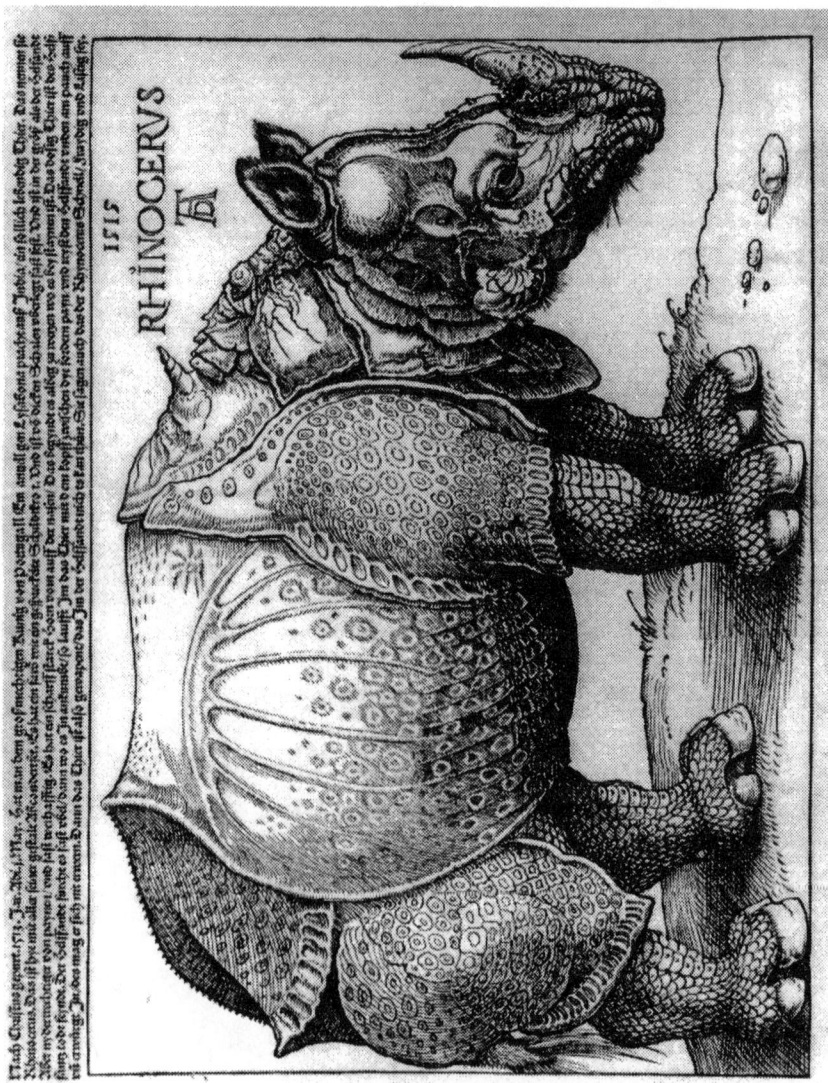

Albrecht Dürer: *The Rhinoceros*, woodcut, first edition, 1515 (British Museum)

Metaphor and Belief in *The Faerie Queene*

Rufus Wood

First published in Great Britain 1997 by
MACMILLAN PRESS LTD
Houndmills, Basingstoke, Hampshire RG21 6XS and London
Companies and representatives throughout the world

A catalogue record for this book is available from the British Library.

ISBN 0-333-61367-8

 First published in the United States of America 1997 by
ST. MARTIN'S PRESS, INC.,
Scholarly and Reference Division,
175 Fifth Avenue, New York, N.Y. 10010

ISBN 0-312-17414-4

Library of Congress Cataloging-in-Publication Data
Wood, Rufus, 1961–
Metaphor and belief in The faerie queene / by Rufus Wood.
p. cm.
Includes bibliographical references and index.
ISBN 0-312-17414-4 (cloth)
1. Spenser, Edmund, 1552?–1599. Faerie queene. 2. Christianity
and literature—England—History—16th century. 3. Christian
poetry, English—History and criticism. 4. Belief and doubt in
literature. 5. Renaissance—England. 6. Allegory. 7. Metaphor.
I. Title.
PR2358.W65 1997
821'.3—dc21   96-53861
                                                               CIP

© Rufus Wood 1997

All rights reserved. No reproduction, copy or transmission of this publication may be made without written permission.

No paragraph of this publication may be reproduced, copied or transmitted save with written permission or in accordance with the provisions of the Copyright, Designs and Patents Act 1988, or under the terms of any licence permitting limited copying issued by the Copyright Licensing Agency, 90 Tottenham Court Road, London W1P 9HE.

Any person who does any unauthorised act in relation to this publication may be liable to criminal prosecution and civil claims for damages.

The author has asserted his right to be identified as the author of this work in accordance with the Copyright, Designs and Patents Act 1988.

This book is printed on paper suitable for recycling and made from fully managed and sustained forest sources.

10 9   8   7   6   5   4   3   2   1
06 05 04 03 02 01 00 99 98 97

Printed and bound in Great Britain by
Antony Rowe Ltd, Chippenham, Wiltshire

For Athanase and Emily

Contents

Frontispiece: The Rhinoceros by Albrecht Dürer   ii

Acknowledgements   ix

Introduction: The Elizabethan Poetics of Metaphor   1
    Figuring Forth   1
    Giddy Metaphors   10
    To Variety Inclined   15
    Heuristic Metaphor and *The Faerie Queene*   19

1 Metaphor as an Act of Faith   28
    Not Seeing the Wood for the Trees   28
    Not Seeing the Man for the Tree   37
    Not Seeing Is Not Believing   50
    Blindness and Insight   62

2 Metaphor as a Process of Change   76
    Metaphor, Metamorphosis and Emblem   76
    Conceiving Metaphors of Love   93
    Mimetic Metaphor   110

3 Metaphor as an Act of Idolatry   127
    Allegory and Idolatry   127
    From Iconomach to Iconoclast   141
    Idylls of Allegory   157

4 Meta-Metaphors   181
    Mutabilitie's Mutation   181
    The Nature of the Poem   188

Notes   205

List of Works Cited   222

Index   229

Acknowledgements

I owe an enormous debt of gratitude to the excellent teachers who have taught me over the years and made the writing of this book possible. My interest in *The Faerie Queene* was initiated by the enthusiasm of Brian Nellist who shared his encyclopaedic knowledge of Renaissance matters with me. The timely assistance of Edward Burns ensured that I did not lose momentum at a point when I was in danger of losing my way. The encouragement and advice of Nick Davis has been a source of continual erudition and inspiration without which I could not have finished what often seemed like an 'endlesse worke'. His expertise in medieval and Renaissance studies is only equalled by his generosity.

I was granted a period of research leave by Liverpool Hope University College which enabled me to progress more rapidly with Chapter 3. I have also received much help from friends and colleagues in the English Department at the College. In particular, I would like to thank Elizabeth Cosnett, Michael Parker and Richard Greaves, all of whom have offered useful advice after reading parts of the manuscript. Two other readers who found time to read the manuscript during particularly busy periods for them both, and made suggestions which have been gratefully incorporated, are Gordon Nichols and Willy Maley. I am also indebted to the editors Margaret Bartley and Charmian Hearne with whom I have had the pleasure of working at Macmillan. Their faith in this project has never wavered.

Finally, I would like to thank all the members of my family who have given me support. In particular, Marcus Wood donated the computer on which the manuscript was written and Beatrice Wood provided much-appreciated assistance with proofreading.

I have relied upon the patience and care of my wife throughout; she, above all, has had a sustaining influence upon me.

Introduction: The Elizabethan Poetics of Metaphor

FIGURING FORTH

In the *Rhetoric*, Aristotle drew attention to metaphor as the most effective means of communicating new ideas. 'Now strange words simply puzzle us; ordinary words convey only what we know already; it is from metaphor that we can best get hold of something fresh.'[1] In *An Apology for Poetry*, Sir Philip Sidney quite naturally turned to metaphor to help elucidate his own interpretation of the Aristotelian poetic: 'Poesy therefore is an art of imitation, for so Aristotle termeth it in his word *mimesis*, that is to say, a representing, counterfeiting, or figuring forth – to speak metaphorically, a speaking picture – with this end, to teach and delight.'[2]

Sidney's adoption of Simonides's phrase, 'a speaking picture', is usually discussed within the wider context of the Renaissance commonplace derived from Horace's dictum *ut pictura poesis*.[3] What is less frequently pointed out, however, is the significance of the metaphoric basis of the analogy between the pictorial and poetic arts. In fact, Sidney's self-conscious introduction of a metaphor into his own most overt statement of poetic principle tells us more about his own attitudes towards metaphor than it does about the precise meaning of the metaphor itself. The rhetorical accumulation of the sentence as it builds up towards the final metaphor endorses the superiority of the figurative over the more literal expressions which precede it, and consequently reveals more than a theoretical reiteration of the Aristotelian doctrine of mimesis. Sidney's definition of poetry here roots itself in a commitment to metaphor as a means of pursuing, encompassing and expressing new ideas.

The implication behind Sidney's use of metaphor is not that metaphor can express things which cannot be said any other way. What it suggests about metaphor is, firstly, that it can say certain things more explicitly than any other form of expression and, secondly, that without metaphoric perception, certain relationships could not be perceived at all and could therefore not possibly be expressed. Aristotle's view of metaphor certainly invests it with inspirational powers:

> It is a great thing, indeed, to make a proper use of these poetical forms, as also of compounds and strange words. But the greatest thing by far is to be a master of metaphor. It is the one thing that cannot be learnt from others; and it is also a sign of genius, since a good metaphor implies an intuitive perception of the similarity in dissimilars.[4]

If, as Aristotle here says, to metaphorize well is a gift of genius, through which hidden relationships can be intuitively grasped, then metaphor becomes instrumental in the processes of invention and discovery. Metaphor is not a mere ornament of language, it is involved in the redefinition of reality that springs from the 'perception of the similarity in dissimilars', which is inconceivable without the metaphoric process.

The search for such an heuristic theory of metaphor underlying the Elizabethan poetic is best directed towards the poets' own self-referential comments when they surface in the literature of the period. A discussion of metaphor, as a means of discovering truths about the world that remain hidden from other forms of discourse, when it does appear, is frequently expressed metaphorically itself. A significant starting point is offered by a particularly deceptive passage in *Antony and Cleopatra*. When the metaphoric implications of Mark Antony's description of a crocodile are drawn out, it can be seen to offer a telling critique of the imaginative sterility of non-metaphoric language:

> Ant. [*To Caesar*] Thus do they, sir: they take the flow
>   o' the Nile
>   By certain scales i' the pyramid; they know,
>   By the height, the lowness, or the mean, if dearth
>   Or foison follow. The higher Nilus swells,
>   The more it promises: as it ebbs, the seedsman
>   Upon the slime and ooze scatters his grain,
>   And shortly comes to harvest.
> Lep. Y'have strange serpents there?

Introduction: The Elizabethan Poetics of Metaphor

Ant.   Ay, Lepidus.
Lep.   Your serpent of Egypt is bred now of your mud by the operation of your sun: so is your crocodile.
Ant.   They are so.
Pom.   Sit, – and some wine! A health to Lepidus!
Lep.   I am not so well as I should be: but I'll ne'er out.
Eno.   Not till you have slept; I fear me you'll be in till then.
Lep.   Nay, certainly, I have heard the Ptolemies' pyramises are very goodly things; without contradiction I have heard that....

Lep.   What manner o' thing is your crocodile?
Ant.   It is shap'd, sir, like itself, and it is as broad as it hath breadth: it is just so high as it is, and moves with it own organs. It lives by that which nourisheth it, and the elements once out of it, it transmigrates.
Lep.   What colour is it of?
Ant.   Of it own colour too.
Lep.   'Tis a strange serpent.
Ant.   'Tis so, and the tears of it are wet.
Caes.   Will this description satisfy him?

(II. vii. 17–35 and 40–49)[5]

The language of the literal, a description of something in terms of itself, is here comically and ruthlessly ridiculed. The central irony is contained in Caesar's incredulity at the drunken Lepidus being taken in by such a transparent and monstrous joke, when Caesar himself leaves the banquet oblivious to the real thrust of Mark Antony's parody. For the prime target of the jest is not really Lepidus at all, but the values the play associates with Caesar's Rome, intoxicated with its belief in the descriptive accuracy of a language capable of reducing things to words. In the eyes of such reductive literalism, language is viewed as an instrument of truth, but only in so far as it has the capacity to describe the world entirely in terms of itself. The heuristic power of language to explore reality imaginatively is completely disregarded.

It is the belittlement of imaginative truth, inherent in such a restricted philosophy, which Mark Antony satirically exposes by taking the rationale of linguistic literalism to its own absurd conclusion. After all, would Mark Antony's description be qualitatively any more satisfactory if he had described a crocodile as 'a large amphibious saurian reptile of the genus *Crocodilus* or other allied genera' (*OED*, 1), estimated its length to be about eight metres, its breadth one metre and described its diet and locomotion as the *Encyclopaedia Britannica* does, in the following terms:

> In their first weeks of life crocodiles eat mostly worms and water insects, then frogs and tadpoles; finally, their main diet is fish. Older crocodiles are more apt to prey upon waterfowl and on mammals, and occasionally a member of one of the larger species eats a human. . . . The principal style of locomotion is that of swimming, in which the crocodile places its legs back against the sides of its body and moves forward by means of lateral wavelike motions of the tail.

No doubt Caesar would have been satisfied, but does the amended definition really reveal more than Mark Antony's tautological simile: that a crocodile is, in the final analysis, all too obviously 'like itself'. Large in comparison to what, we might ask? What does a crocodile's leg look like? There are any number of comparative questions left unanswered. But then, it is precisely the comparative element which is so conspicuous by its absence from the phrasing of Lepidus's questions: 'What manner o' thing is your crocodile?' and 'What colour is it of?' The implicit denial here of the propriety of analogy or metaphor for the determining of a crocodile's nature, rests on the assumption that the crocodile is a thing which can be reduced to a catalogue of its individually itemized parts. It is an assumption which Mark Antony must of necessity frustrate, not just because it overlooks the inevitable selectivity of even the most expansive catalogue, but because ultimately it imposes intolerable limitations on the nature of human perception, and consequently on the reaches of human understanding.

In the above description of a crocodile, it is immediately apparent that the most graphic information is conveyed by the adjectively-disguised simile 'wavelike', which alone enables us to begin to visualize the dynamics of a swimming crocodile. Without it, the whole passage tends towards the literal and self-defining and becomes like Mark Antony's description, self-limiting and pointless. The ideal of a universe entirely explicable in terms

Introduction: The Elizabethan Poetics of Metaphor

of mathematical or scientific definitions might seem realizable so long as the subject in question can be treated analytically, as with Mark Antony's description of Egyptian agriculture in the Nile Valley. Unfortunately for the analysts, however, not everything is without contradiction – not even 'Ptolemies' pyramises', as the ambiguity of Lepidus's statement makes all too clear: are they goodly things without contradiction? Are they goodly things because they are without contradiction? Or has Lepidus heard, without contradiction, that they are goodly things? Mathematical and scientific certainty dissolves into the confusion of second-hand report, subjectivism and linguistic ambiguity. It is the inability of rational systems of thought to come to terms with even the most tangible of objects which leaves them so helplessly bewildered when confronting realities whose existence grows out of paradox or enigma.

Mark Antony therefore directs his attack against the obvious shortcomings of practical philosophies, which in their dissection of reality construct false or incomplete forms of knowledge. The failure of such investigations is seen to be built into the process of their conceptualization of the nature of the world. In their place he proposes the liberation of the intellect by the enlargement of its compass, to include metaphoric systems of thought that can alter and redefine perceptions of reality, by creating new ways of looking at it. Armed with metaphor, the intellect thus has at its disposal a means of discovering and representing the world around it, that is as limitless as creation itself.

As we have seen, the necessity of metaphoric thought to begin to comprehend the infinite mysteries of the universe, underlies Mark Antony's description of a crocodile. The description, however, does not just discuss metaphor, it inevitably functions metaphorically, mirroring in its own structure the argument it is asserting. The crocodile, the serpent of the Nile, as Cleopatra has revealed earlier, is one of Mark Antony's pet names for her: 'He's speaking now, / Or murmuring, "Where's my serpent of old Nile?" / For so he calls me' (I. v. 24–6). Unbeknown to the Romans, when Mark Antony refers to the crocodile, the metaphorically submerged subject of his discourse is Cleopatra – the woman of 'infinite variety' – and the impossibility of understanding or describing her in terms that refuse to recognize the full complexity of her nature. The imaginative, the mystical and the theatrical constitute a closed world to the literal, the reductive and the practical, unless they can first liberate themselves from the restrictions of their own methodology.

Significantly, Lepidus develops a taste for the fabulous and strange in proportion to the quantity of wine he imbibes. The hold of his Roman sobriety, nevertheless, remains perceptible in the curiously pedantic tone of his questions; for as Enobarbus ironically suggests, a Roman can only abandon his earnestness in his drink or his dreams. Lepidus's drunken transmigration is consequently incomplete, transforming him literally into a general figure of fun and metaphorically into a symbol of the blindness of the Roman interpretation of reality.

In the light of a metaphoric reading of the passage, the comment of a servant which precedes the banquet scene takes on an entirely new significance:

> To be called into a huge sphere, and not to be seen to move in't, are the holes where eyes should be, which pitifully disaster the cheeks.
>
> (II. vii. 14–16)

Uttered as a denunciation of men like Lepidus who fail to take the responsibilities of their social and political position seriously, the statement, itself overtly metaphoric, carries a second metaphoric interpretation that goes beyond the speaker's intended import. There is a veiled criticism which condemns the blinkered vision of men who destroy the beauties of the world by disfiguring their means of perceiving them. In the last analysis it is a man like Octavius Caesar, whose practicality can reduce the death of Cleopatra to something resembling a coroner's post mortem, who leaves the audience asking: 'Will this description satisfy him?'

In the end, this is all literal-minded discourse can hope for, since as Aristotle said, 'ordinary words convey only what we know already; it is from metaphor that we can best get hold of something fresh.' If reality is to be grasped at all it must be grasped via metaphor, for metaphor, like poetry itself, is not 'compassed within the circle of a question according to the proposed matter' (*Apology for Poetry*, p. 100). Metaphor imaginatively releases the intellect from such strictures, 'disdaining to be tied to any such subjection' (*Apology for Poetry*, p. 100). When the poet cultivates metaphor, then he is able to encompass Sidney's highest ideal 'so as he goeth hand in hand with Nature, not enclosed within

Introduction: The Elizabethan Poetics of Metaphor

the narrow warrant of her gifts, but freely ranging only within the zodiac of his own wit' (*Apology for Poetry*, p. 100). Here, a direct link between the creative aspects of poetry and metaphor has been implied which, it might be objected, goes beyond the argument Sidney presents in *An Apology for Poetry*. To see if any such underlying correlation between the two exists there, it is necessary to return to Sidney's text and the metaphor of the speaking picture with which this investigation began.

The example quoted earlier is not the only occasion when Sidney adopts the metaphor of 'the speaking picture'. Quite apart from the many references to painting and paintings which are found throughout *An Apology for Poetry*, there is a second passage where, talking of the superiority of the 'peerless poet' over the philosopher, Sidney extends his discussion of the precise meaning of the phrase 'the speaking picture of poesy':

> For as in outward things, to a man that had never seen an elephant or a rhinoceros, who should tell him most exquisitely all their shapes, colour, bigness, and particular marks; or of a gorgeous palace, the architecture, with declaring the full beauties might well make the hearer able to repeat, as it were by rote, all he had heard, yet should never satisfy his inward conceits with being witness to itself of a true lively knowledge; but the same man, as soon as he might see those beasts well painted, or the house well in model, should straightways grow, without need of any description, to a judicial comprehending of them: so no doubt the philosopher with his learned definition – be it of virtue, vices, matters of public policy or private government – replenisheth the memory with many infallible grounds of wisdom, which, notwithstanding, lie dark before the imaginative and judging power, if they be not illuminated or figured forth by the speaking picture of poesy.
>
> (*Apology for Poetry*, p. 107)

Several things are notable in this passage. Firstly, it is worth pointing out how closely Sidney's list of the outwardly describable features of a strange animal mirrors Mark Antony's parodic portrayal of the crocodile. Secondly, Sidney attributes to poetry the same capacity to illuminate abstract concepts that painting has for describing the physical world. Thirdly, and most importantly, Sidney claims that poetry, like art, satisfies the 'inward conceits' by providing 'a true lively knowledge'. On this claim rests the power of poetry to 'teach and delight' by appealing to 'the imaginative and judging power'.

At this point in the argument it is useful to consider how an artist sets about constructing a representation of the physical world, before returning to Sidney's concern with poetry's representation of abstract concepts. To assist in this matter, and to maintain the theme of 'exotic' beasts, I have selected Dürer's woodcut of a 'rhinocervs', with which Sidney may have been familiar in one form or another (see frontispiece).

Dürer's woodcut is one of the most renowned images in the history of art – partly for the way in which, despite its 'realistic' inaccuracies, it manages to capture what can only be described as the essence or spirit of a rhinoceros, but mainly for the influence it had for hundreds of years on innumerable pictures of the rhinoceros. Paintings and illustrations, including many reputedly drawn from life, can be shown to have features which can only have been 'borrowed' from, or influenced by, Dürer's original.[6] This long-running tradition itself displays the extraordinary power of an artist's image to shape reality by making an observer see, or think he sees, certain features at the expense of others, even when the 'reality' is present before him. In this respect, the effect of an established image is very similar to that of conventional metaphors which shape our conceptual system for us, thereby imposing assumptions about concepts which prevent us seeing them afresh for ourselves.

There is a level then at which an artist's representation can be said to function like metaphor; but what about the creation of a primary or new image, like Dürer's? Is that too constructed in a similar manner to the creation of a new metaphor? When Dürer drew his 'rhinocervs' (admittedly not from life, although the point is irrelevant here) how did he produce the image now before us? If E.H. Gombrich is correct in assuming that Dürer was assisted 'by what he had learned of the most famous of exotic beasts, the dragon with its armored body',[7] then we can see that the artistic process, the means of rendering the unfamiliar or new, relies upon first relating it to the familiar and known. This should come as no surprise, for after all, this is the manner in which an understanding of something strange or unknown is always gained: by a gradual process of categorization via an existing system of classification, out of which emerges a redefined

Introduction: The Elizabethan Poetics of Metaphor

but graspable comprehension. A further quotation from E.H. Gombrich on the subject illustrates the point perfectly and establishes a firm link between the artistic and metaphoric processes:

> He [the artist] begins not with his visual impression but with his idea or concept ... The individual visual information, those distinctive features I have mentioned, are entered, as it were, upon a pre-existing blank or formulary. And, as often happens with blanks, if they have no provisions for certain kinds of information we consider essential, it is just too bad for the information.
>
> The comparison, by the way, between the formularies of administration and the artist's stereotypes is not my invention. In medieval parlance there was one word for both, a *simile*, or pattern, that is applied to individual incidents in law no less than in pictorial art.[8]

The use of the term *simile* significantly establishes a comparative creational link between the processes of figurative language and the artist's visual representation and, by extension, between metaphor and all attempts to attain a judicial comprehension of reality, physical or abstract. Metaphoric thought is not only natural to the human mind, it is necessary for the mind to function. Understanding is based upon a conceptualization that relies upon the integration of the new into the old; a process that is essentially metaphoric. Thinking metaphorically, far from being unusual, is natural, and something we do all the time at a subliminal level without consciously considering it. Art makes metaphor seem strange by confronting us with it, by removing it from the subconscious level at which it usually works and self-consciously examining its processes in an attempt to recover the latent power in metaphor that allows us to 'get hold of something fresh.'

There is a connecting thread linking Sidney's conception of creativity, despite its evident differences, with more contemporary views. That link is the importance placed upon metaphor as a means of discovering and transmitting knowledge. Poetry and painting are consequently united in and by the comparative act that underlies metaphor, since to be creative at all, to see things anew, is virtually synonymous with what Aristotle referred to as the ability 'to metaphorize well'. Creativity, like metaphor, is a conscious perception of 'the similarity in dissimilars', and it is this that led Aristotle to call metaphor a thing of genius and Sidney to see in a painting's representation of the physical, the same essential function that he found in poetry's representation of the abstract. For Sidney, it is the poet's recourse to metaphor that constitutes the origin of the real difference between the poet and the philosopher. The philosopher can replenish the memory ('convey only what we know already'), but the poet is able to speak through metaphor to 'the imaginative and judging power', which remains untouched by the learned definitions of the philosopher's words. Thus Sidney's poetic is effectively a metaphoric, rooting poetry in the single most creative and inspired feature of language.

GIDDY METAPHORS

The embedding of metaphor in the defence of poetry is not without its attendant dangers. Aristotle considered metaphor to be more appropriate to poetry than prose, but he still dealt with it in both the *Rhetoric* and *Poetics*. When Sidney asserts that the poet 'nothing affirms, and therefore never lieth' (*Apology for Poetry*, p. 123), he is trying to keep poetry separate from the rhetorical disciplines of persuasion and proof. Metaphor, as a feature of language appropriate to both these domains, threatens to bring the purity of poetry into contact with the violence and deception of rhetoric. This may explain why Sidney, despite his insistence that the art of poetry cannot be blamed for the actions of those who abuse it, includes the word 'counterfeiting' alongside 'representing' and 'figuring forth' in his definition of poetry. To counterfeit means to imitate, although it may or may not carry with it the sense of an intent to deceive. In the context of Sidney's overall argument in *An Apology for Poetry* we assume no such indication of the poet's power to conceal as well as to reveal. Yet, the ambiguity of the word, rather like the pun in the opening line of the first sonnet in *Astrophil and Stella*, alerts us to the close proximity of truth and lies in poetic discourse: 'Loving in truth, and faine in verse my love to show'. Here, as in *An Apology for Poetry*, a word suggests a meaning that points to the paradoxes at the heart of poetry and of the poet's professed desire to discover and tell the truth.

Introduction: The Elizabethan Poetics of Metaphor

In this respect, metaphor embodies both the highest aspirations of poetry and its worst fears; for at the very moment of its perception of 'the similarity in dissimilars' it also brings about a masking of some aspects of the subject it seeks to illuminate. Its perception, no matter how enlightening, must still be limited and therefore distorted for the reasons Lakoff and Johnson explain:

> New metaphors, like conventional metaphors, can have the power to define reality. They do this through a coherent network of entailments that highlight some features of reality and hide others. The acceptance of the metaphor, which forces us to focus *only* on those aspects of our experience that it highlights, leads us to view the entailments of the metaphor as being *true*.[9]

Metaphor is doomed to reveal truths only at the expense of truth. The poet may never lie, but neither can he tell the whole truth. The masking of reality and the power to deceive are potentially just as much features of metaphor as its ability to expose reality and discover truths. It is a dichotomy that never really surfaces in *An Apology for Poetry* which, as a rhetorical text of defence, can freely hide behind the deception of its own rhetoricity. Nevertheless, as a tension inherent in the metaphoric conception of poetry, it regularly surfaces as an issue elsewhere in the poetry of the period. Michael Drayton's ninth sonnet in his *Idea in Sixtie Three Sonnets* explores this interplay between metaphor, poetry, truth and lies.

> As other Men, so I my selfe doe Muse,
> Why in this sort I wrest Invention so,
> And why these giddy Metaphors I use,
> Leaving the Path the greater part doe goe.
> I will resolve you; I am Lunaticke,
> And ever this in Mad-men you shall finde,
> What they last thought of, when the Braine grew sicke,
> In most distraction they keepe that in Minde.
> Thus talking idly in this Bedlam fit,
> Reason and I (you must conceive) are twaine;
> 'Tis nine yeeres now since first I lost my Wit;
> Beare with Me then, though troubled be my Braine:
> With Diet and Correction Men distraught
> (Not too farre past) may to their Wits be brought.[10]

The main emphasis of the sonnet is on the madness and folly of love: the state of mind it induces in the poet and the style of poetry which results. In the opening quatrain the reader is consequently invited to question the poet's style and intention. A healthy scepticism is encouraged by the suggestion that a critical attitude is held by other men as well as by the poet himself. The implied criticisms of poetic excess contained in the phrases 'wrest Invention so' and 'these giddy Metaphors' further indicate a discerning, if not openly hostile, stance towards the sonnet which is carried over into the commentary on the madness of erotic mania presented in the rest of the poem.

On the surface this provides a straightforward explanation of the excesses and metaphoric confusions thrown out in insane profusion by the love-sick brain of a bewildered man. The poet's account of his poetic inventiveness initially invites this sort of rational paraphrase, but it gradually becomes apparent that there is more going on in the sonnet than such a superficial reading allows. For, while the tone of the sonnet is relaxed and humorous, the numerous ambiguities and ingenious ironies reveal a sharp wit at work just beneath the surface, giving vent to a disguised but caustic attack on the criticisms voiced by Drayton's detractors. In the opening line, for instance, he toys with the meanings of 'Muse'. Placed at the end of the line and capitalized, the word draws attention to itself. It is impossible to ignore the inherent pun that associates the poet's Muse – his source of poetic inspiration – with a state of bewildered meditation. This suggestion that perplexity and even insanity are deeply rooted in the poetic genius, offsets the all too glib responses the sonnet ostensibly invites, and instigates a radical reassessment of the proposed disjunction between truth and figurative poetic language.

This sonnet represents an attempt, with all the attendant dangers, to construct a defence of poetry and figurative speech out of the very language that is used to attack and belittle them. The stakes are high: should the ironic subject fail to surface, the poet will be condemned by his own words, while, if the counter-argument is stated too dogmatically, the subtle suggestiveness of poetic language will appear to have been discarded in favour of a more robust discourse when it comes to expressing ideas clearly and convincingly. Everything depends upon the structuring of the sonnet's self-criticism; it must develop naturally and logically while also exposing the inadequacies of its own conclusions. Not

Introduction: The Elizabethan Poetics of Metaphor

surprisingly then, we find the sonnet is structured in three distinct parts. The opening quatrain poses the central question: why does the poet use such extravagant images and complex metaphors? Then comes the answer, given in the opening line of the second quatrain: 'I am Lunaticke'. This answer is then extended on into the third quatrain. Finally, the poet begs patience from the reader, proffering the future prospect of a more controlled poetic when his sanity returns.

Embedded within the tripartite progression of the sonnet, however, is a structure of disorientating contradictions, metaphoric correspondences and semantic equivocations which force the insanity of the self-professed lunatic to be brought into question. The fifth line's authoritative assertion – 'I will resolve you' – is a statement on which the reader must reserve judgement. It is natural to assume that the answer is contained in the second half of the line, 'I am Lunaticke', but then the resolution is being provided by a madman whose poetic logic has been questioned from the outset. Alternatively, the assertion can be taken to refer to a time in the future when he 'will' be able to resolve matters, if only we, as readers, bear with his deranged ramblings until his sanity returns and he can free his mind from its obsession with love. Either way, the statement is developed with a coherence which belies the poet's declared insanity and points to a clarity of vision that is only accessible through a profusion of ideas and 'giddy Metaphors'. The second quatrain reinforces the notion of the single-mindedness of the madman, whose thoughts, no matter how distracted they might appear, are always linked back to the same original source.

The close relationship Drayton's sonnet has developed between the traditionally associated figures of the lover, the lunatic and the poet now begins to disentangle itself to reveal the poet's distracted metaphors and congenital inventiveness as rather more than idle talk. They provide him with the means of exploring his world to ascertain profound truths. The love-poet's duty is to understand *eros* fully and to do so he must utilize the conventional postures and conceits available to him, until love's multiple secrets have been divulged. If love is sickness, the poet must fall ill; if love is a journey, that journey must be undertaken; if love is madness, then the poet must become insane. Here, in the desire to understand the concept of love as fully as possible, the necessity for the multiplication and extension of metaphor can be pinpointed. Metaphoric variety enables the poet to encompass the diversity of love, presenting composite perspectives in an effort to construct a kaleidoscopic vision with the versatility to shift and change like love itself. The ideal philosophical investigation must be conducted in harmony with its subject, terminating only when all the investigative possibilities have been exhausted.

Drayton's awareness of the inherent problems involved in such a scheme are evident in this ninth sonnet. The difficulty of maintaining a visible centre to the fluctuating poetic structure is emphasized. The disorder, chaos and insanity are all graphically exhibited and satirically confessed: 'Reason and I (you must conceive) are twaine'. But, what do we take 'twaine' to mean in this context? Is the poet divorced from reason or indistinguishable from it? The success, not just of this sonnet but of the whole sequence, relies upon Drayton's ability to put his sanity and reason beyond doubt. When he plays the madman, he must do so with the inspiration of the poet, to display the perplexity of the lover. By the time the final couplet talks of curing the poet's diseased mind, the reader should have been alerted to the ironic voice of the bracketed phrase: '(Not too farre past)' and the sly humour of the references to medical and moral cures for his disposition.

Yet, just as the sonnet drives to its apparent conclusion, the reader's perception of the dynamism of the form is tested once more. The metaphor of sickness and cure is most obviously to be associated with the traditional description of the lover's melancholy and its remedy as described in Elizabethan medical commentaries:

> The patient must revise his diet and habits: 'As an idle sedentary life, liberal feeding, are great causes of [love], so the opposite, labour, slender and sparing diet, with continual business, are the best and most ordinary means to prevent it.' The lover may subdue the flesh 'by earnest studie and meditation, by often fasting, by much labour, by hard fare, by hard lodging, and such like.'[11]

In the reference to 'Diet and Correction', however, there is the suggestion of spiritual disease which points back to the fourth line of the sonnet: 'Leaving the Path the greater part doe goe.' The path is no longer just the beaten track of poetic commonplace; it is also the spiritual path of righteousness. The final couplet awakens the poet's latent fear of a corruption that may lie at the heart of his love and be infecting his poetic inspiration. His desire to dispose of his critics once and for all in the final couplet, where the ironic tone reaches its climax, thus backfires, leaving the poet with a far more serious and disturbing awareness of the lurking danger in poetry.

This is typical of the metaphoric complexities written into Elizabethan sonnets, enabling them to reflect the convolutions of the human mind and the contradictions of lived experience. Truth is not simple and cannot be simply represented. Sonnets, therefore, explore experience using metaphors that refuse to reduce the world to a lifeless shadow or a stereotypical parody of itself. Individual sonnets shift and adapt metaphors in the belief that this exploratory method is best able to capture the complexities of reality.

TO VARIETY INCLINED

The Elizabethan commitment to metaphor as a means of moving towards a more comprehensive understanding of a subject begins to explain the structure of imagery within single lyrics. The poet must treat metaphor expansively, allowing it to develop in a variety of directions at the same time, if he is to encompass the layerings of meaning that constitute poetic truth. The importance of metaphor in the Elizabethan poetic goes some way to explaining the intricate interplay of imagery typical of Elizabethan sonnets at a local level. What remains to be asked is whether it also influences the structure of larger poetic units.

The structure of Elizabethan sonnet collections provides a natural point of departure. The terms most commonly applied to collections of sonnets like Sidney's *Astrophil and Stella*, Daniel's *To Delia*, Drayton's *Idea in Sixtie Three Sonnets*, Spenser's *Amoretti* and Shakespeare's *Sonnets* are 'sonnet sequence' and 'sonnet cycle', although there is no generally agreed definition of the generic features of such literary phenomena.[12] Maurice Evans has tried to use the terms themselves to imply a sense of structure underlying a unified collection of sonnets:

> The difference, indeed, between a genuine sonnet cycle and a mere sequence of sonnets depends upon the ability of the poet

to impose a common structure or tone upon a collection of individual units, and there are very few genuine cycles among the Elizabethans. Sidney and Shakespeare impose a dramatic unity upon their sequences, Spenser a common mood, Drayton a common quality of immediacy, but the rest are mostly memorable for good sonnets rather than for significant groupings.[13]

At best, therefore, Evans can evoke a vague sense of unity or common purpose underlying such sonnet collections, though the precise features of these structures are not made any more explicit than his reasons for distinguishing the terms in the first place.

A more detailed examination has been undertaken by Germaine Warkentin who has argued that the flexible structure found in Elizabethan sonnet sequences was derived from Petrarch's *Canzoniere*, which established an aesthetic frame of reference for subsequent generations of sonneteers. 'This structuring principle', she says, 'is the concept of *variatio*, variety.'[14] The relationship between the individual sonnets and the structural features of the whole collection is seen by her to grow naturally out of conventional Renaissance views of love-melancholy. Erotic mania produces a variety of moods in the lover and it is these which are reflected in the varied passions presented in the sonnets. Variety accounts for the fluid appearance of Elizabethan sonnet sequences as the natural consequence of the poet's intention of presenting a conventional picture of the 'unstable fury of lovers'. Variety is therefore a means of imitating the passion of lovers, but does not constitute a formal structuring principle for collections of sonnets; it merely coincides with the plasticity of their organization. A structural principle, if it is to be established, must be found more deeply rooted in the Elizabethan poetic. It must infuse both the parts and the whole, generating variety itself as an aesthetic and intellectual principle beyond its mimetic function.

This is not to deny the presence of variety in sonnet collections, or its importance to the genre as a whole, but instead of treating variety as the source of structure, to view variety as a product itself of more basic structuring forces. Fortunately, we do not have to search too far, for in a general comment on Elizabethan imagery Rosemond Tuve points back to metaphor itself as the generator of variety:

Introduction: The Elizabethan Poetics of Metaphor

images are delightful if they make for a greater intellectual richness. This is one of the most important implications of the demand for variety. Metaphor is the major trope for the accomplishment of this end.[15]

Rosemond Tuve goes on to quote the following comment from John Hoskins's *Directions for Speech and Style*: 'Besides, a metaphor is pleasant because it enricheth our knowledge with two things at once, with the truth and with similitude'.[16] These two statements taken together attach to metaphor two significant and complementary functions as the trope of variety through which our knowledge of the truth is developed. Variety in sonnet collections is the result of the metaphoric quest to define the true nature of love – a project than can only be accomplished by a sequence or series of sonnets that allows the similitude to be constantly changed. Metaphor is therefore responsible for the flexible structure of individual sonnets and of whole sonnet collections, where the variety which it naturally produces is also the means by which it can fulfil its own desired end of expressing truth.

In the prefatory address 'To the Reader of These Sonnets', Michael Drayton begins his *Idea in Sixtie Three Sonnets* with an explanation of the nature of the sonnets which are to follow. When it first appeared in 1599 it was then only placed second in the collection, but its gradual emergence into a more prominent position in subsequent editions suggests Drayton's awareness of its suitability as a comment on the collection's poetic intentions. The sonnet performs the function of a formal *excusatio*, announces the purging of excessive passion, an avoidance of elaborate, exaggerated or fantastic complaints, and also expresses the nature of its commitment to truth in the sestet:

> My Verse is the true image of my Mind,
> Ever in motion, still desiring change;
> And as thus to Varietie inclin'd,
> So in all Humors sportively I range:
> My Muse is rightly of the English straine,
> That cannot long one Fashion intertaine.

At the very outset, Drayton establishes his poetic commitment to intellectual inventiveness at the expense of passionate entreaty.

His verse adheres to truth, an intellectual truth of the mind, rather than an emotional truth of the heart. The collection, as the title suggests, is to be about ideas, or an Idea, and not emotions: a philosophical investigation of the metaphysical conceptions of love which lie behind the physical and emotional responses it arouses. Its structure must therefore allow for the free flow of ideas if the enterprise is to succeed, and as such it must be flexible enough to allow the poet to shift and change his approach as each new investigative possibility presents itself. The fluid structure of his sonnet collection is integrally linked to the logical structure of the probing units of which it consists; together they create the ideal poetic form with which to conduct an exploration of love.

What Drayton is describing in the Proem is the pliable poetic structure which will give rise to the dynamic process of metaphoric discovery: 'Ever in motion, still desiring change'. The line encapsulates the tension between stasis and motion, the constant and the variable which energizes Elizabethan sonnet collections. The ambiguity of the word 'still' allows the meaning to shift from emphasizing the stability underlying alteration, to the ceaseless quest for variation. Variety is the inevitable consequence of the latter, but it is a variety which serves a single-minded purpose: the discovery and interpretation of the multiple dimensions of love. Variety is not just a means of generating poetic multiplication for its own sake; along with *inventio* (invention) it is one of the poet's main tools for discovery – a means of penetrating human actions, thoughts and emotions.

The final couplet of the introductory sonnet makes a further significant claim. Far from presenting the pursuit of intellectual truths as the preserve of his own sonnets, Drayton places himself in this respect within the established tradition of the English sonnets. He clearly perceives his own exhibition of metaphoric freeplay to exist generally among other Elizabethan sonneteers. The last line focuses directly on the restlessness of such a design that cannot be trapped within a single vein. Drayton's statement liberates the poet, enabling him to range freely 'in all Humors', exploring all the complexities of abstract love by exploiting existing conceptual metaphors, or where they prove inadequate, inventing new ones. Similes, comparisons, analogies, in fact the whole corpus of metaphoric discourse is the generative force producing variety and shaping the style and structure of Elizabethan sonnet collections. Metaphors are therefore adopted anew in

Introduction: The Elizabethan Poetics of Metaphor 19

successive sonnets, but also shifted and adapted in each individual poem. The extension of ideas and the perpetuation of the poetic process which produce the protean structure of sonnet collections are founded on the Elizabethans' commitment to the comprehensiveness of metaphoric discourse as a means of comprehending ultimate truths. It is a dynamic poetic which generates variety as an heuristic enterprise and which explains the 'loose structure' of this Elizabethan literary form.

HEURISTIC METAPHOR AND *THE FAERIE QUEENE*

The Elizabethan perception of metaphor has so far been examined to establish its significance as an instrument for discovering, exploring and presenting the truth through figurative representation. In practice this has been seen to give rise to particular forms of poetry that are characterized by a delight in the intricate interplay of imagery within individual poems and a structural principle of metaphoric substitutions typical of larger structures. In both cases the organization of the whole is governed by the need to allow metaphor to express itself as expansively as possible. The result is the production of open-ended, fluid structures which resist moving towards partial or incomplete definitions that would amount to a premature and false image of truth.

So far, the test ground has been Elizabethan sonnets, where there was no initial expectation of overall coherence and a metaphoric of variation matched a flexible principle of structure to a puzzling literary genre. If the commitment to metaphor as a means of discovering truth is really a major part of the Elizabethan poetic it should be possible to observe its influence in the work of a major author such as Spenser.

Spenser's own sonnet collection *Amoretti* certainly conforms to the metaphoric variety of other Elizabethan collections. A narrative thread can be detected in occasional references to the passage of time such as in sonnet 4: 'New yeare forth looking out of Janus' gate' and sonnet 62: 'The weary yeare his race now having run'. The development of the lover's suit, however, is not primarily presented as a narrative event but as a process of metaphoric comprehension. Where his progress is seen, it takes place through the extension or transfer of metaphoric understanding. A. Leigh DeNeef has shown how Spenser's sonnets display 'the rhetorical interplay between metaphors that close by literal reduction and those that open by metaphoric extension'.[17] DeNeef traces through what he terms a 'mini-sequence' of sonnets, exploring ideas of capture and captivity, where the poet's initial metaphor, through misunderstanding, becomes a 'literal place from which he wishes to escape'.[18] It is only after the discovery of the metaphoric levels of the original terms that the sequence is able to move towards a more complete understanding of the nature of love.

A radical example of Spenser's ability to reinterpret his own metaphors can be found in sonnet 67, where the initial metaphor of the hunt double backs on itself:

> Lyke as a huntsman after weary chace,
>   seeing the game from him escapt away,
>   sits downe to rest him in some shady place,
>   with panting hounds beguiled of their pray:
> So after long pursuit and vaine assay,
>   when I all weary had the chace forsooke,
>   the gentle deare returnd the selfe-same way,
>   thinking to quench her thirst at the next brooke.
> There she beholding me with mylder looke,
>   sought not to fly, but fearelesse still did bide;
>   till I in hand her yet halfe trembling tooke,
>   and with her owne goodwill hir fyrmely tyde.
> Strange thing me seemd to see a beast so wyld,
>   so goodly wonne with her owne will beguyld.

Here, the terms of the metaphoric and literal environments of the sonnet are not easily disentangled. The opening quatrain establishes the hunting simile using the third person for the terms of the comparison. The introduction of the first person pronoun in the second quatrain ostensibly presents the subject of the simile: the lover's pursuit of his lady. The vocabulary of the hunt, far from receding, remains powerfully present and the only phrase that suggests the literal environment is 'the gentle deare', which ambiguously alludes to both the forest animal and the poet's beloved. The shift from third to first person continues throughout the sonnet but the metaphoric terms of the hunting comparison are never replaced by terms solely associated with the poet's pursuit of his lady. There is an uneasiness about the applicability of the comparison which surfaces directly in the couplet, where the poet refers to the outcome as 'Strange'. The strangeness derives from the sudden transformation of the hunted animal into a willing captive. The terms of the comparison cannot adequately accommodate such a transformation that is inexplicable in terms of the behaviour of a chased deer. The dangers of imposing a metaphor, or of over-extending it, are foregrounded in this sonnet. If the poet's conception of love as a chase or hunt was appropriate when his lady seemed aloof, it does not easily translate when she returns the poet's advances. Clearly the attempt to match the metaphor to the changing circumstances of the poet's situation has become strained. The only solution is therefore to abandon the metaphor of the hunt and to adopt a new metaphor in its place.

This transformation and replacement of metaphor in an attempt to move towards an adequate expression of the poet's awareness of love is characteristic of the development of imagery running throughout the *Amoretti*. Spenser's metaphoric honesty places him at the centre of the Elizabethan sonneteers' heuristic quest to define the nature of *eros*. There is no place in *Amoretti* for dishonesty or self-deception, metaphors must be used to explore, but must be willingly abandoned and replaced if their potency becomes exhausted. This commitment to metaphor as a means of discovering and capturing truths through the gradual illumination of their parts is readily included into the open-ended structure of a sonnet sequence. Here, the metaphor can be changed, or new metaphors added, without interfering with character portrayal or narrative development. It is less clear how such metaphoric fluidity could be adapted to the demands of poetic narrative.

A more fluid narrative could hardly be imagined than what G. Wilson Knight once referred to as 'the baggy, bulgy, loose effect' of *The Faerie Queene*.[19] In a telling passage, he reveals the cause of his deep-rooted dissatisfaction with what he sees as Spenser's lack of discipline:

> His poem does not quite live the gospel it preaches. It lacks architectonic strength. It is fluid. Of the two qualities needed, that of a time-sequence and a strong, controlling, spatial design, it valuably possesses only the first. Its spatialized scheme, though

vast, is unsubstantial.... The nature of his creation changes indecisively. Aristotle's idea that the constructing of a weighty central plot is a greater art than characterization or rhetoric comes to mind. Spenser's fluid, shifting significances make a boneless, piecemeal work. There is a lack of tough moral fibre in his constructional technique.[20]

The fluid structure certainly does suggest that Spenser's narrative is not driven by a sense of unifying plot. But fluidity of structure is not necessarily the same thing as absence of structure. What G. Wilson Knight assumes to be a 'piecemeal work' is an exploratory, metaphorically structured narrative. It does not conform to dramatic conceptions of character or plot because these are not part of its allegorical nature. *The Faerie Queene* does not comply with the expectations of dramatic narrative, not because it fails to, but because it never tries to. The poem demands a different set of expectations, which interpret its structure in terms of the changing metaphors it freely adopts in its advance towards an ever more meaningful expression of its theme.

The function of metaphor, once it is transformed from a mere figure of speech or rhetorical ornament into a principle of structure, implies a controlling influence on the literary work that requires more thorough investigation. *The Faerie Queene* is an ideal text to study since, not only does its metaphoric plot produce the expansive, serpentine structure so radically different from more linear forms of narrative, but its own plot is frequently metaphoric in another sense. Episodes which grow externally out of the proliferation of metaphor have a tendency to turn inwardly to reflect on their own metaphoric status. The exploration of the poem's self-referential discussion of metaphor accounts for the selection of material in this study.

Chapter 1 looks at a metaphoric plot across a whole book of the poem. Book I, as the opening encounter with an extended metaphoric plot, must gradually educate the reader in the processes involved in the interpretation of such a text. The parallel drawn between the protagonist's quest for spiritual understanding and the reader's search for hermeneutic comprehension focuses attention directly on the text's metaphoric status as an investigation of exegesis. The metaphoric environment in this, the Book of Holiness, creates an unusually clearly defined narrative framework around the metaphoric plot. The text of the poem can never stray too far from its sense of the external narrative influences of the Bible and Christian history. The metaphoric correspondences here function within a system that contemplates the eventual termination of its own activity. This projection towards a moment of ultimate fulfilment provides metaphor with a vision of the union with truth it seeks through its own evolution.

Book I allows the metaphoric plot to develop its faith in its own activity through its association with Christian belief. Metaphor in this environment functions as an instrument of truth, capable of producing moments of pure revelation. In aligning its own metaphoric expansiveness with truth, the poem implies that any movement towards the limiting or literalizing of its expression amounts to falsehood. The metaphoric plot will be fought out between the metaphoric forces of good and the literal forces of evil. The central religious metaphor creates a polarization of the discussion that in establishing a system of oppositions begins to reduce the complexity of the real metaphoric struggle. There is no difficulty in the religious environment of Book I in realizing the inherent conflict between icons and metaphor. An icon to the Protestant court of the Elizabethans was a false image, standing in place of, and consequently obstructing communion with, the true, living God. The construction of false metaphor assumes the characteristics of idolatry, the worship of an image as truth, instead of the image serving to illuminate truth.

The conflict that emerges in Book I between proper and improper uses of figurative language should surface elsewhere in the text of the poem, if it is to be seen as descriptive of Spenser's own view of metaphor throughout *The Faerie Queene* and not just as a product of the religious terminology naturally related to the Knight of Holiness. Various episodes suggest themselves as potentially fertile sources of metaphoric plots for such an investigation. In each book of *The Faerie Queene* metaphoric plots develop in comparatively self-contained episodes to re-examine the issues raised in Book I. In Book III, however, a sequence of narrative episodes occurs, virtually concurrently across five cantos, providing the poem's most prolonged investigation of the distinctions between good and bad metaphors in a secular context. Cantos six to ten of Book III are the narrative plots which will be the focus for the textual analysis of Spenser's self-referential discussion of metaphor in Chapter 2. This chapter does not follow the order in which the episodes appear in the poem. To clarify the distinctions that are being defined it begins by examining the narrative plot that on the surface might seem to offer an ideal example of fluid, metaphoric change. The narrative which produces the final metamorphosis of Malbecco creates an illusion of change through a systematic reduction of metaphoric possibility in the form of the final emblem of jealousy. There is a disturbing inconsistency in interpretations like Harry Berger Jr's, which see the transformation of Malbecco as the energetic conversion of a 'dead stereotype into a living archetype' only to argue that Spenser then 'presents himself as eager to leave the whole problem behind'.[21] It is precisely because Malbecco becomes a too rigid definition of jealousy that he must be abandoned.

The second section of Chapter 2 turns from Malbecco, an extreme example of the limiting of metaphor, to the metaphoric plot which sets the whole sequence in motion. The Garden of Adonis offers an environment which constitutes a poetic space rather than a narrative progression. The ideal metaphoric plot turns out to prefer a world of shifting spatial correspondences to a linear narrative development. Here, the presentation of overlapping images of love and generation provide a perfect metaphor for the activity of metaphoric creativity. The episode displays in its own metaphoric and mythological substitutions the ceaseless activity of heuristic metaphor. The Garden of Adonis is for Spenser, as it was for Plato in the *Phaedrus*,[22] a pleasant setting (a *locus amoenus*)[23] in which the discussion of the proper use of writing could be cultivated using the metaphors of planting and sowing. Metaphor is consequently both the subject and the structuring principle of Spenser's own version of this delightful garden. To function properly, metaphor requires the freedom to express its infinite variety that can only be accommodated within the expansive grounds of such a mythological paradise.

The fluid transfer from image to image in search of an ever more comprehensive understanding, however, is only free from potential abuse in an idyllic setting such as the Garden of Adonis. Chapter 2 concludes with an examination of another distinctive corruption of metaphor. Malbecco enacted the confinement of metaphor, but the narrative of the creation of False Florimell acts as a parody of the generative openness of metaphor in the Garden of Adonis. Here, it is the literalization of figurative language which inverts true metaphor by substituting a false image in the place of the original it should seek only to describe. The

Introduction: The Elizabethan Poetics of Metaphor

narrative of False Florimell extends beyond Book III into two further episodes in Book IV and Book V which plot her eventual demise.

The metaphoric plots of Book III develop the conflicts between the forms of true and false figurative language outside the immediate context of theology. The narrative of False Florimell, however, highlights a serious problem for the Christian poet whose defence of allegory as an instrument of truth, capable of attaining moments of divine revelation, relies on maintaining the figurative purity of his metaphoric discourse. Once acts of figurative abuse in poetry are perceived as analogous to acts of idolatry, then the duty of the faithful poet to protect his own metaphors from idolatrous disfigurement becomes ever more pressing.

Chapter 3 focuses on episodes in which the poem reflects on the dangers of allegory becoming corrupted by the transgressive tendencies of its own poetic figures. The first section of the chapter continues to investigate links between allegory and idolatry in terms of the way in which both can be said to embody abstract concepts. Where the allegorical embodiment, or sign, comes to replace the thing signified, then the poem is in danger of committing an act of idolatry. It is no longer so easy to separate the secular from the sacred in *The Faerie Queene* when the discourse of allegory is seen to have such theological implications. The Bower of Bliss is a particularly fruitful site for further exploration of the idolatrous potentialities of allegory. There has been a long tradition of criticism viewing Guyon's temptation within Acrasia's bower as a self-reflexive episode representing the intoxicating allurements of Spenser's own lyrical poetry. Once the bower's evocation of sensual pleasure is seen to be not just a representation of the seductive qualities of poetry but is also associated with the traditional analogies between idolatry and carnality, then the metaphoric reverberations of the passage can be better understood.

If idolatry is viewed as the replacement of the spiritual love of God with the physical love of earthly and fleshly pleasures, then the dangers of a poetic discourse which appeals sensually and sexually to the ear and eye of the reader becomes much more obviously akin to idolatry. Mammon and Acrasia are consequently likened and at the same time differentiated in terms of their idolatrous appeal; likened in so far as they both offer Guyon forms of temptation which replace heavenly bliss with an earthly substitute, but differentiated in so far as Mammon's appeal to both Guyon and the reader is more readily resisted. The aesthetic and erotic attractions of the Bower of Bliss have a disorientating effect precisely because metaphor is used transgressively to blur theological distinctions and to confuse moral judgements. The poem's iconoclastic responses to the overwhelming experience presented in the Bower of Bliss cannot destroy the realization that no matter how hard the poet strives to sanctify the language of allegory, it may still elicit an idolatrous response in the reader.

The last section of Chapter 3 develops the discussion of temperate and intemperate reading to look at the further exploration of the carnal appeal of allegory in Book VI. The repeated cynosural motifs become a focus of the struggle to define appropriate responses to revelatory disclosure in *The Faerie Queene*. On Mount Acidale, where it is essential that the visionary moment is protected from the abuse of idolatrous misreading, Calidore's transgressive intrusion is an untimely reminder that the allegorical quest for visionary fulfilment is all too easily defiled by the misappropriation of misinterpretation. The positioning of the attempted sacrifice of Serena directly before Calidore's pastoral excursion presents a perturbing analogy. The cannibals' carnal appetites generate an idolatrous literalization of the figurative language traditionally associated with the love poet's courtly blazon. Their grotesque enactment of the moral and spiritual degeneration of metaphoric discourse has disconcerting affinities not only with Calepine's inconclusive reunion with Serena but also with Calidore's response to the Dance of the Graces. The defence of the language of allegory necessitates an attempt to resurrect the poem's faith in metaphor as a means of acknowledging the absence of divine presence while sustaining a belief in the revelatory truths figured forth in the 'continued Allegory' of *The Faerie Queene*.

Chapter 4 looks at a further threat to metaphor, which instead of subverting or limiting its power in the manner of previous false figures, represents an over-extension of the powers of metaphor. The figure of Mutabilitie in the Mutabilitie Cantos, in seeking to raise metaphor to the status of a self-defining principle, divorces it from its true function of descriptive discovery. Unlike previous figures of abuse, Mutabilitie cannot simply be defined in terms of oppositions between true and false. She bears witness to a more fundamental issue that brings into question the ability of metaphor to refer to anything beyond itself. The poem's own self-referential concerns, and its faith in the power of metaphor, demand that Mutabilitie is corrected rather than dismissed. The tentative solution the poem offers to the problem stands as a last testimony to Spenser's belief in metaphor as an heuristic instrument of truth.

1
Metaphor as an Act of Faith

NOT SEEING THE WOOD FOR THE TREES[1]

No more literal representation of a proverb's metaphoric implications is to be found than in Spenser's treatment of the rhetorical commonplace of the catalogue of trees in the opening canto of *The Faerie Queene*. Secure in their knowledge of the physical and symbolic meanings of trees, Redcrosse and Una readily set about naming all those they find in the forest. Each one in turn is designated a well established literary connotation; the traditional list lengthens and the narrative environment is comfortably placed as a well known allegorical plot:[2]

> Much can they prayse the trees so straight and hy,
> The sayling Pine, the Cedar proud and tall,
> The vine-prop Elme, the Poplar neuer dry,
> The builder Oake, sole king of forrests all,
> The Aspine good for staues, the Cypresse funerall.[3]

(I. i. 8)

Suddenly the rhetorical order vanishes. Redcrosse's and Una's confident interpretation, delightful as it seemed, was misplaced. They have mistaken the nature of this particular plot of land and consequently find themselves lost in a bewildering maze of paths and by-ways. The contrast between the well-balanced, controlled lines of the catalogue and the directionless confusion of the now physically and mentally displaced wanderers that follows, reinforces this first drastic misreading of the text:

> When weening to returne, whence they did stray,
> They cannot finde that path, which first was showne,
> But wander too and fro in wayes vnkowne,
> Furthest from end then, when they neerest weene,
> That makes them doubt, their wits be not their owne:
> So many pathes, so many turnings seene,
> That which of them to take, in diuerse doubt they been.
>
> (I. i. 10)

Single-minded certainty has given way to 'diuerse doubt' and all because of an initial failure to see the wood for the trees. Only when it is 'too late' (I. i. 13) does Una (ever a more able interpreter than Redcrosse) begin to appreciate 'the perill of this place' (I. i. 13), as she recognizes the symbolic meaning of the trees collectively, rather than individually:

> This is the wandring wood, this *Errours den*,
> A monster vile, whom God and man does hate:
> Therefore I read beware.
>
> (I. i. 13)

This is the first lesson of *The Faerie Queene*, and one which unites protagonist and reader in a common hermeneutic quest: 'Therefore I read beware.' Una, in interpreting the danger signals of her world, alerts the reader to the dangers of the activity of reading itself. It was by misreading the signs that Una became lost in the first place, and now, in her reassessment of her position, she unwittingly warns us to beware of reading. Unfortunately, it is 'too late' for us as well, for having entered the text of the poem we cannot turn back unscathed. We may choose to be more careful next time and try not to rush into things with the haste of Redcrosse, but we have already wandered far from 'that path, which first was showne', and now there is no longer an easy way out again. Once in the textual maze, the only option is to go on – to follow the path most 'like to lead the labyrinth about' (I. i. 11): a path that will necessitate a wearisome journey full of false starts, dead ends and meandering detours.

Right from the start, the plot of *The Faerie Queene* implicates the reader in the characters' misreadings. The opening stanzas of the poem constitute a paradigm for the hermeneutic crisis to be confronted on every page: how do we know if we are reading correctly? When should we 'read beware'? *The Faerie Queene* offers no simple solutions to such problems; on the contrary, it stands as a monument to the unending quest for hermeneutic certainty. Only by first entering the forest of textual deception, can we ever hope to learn to read our way out again. Not reading the text is no answer; ignorance is not bliss, it is merely a more entrenched form of self-deception. The poem raises the problem of correct interpretation time after time, perpetually drawing attention to the fact that right reading implies its opposite, wrong reading. Unfortunately, no hard and fast rule for distinguishing between them is provided. Learning from our mistakes is perhaps the best we can hope for, but for that to happen, we must first recognize our mistakes. Seeing the wood for the trees is easy enough once we are told it is a wood, but how many trees make up a wood – one, two, three, etc.?[4] The point at which we should cease cataloguing them individually and recognize their collective status is not clearly defined. In the end, it seems to rely upon an intuitive knowledge – 'This is the wandring wood' – a knowledge which is not easily taught or learnt.

There is, however, an important distinction to be made between the world of *The Faerie Queene* which the characters of the poem inhabit and the text of the poem which represents that world to the reader. Readers, it is true, frequently identify with the plight of Redcrosse and Una, but they are also expected to distance themselves to some extent from the characters' moral indiscretions. Looking back at the initial description of the 'shadie groue' (I. i. 7), a subtext can be perceived beneath the poem's narrative surface providing a series of signs or clues to assist the reader with the moral interpretation of the wood:

> Whose loftie trees yclad with sommers pride,
> Did spred so broad, that heauens light did hide,
> Not perceable with power of any starre.
>
> (I. i. 7)

It is a narrative device which Spenser utilizes throughout *The Faerie Queene*, allowing apparent description to pass effective moral judgement. The key words are clearly 'pride' and 'heauens' which, if replaced by the blander words 'green' and 'the bright', would remove the effect of moral commentary and leave the words 'loftie' and 'hide' free from any adverse implications. The trees' proud opposition to God's light along with such other pointers as 'the birdes sweete harmony'[5] (I. i. 8) thus privilege the reader's interpretation of the text over the protagonists' experience of their world. In self-consciously drawing attention to the text's privileging devices, however, far from solving the hermeneutic crisis, the poem raises further doubts concerning the self-sufficiency of an autonomous reader, were the textual indicators to be made less obvious, or worse still, taken away completely. The potential for misinterpretation would then leave the reader no better off than Redcrosse himself, whose tendency to plunge headlong into error perhaps parodies the reader's own self-confident interpretation of the text.

The opening of *The Faerie Queene* thus establishes one of the poem's central dynamics: the problem of seeing or reading aright.[6] The moment reading begins, the moment we follow Redcrosse into the wandering wood, confrontation with this primary textual crux is unavoidable. The disarmingly simple question lurking in Errour's den is quite simply how do we read Errour? Redcrosse's encounter with the dragoness Errour has been interpreted as a paradigm of 'the overarching structural function wordplay serves in the first book'.[7] The etymology of the word error, from the Latin *errare*: to wander, links the errancy of Redcrosse, the errant knight in his wanderings throughout Book I, with Spenser's 'investigation into the meaning of one particular word: error.'[8] Allegory, as the title of Maureen Quilligan's book *The Language of Allegory* suggests, is all about words: an investigation in words into the meaning of words. The approach provides many insights into the relationship between wordplay and narrative structure in *The Faerie Queene*, but ultimately it finds itself trapped by the circular nature of its own arguments. One word is to be understood in terms of another word without reference to a metalanguage which controls meaning. Viewed in this way, allegory is nothing more than a form of extended pun, as Quilligan herself implies when she refers to 'the essential affinity of allegory to the pivotal phenomenon of the pun, which provides the basis for the narrative structure characteristic of the genre.'[9] The problem is that puns, by definition, do not provide meaning, they provide homonymic associations. The usefulness of these for establishing a word's original or true meaning is haphazard and unrealiable. Puns, far from supporting the etymological search for the precise historical meaning of a word, threaten to disrupt the progress of that search by suggesting a potentially limitless supply of associated words. Each new word is then capable of enacting its own narrative exploration of itself, leading the narrative on a path of infinite digression. Pun and etymology do not constitute a single unified approach to the meaning of words. They constitute two very different tendencies inherent in the nature of language, the interaction of which generates the conflicting desires of the text of *The Faerie Queene*. The poem's etymological search is to be associated with the diachronic desire that launches *The Faerie Queene* on its Virgilian style epic quest towards finality and closure, while its punning playfulness is to be seen in terms of the textual synchronicity creating the self-perpetuating narrative of unending Ariostan romance.[10]

Error, then, is not to be understood simply in terms of its etymological root, which in any case does not give rise to a single narrative sequence leading to a final truth, but to a convoluted history of misguided wanderings or errors. Errour is a far more complicated monster, whose meaning is to be found not in an investigation of one word, whose very spelling is duplicitous (is Errour Error?), but in the narrative presentation of the entire episode and those features of Errour which are made most prominent.[11]

Returning to the text, Spenser's Errour is seen to possess three distinct weapons which she uses in the battle against Redcrosse: her 'hideous taile' (I. i. 16), her 'floud of poyson horrible and blacke' (I. i. 20), and her 'cursed spawne of serpents small' (I. i. 22). At first glance, there is nothing to connect these different aspects of her armoury, but if the narrative pointers are examined more closely, a common feature can be discovered in the description of them all. To start with, Errour's vomit and her progeny both issue from her mouth, and are secondly both linked to ideas of the written word; what she spews forth is 'full of bookes and papers' (I. i. 20) while her 'yong ones' are 'fowle, and blacke as inke' (I. i. 22). The details are not superfluous (with Spenser, they never are); they are designed to draw attention to the specific type of error Errour represents. The deformed monsters and inky poison that issue forth from Errour's mouth constitute the deformation and defilement of the spoken and written word. Errour's primary weapon, her 'huge long taile' (I. i. 15), can now be figuratively reinterpreted as its own homonym. Errour's 'taile' is an erring tale: an erroneous narrative that threatens to overwhelm the unwary reader.

Redcrosse's confrontation with Errour presents a literal plot which maps onto a figurative analysis of misinterpretation, both of which progress logically through the battle. The mistaken assumptions with which Redcrosse entered his narrative environment have already been discussed, but throughout the ensuing conflict with Errour, it is an interpretational problem which confronts him: to see 'the vgly monster plaine' (I. i. 14). Errour's natural habitat, 'the darksome hole' (I. i. 14), is a place where she can hide from the light of figurative insight, hoping 'in desert darknesse to remaine, / Where plaine none might her see, nor she see any plaine' (I. i. 16). Errant narrative is not just difficult to see for what it is, it is also incapable of proffering any insights of its own. Redcrosse already thinks he has seen the monster clearly, but the light he brought with him was 'A litle glooming light, much like a shade' (I. i. 14), enough to show Errour 'horribly displaide' (I. i. 14) but not to expose her real nature. Once engaged with, false narrative does not shrink from the encounter but rushes forth:

> hurling her hideous taile
> About her cursed head, whose folds displaid
> Were stretcht now forth at length without entraile.
>
> (I. i. 16)

It is now, with the narrative unfolding itself, that the struggle begins, for Errour is not a passive form of narrative abuse but strident and loud:

> Therewith enrag'd she loudly gan to bray,
> And turning fierce, her speckled taile aduaunst.
>
> (I. i. 17)

The advance of the false 'taile', Errour's most dangerous weapon, threatens to subdue Redcrosse's resistance. He finds himself suddenly immobilized as the 'taile', '*Errours* endlesse traine' (I. i. 18), wraps around him. The climax of the fight now requires that the figurative interpretation of Errour's literal monstrosity is clearly brought to light. Spenser's solution is to introduce Redcrosse's attempted strangulation of the dragon:

> Wherewith he grypt her gorge with so great paine,
> That soone to loose her wicked bands did her constraine.
>
> (I. i. 19)

At first, the lines seem to represent a purely physical action, until in the following stanza Spenser draws out the figurative import carried by the word 'grypt'.[12] Redcrosse is, in fact, on the verge of getting to grips with Errour, of grasping hold of her meaning. Not surprisingly, it is at this precise moment that she therefore disgorges her flood of poisonous 'bookes and papers', shortly followed by her ink-black brood, in an attempt to force Redcrosse to 'slacke / His grasping hold' (I. i. 20). The phrase encapsulates the involved nature of the struggle, emphasizing the importance of the mental activity involved in perceiving hidden things, of grasping hold of figurative meanings. The simultaneous conflict and coexistence of the literal and figurative is essential to the success of Spenser's allegory.

Momentarily, however, Spenser now chooses to explode that coexistence by showing the tide of the battle turning, not as a result of any action on the part of Redcrosse, but as the result of a sudden metaphoric retranslation of the entire scene:

> As gentle Shepheard in sweete euen-tide,
>   When ruddy *Phoebus* gins to welke in west,
>   High on an hill, his flocke to vewen wide,
>   Markes which do byte their hasty supper best;
>   A cloud of combrous gnattes do him molest,
>   All striuing to infixe their feeble stings,
>   That from their noyance he no where can rest,
>   But with his clownish hands their tender wings
> He brusheth oft, and oft doth mar their murmurings.
>
> (I. i. 23)

This is one of the most extraordinary stanzas to be found anywhere in *The Faerie Queene*. Suddenly, the scene is no longer threatening; we enter an extended simile of pastoral simplicity where Errour's offspring become nothing more than troublesome gnats whose desire 'to infix their feeble stings' is a pale shadow of the 'mortall sting' (I. i. 15) of their progenitor's tail. The clownish rustic with his natural honesty is untroubled by what are no longer monstrous distortions of language but quiet 'murmurings'. What the stanza thus reveals is a glimpse of the restorative powers of figurative language properly used. The voices of detractors are reduced to 'murmurings' and the power of Errour vanquished, as the poem momentarily discovers its own source of salvation in a pastoral language that is all the more resonant because of its religious connotations in this, the Book of Holiness. The stanza effects an early prefiguration of the vision of 'The new *Hierusalem*' (I. x. 57) Redcrosse is to receive in the tenth canto, when the narrative of his own life is to be figuratively revealed to him. Inevitably, the poem must immediately return to finish the actual battle with Errour, just as Redcrosse must return from his vision to complete his earthly quest, with the final defeat of the dragon in the eleventh canto. After such visions, however, the dangers of misinterpretation are reduced by the knowledge of the transformative and salvific powers of figurative language.

The encounter with Errour thus places at the threshold of the poem a symbolic episode dealing with the problems of learning to read properly. Una's initial exclamation at the mouth of Errour's den, 'Therefore I read beware', turns out to be a prophetic warning. It also has much in common with another cautionary exclamation about a linguistic monster that has a certain kinship with Spenser's Errour, derived from the tendency to disfigure man by falsifying the figurative significance of his language. '"Beware the Jabberwock, my son!"' is the warning given to the youthful dragonslayer by his father in the poem 'Jabberwocky' in Lewis Carroll's *Through the Looking-Glass*. The Jabberwock is the dangerous creature which inhabits a nonsensical poetic environment which represents an alternative linguistic universe to both literal and metaphoric language. It is, however, only an extreme version of the erroneous metaphoric discourse which Spenser's false poets seek to foster throughout *The Faerie Queene*: a language of deceit that is only one step away from a meaninglessness that still sounds frighteningly like, and threatens to pose as, good sense.[13]

'Jabberwocky', as Carroll meticulously reveals, is, from the start, a mirror poem that attempts to invert order and usurp meaning. Where Spenser's Errour threatens to falsify language by hiding its correct figurative meaning, Carroll's Jabberwock threatens to annihilate figurative language by destroying all meaning. These linguistic monsters must therefore be slain literally within the text by dragonslayers, and figuratively by the reader. Carroll uses Alice to expose the hermeneutic problem and the dangers of self-deception raised by 'Jabberwocky':

> 'It seems very pretty,' she said when she had finished it, 'but it's *rather* hard to understand!' (You see she didn't like to confess, even to herself, that she couldn't make it out at all.)[14]

Alice, however, is not the only character to provide a commentary, for later, the book's own self-satisfied critic, Humpty Dumpty (who attempts to master language in his own fashion by trying to make the poem mean 'just what I choose it to mean'),[15] offers his reading of the first stanza of 'Jabberwocky'. The problem with Humpty Dumpty's interpretation is that he has forgotten that it is not necessarily his meaning he should be seeking, but the text's. Carroll ironically deflates Humpty Dumpty's bigotry when his confident interpretation, despite its magnanimous inclusion of the 'portmanteau' theory of ambiguity (there are two meanings packed up into one word), turns out to have little more relation to the real world than the poem itself, as Tenniel's illustration makes abundantly clear.

Once the connection has been made between the abuse of metaphor and nonsense, it is possible to see why allegory presents its own particular dangers to the unwary reader. J. Nohrnberg has suggested a possible allusion in the description of Errour to the Delphic pythoness and the riddles of oracular utterance.[16] There is, however, a major difference between the structure of allegory and riddle that makes allegory potentially more illusive. Riddles function by presenting a first-level description that only makes sense when a second-level interpretation is provided. To remain on the first level is deeply dissatisfying since only when the interpretation is provided are various incongruities and illogicalities removed. Riddles set puzzles which demand that their solutions are found. Allegory is quite different; allegory provides a first-level description in the literal narrative that is perfectly logical. The reader senses no immediate cognitive loss and is not directly invited to construct an interpretation at a secondary level. Expressed in a slightly more technical vocabulary, riddles present a system of signs or signifiers, that only make sense when mapped onto a single system of signifieds not immediately apparent, but which, once discovered, are the riddle's solution. Allegory, on the other hand, presents a system of signs which maps easily onto a literal system of signifieds, which in turn constitute a secondary system of signs which map onto at least one (and frequently more than one) secondary system of signifieds. The literal narrative is thus simultaneously both the signified in a first system and the signifier in a second system.

It is this double function of the literal in allegory which raises major problems for readers. Firstly, they may fail to progress from the first level of literal signification to the second level of figurative signification without realizing the limitations of their reading of the text. Secondly, they may become confused as to the nature of the secondary signification, since it is not a closed but an open system, and consequently furnish themselves with an incomplete or false figurative interpretation. It was precisely this mistake which initially led Redcrosse into Errour's den: his failure to see the wood for the trees. Essentially, it is the same problem he confronts throughout Book I as he struggles to read his world metaphorically. It is a problem he has clearly not overcome when he meets Fradubio in the second canto.

NOT SEEING THE MAN FOR THE TREE

Redcrosse's encounter with Fradubio (I. ii. 28–45) provides a particularly useful opportunity to examine Spenser's commitment to metaphoric discourse by comparing his presentation of the episode with its primary source in Ariosto's *Orlando Furioso*. Spenser's passage is modelled on Ariosto's account of Ruggiero's meeting and conversation with Astolfo.[17] In Ariosto's more extensive version Ruggiero arrives on Alcina's island alone and is refreshing himself by a spring when his horse accidentally gets entangled in the branches of a myrtle bush. To his astonishment the myrtle begins to moan with pain and begs Ruggiero to free his horse. Ruggiero immediately complies, proffering his services if he can be of further help, and asking the myrtle to inform him of its true identity. The myrtle tells him that its name is Astolfo and then relates the story of his metamorphosis. He tells how he had been travelling home when the beautiful enchantress Alcina had fallen in love with him, luring him away from his friends and taking him back to her island to be her lover. Here, she had kept him in luxury until, becoming infatuated with a new lover, she had turned him, like many before, into a tree. When he has finished his tale Astolfo then warns Ruggiero that a similar fate awaits him on Alcina's island, and that despite being warned he will be unable to resist Alcina's charms. Duly forewarned, Ruggiero proceeds on his way, shortly to be seduced by Alcina.

This summary indicates the extent to which Spenser drew on Ariosto for his own more condensed story of Fradubio's metamorphosis. It also reveals a significant inversion of Ariosto's narrative sequence which is symptomatic of Spenser's subtle transmutation of the tale. Whereas in *Orlando Furioso*, Ruggiero meets Alcina only after he has spoken with Astolfo; in *The Faerie Queene*, Redcrosse is already with Duessa when his meeting with Fradubio takes place. The conversation which Ariosto presents as a warning of the dangers awaiting Ruggiero in the near future is turned by Spenser into an ironic reflection of Redcrosse's own situation at the time it takes place. What is technically a structural change clearly affects much more than just the structure of the narrative sequence. This shift in emphasis away from culpability and onto nescience, reveals Spenser's interest once again in matters of interpretation. Redcrosse, as he did in his encounter with Errour, is confronting a hermeneutic challenge; understanding the nature of his own narrative quest relies upon his first learning to read the allegorical significance of the characters he meets and the stories they tell him. Interpretation, however, demands an imaginative leap, a willingness to read the allegory for what it signifies, not what it says, and to see the narrative signs as metaphoric significations with which to decode the 'darke conceit'.

Unfortunately, Redcrosse remains naive, still trying to understand his world literally and ignoring its symbolic implications. The very reason he abandoned Una and adopted Duessa in her place was the result of misinterpreting their allegorical characters. Redcrosse assumed 'truth' would be openly displayed, not concealed like Una:

> Yet she much whiter, but the same did hide
> Vnder a vele, that wimpled was full low,
> And ouer all a blacke stole she did throw.
>
> (I. i. 4)

Una – like allegory, itself the figure of 'false semblaunce' – is a 'darke conceit', a veiled truth. This paradoxical representation of truth as a hidden beauty awaiting disclosure does not correspond with Redcrosse's simplistic expectations. When he meets Duessa, whose openness and lavish show are more in keeping with his concept of a 'goodly Lady' (I. ii. 13), he welcomes her company, not recognizing her deceitfulness because she seems so superficially attractive. It is this same inability to penetrate literal appearances and gain the spiritual enlightenment embedded in the metaphoric referents of the discourse which Redcrosse displays throughout his encounter with Fradubio. Nothing illustrates the limitations of his literal perception better than the interplay of the verbs 'to see' and 'to seem'.

It is worth noting, first of all, that although the word 'seem' occurs eight times in the passage, it is never uttered by Redcrosse. He remains convinced throughout that his sight is a reliable window onto the external world, so that even when what he sees is extraordinary, he only desires to have an explanation for such phenomena, regardless of what their implied meaning might be:

> Quoth then the knight, by whose mischieuous arts
> Art thou misshaped thus, as now I see?
>
> (I. ii. 34)

Fradubio whose own situation makes him aware of the discrepancy between what he appears to be in the sight of others, and what he knows himself to be beneath his misleading exterior, in contrast to Redcrosse, never uses the verb to see, unless it is to reveal the limitations and misconceptions of visual impressions:

> To loue this gentle Lady, whom ye see,
> Now not a Lady, but a seeming tree;
>
> (I. ii. 35)

or alternatively to refer to a form of perception amounting to an interpretation of events which is not based on sight at all:

> The wicked witch now seeing all this while
> The doubtfull ballaunce equally to sway.
>
> (I. ii. 38)

Fradubio's attempt to render the deceptiveness of appearances reaches its climax in his confused description of his past inability to distinguish visually between the 'false' Duessa and the 'faire' Fraelissa:

> So doubly lou'd of Ladies vnlike faire,
>   Th'one seeming such, the other such indeede,
>   One day in doubt I cast for to compare,
>   Whether in beauties glorie did exceede;
>   A Rosy girlond was the victors meede:
>   Both seemde to win, and both seemde won to bee,
>   So hard the discord was to be agreede.
>   *Fraelissa* was as faire, as faire mote bee,
> And euer false *Duessa* seemde as faire as shee.
>
> (I. ii. 37)

Fradubio's dilemma recalls the well-known 'choice of Hercules' that Hallet Smith has suggested had a powerful influence on the Renaissance concept of the heroic.[18] Hercules seated himself at a crossroads and listened to the arguments of two goddesses (Venus representing pleasure and Diana virtue) and eventually chose virtue; Fradubio, because he based his decision entirely on the appearances of Fraelissa and Duessa, fails to make the correct moral choice. It is true that Fraelissa does not represent an ideal image of virtue or truth as Diana and Una do, but she is undeniably morally preferable to Duessa.[19] Fradubio, who with hindsight, has begun to understand the extent of his moral blindness, attempts to render the difficulty he had in penetrating Duessa's disguise. His reiteration of 'seeming' and the sequence of comparative constructions in which the respective qualities of Fraelissa and Duessa are used to balance the lines of verse, actually transform Fradubio's own indecision into part of the experience

Metaphor as an Act of Faith 41

of reading the stanza. When Fradubio does see Duessa 'in her proper hew' (I. ii. 40), what he describes, ironically, turns out to be the features which he could not in fact see:

> Her neather partes misshapen, monstruous,
> Were hidd in water, that I could not see,
> But they did seeme more foule and hideous,
> Then womans shape man would beleeue to bee.
>
> (I. ii. 41)

What we 'see' here is not a fixed visual image, indeed is not a visual image at all, but the fluctuating process by which an image is interpreted, and in the process transformed, by a character's critical understanding. What Fradubio says he saw is only what he imagined he would have seen, so that by the end of the stanza he has ceased to differentiate at all between what he sees and what he thinks and understands, since for him they are no longer separate actions, but simultaneous and effectively synonymous parts of his conscious experience.

Redcrosse has yet to learn that how we see the world depends on how we look at it. His literal-mindedness shuts him off from the comparative and metaphoric interpretations which will eventually lead him towards the salvific experience of spiritual revelation. He still behaves like the characters in *Orlando Furioso* for whom seeing is regarded as the essential means of human knowledge. Alcina falls in love with Astolfo because 'she liked what she saw' (VI. 38) and Astolfo likewise 'burned for her no less ardently, seeing how beautiful she was' (VI. 46) and forgets his responsibilities because he is 'Lost in contemplation of her looks' (VI. 47). Ruggiero is unmoved while listening to Astolfo's verbal account of his metamorphosis but is 'deeply afflicted on seeing the change the knight had undergone from his true self into a scrawny, sterile shrub' (VI. 54). In a context where seeing is believing, it is no surprise that the introductory stanza to the seventh canto of *Orlando Furioso*, coming after Astolfo's description of Alcina but before Ruggiero has seen her in the flesh, is concerned with the human desire for visual and physical proof of things which have been reported:

> Chi va lontan da la sua patria, vede
> cose, da quel che già credea, lontane;
> che narrandole poi, non se gli crede,
> e stimato bugiardo ne rimane:
> che 'l sciocco vulgo non gli vuol dar fede,
> se non le vede e tocca chiare e piane.
> Per questo io so che l'inesperienza
> farà al mio canto dar poca credenza.

He who travels far afield beholds things which lie beyond the bounds of belief; and when he returns to tell of them, he is not believed, but is dismissed as a liar, for the ignorant throng will refuse to accept his word, but needs must see with their own eyes, touch with their own hands. This being so, I realize that my words will gain scant credence where they outstrip the experience of my hearers.

(VII. 1)

The central irony of the whole episode has been extended to Ariosto's own predicament as the writer of a fictional discourse. Just as Ruggiero does not believe Astolfo because his own observations are apparently contradictory, so the reader will not comprehend the inherent truth of Ariosto's poem where it is beyond his practical experience. Ariosto's solution is to turn to metaphors, particularly metaphors of everyday observations, in an attempt to present concrete, realistic descriptions of events in the poem, especially those of an unrealistic or magical nature. The very use of the metaphor of a traveller returning and not being believed is designed to bring Ariosto's own thoughts as writer within the common experience of the reader. The noise issuing from Astolfo when his branches are torn is compared to the hiss of a log on a fire (VI. 27) and the perspiration he sweats is like the sap of a heated log (VI. 32). Again when Ruggiero is given Bradamant's magic ring which enables him to see through Alcina's veneer of beauty, his reaction is likened to a child rediscovering a once ripe fruit in a state of putrefaction (VII. 71).

Spenser does not use metaphor, like Ariosto, to describe the magical or unimaginable. In the case of Fradubio, as elsewhere in *The Faerie Queene*, Spenser is not concerned with metamorphosis as an actual event but as a psychological, moral and spiritual reality. This is why it is so much harder for Redcrosse to understand the implications of Fradubio's narrative than it is for Ruggiero to learn from Astolfo's. Ruggiero is technically always in a position to understand his own condition fully. Ariosto draws attention to this fact, showing Ruggiero's full awareness of what he is doing even as he is about to disregard Astolfo's warning:

> Anzir pur creder vuol che da costei
> fosse converso Astolfo in su l'arena
> per li suoi portamenti ingrati e rei,
> e sia degno di questa e di più pena:
> e tutto quel ch'udito avea di lei,
> stima esser falso; a che vendetta mena,
> a mena astio et invidia quel dolente
> a lei biasmare, e che del tutto mente.

On the contrary, he preferred to believe that if she had changed Astolfo into a myrtle by the sandy shore, it was because he had treated her with stark ingratitude, and so deserved his fate and worse. Everything he had been told about her he dismissed as false, deeming rather that the wretch was moved by spite and envy and was a shameless liar.

(VII. 17)

Ruggiero has not misunderstood Astolfo, he simply refuses to believe him. He is clearly wrong to do so, but unlike Redcrosse he is not ignorant of his moral position, but chooses to disregard the information he has received and to indulge in the sensual pleasures Alcina offers him. Alcina's physical beauty overrides all other considerations for Ruggiero, who is more willing to give credence to what he sees for himself, than what he is told by others. Ruggiero is a literalist, living in a literal world and, consequently, makes his choices with his eyes open. Redcrosse is a literalist living in a metaphoric world and inevitably makes most of his moral choices with his eyes effectively shut. He must acquire a new faith, a faith in Christian metaphors and their power to reveal the true path to salvation.

Right from the start of the episode, Spenser puts readers on their guard against simplistic readings of the text:

> Till weary of their way, they came at last,
> Where grew two goodly trees, that faire did spred
> Their armes abroad, with gray mosse ouercast.
>
> (I. ii. 28)

The trick, which only appears retrospectively, is that the trees' 'armes', that initially appear to be catachrestically described, in the cases of Fradubio and Fraelissa are simultaneously both literal and metaphoric arms. This is a narrative where relationships between the literal and metaphoric are never straightforward, where dead metaphors are liable to come back to life, and where only alert, perceptive involvement with the text will avoid mistakes. Unfortunately for Redcrosse, he is not a very attentive reader of the textual world he inhabits. He has, moments before, failed to listen carefully to Duessa's personal history because his mind was an other things:

> More busying his quicke eyes, her face to view,
> Then his dull eares, to heare what she did tell.
>
> (I. ii. 26)

Now quick to see all the wrong things, he is once again in the wrong frame of mind to gain much insight from Fradubio:

> And in his falsed fancy he her takes
> To be the fairest wight, that liued yit;
> Which to expresse, he bends his gentle wit,
> And thinking of those braunches greene to frame
> A girlond for her dainty forehead fit,
> He pluckt a bough; out of whose rift there came
> Small drops of gory bloud, that trickled downe the same.
>
> (I. ii. 30)

Spenser here contrives to take us inside the consciousness of Redcrosse, to see the intentions behind his actions. What we see are the thoughts 'in his falsed fancy', although the illusion that we are observing physical actions is still created by the prominent position of the verb 'takes' at the end of the line, typographically disunited from the following line which places it grammatically back within Redcrosse's thought process. The appearance of a narrative event taking place is achieved by the infinitive 'to expresse' which necessitates an action to satisfy the thought desiring expression. But this action is delayed for two lines by the extension of the thought process into the following two verbs: 'bends' which is applied to Redcrosse's 'gentle wit' and 'thinking'. When the verb 'pluckt' finally does arrive, it is consequently seen as the product of the mental activity taking place in the rest of the stanza. The sudden revelation in the alexandrine of the 'Small drops of gory bloud' comes as a dramatic shock, precisely because the rest of the stanza has moved us so far inside Redcrosse's imagination that we too are expecting to see Duessa crowned. The sheer physicality of the line thus renders Redcrosse's terror at the result of his action as part of our reading experience, thereby alerting us to the deception our own 'falsed fancy' had succumbed to by associating itself too closely with Redcrosse's psychological desires.

Reading demands active involvement, but not blind devotion. *The Faerie Queene* is paved with such traps for unwary readers to fall into the moment they relax their critical grasp of the text. Redcrosse's aims and intentions are, as yet, far from consistent with those demanded for the fulfilment of his quest; identifying too closely with them is a textual temptation liable to produce fallen readers. Fortunately, the way back is never closed. Spenser, the benign creator of the poem, only ever requires a willingness to do better, to learn from experience, to read more carefully, and to interpret more astutely in the future. Redcrosse, having strayed much further than the reader from 'that path, which first was showne', has a far more arduous return journey to make. His desires, having led him into the presence of Fradubio, have produced within him a spiritual proximity to the tree-man which Spenser's description of his horror wittily reveals:

> Astond he stood, and vp his haire did houe,
> And with that suddein horror could no member moue.
>
> (I. ii. 31)

Rooted to the spot, the petrified Redcrosse momentarily experiences the physical rigidity and stasis induced by spiritual doubt and symbolized by Fradubio's bodily 'arborization'.

The rest of the episode now explores Fradubio's past experience in relation to Redcrosse's present situation, missing no opportunity to point out the extent of his blindness to the metaphoric significations it contains. Just before Fradubio reveals his name, for instance (Fradubio means Brother Doubt, a meaning made explicit in the thirty-seventh stanza), there are two references to doubt in Redcrosse: firstly, 'my doubtfull eares' (I. ii. 32) and secondly, 'And doubting much his sence' (I. ii. 32). In the latter example, the pun is on the alternative meanings of the word 'sence', only one of which is intended or comprehended by Redcrosse. 'Sence' can either refer to 'the senses viewed as forming a single faculty in contradistinction to intellect, will, etc.; the exercise or function of this faculty, sensation' (*OED*, I. 3) or to the 'mental apprehension, appreciation, or realization of (some truth, fact, state of things). Also comprehension, perception of the meaning of' (*OED*, II. 15). Redcrosse suspects his physical senses, which are not in fact at fault, when what is lacking is his ability to realize the moral and spiritual truth of the information his physical senses provide him with.

At every stage of the narrative his spiritual blindness prevents him from discovering the truth about himself and the characters around him. Just as in the first canto Redcrosse failed to see the wood for the trees, so now he fails to see the man for the tree. Fradubio's essential humanity is brought out throughout his narrative in his impassioned outbursts:

> Therewith a piteous yelling voyce was heard,
>   Crying, O spare with guilty hands to teare
>   My tender sides in this rough rynd embard,
>   But fly, ah fly far hence away, for feare
>   Least to you hap, that happened to me heare,
>   And to this wretched Lady, my deare loue,
>   O too deare loue, loue bought with death too deare.
>
>   (I. ii. 31)

Fradubio's intense physical pain produces a frenzied expression of confused fears and desires which draws attention to the most significant aspect of his metamorphosis: the conflict between his rigid external appearance and his all too human internal feelings of anguish and remorse. Fradubio still thinks and feels like the man he was, not the tree others see him as, which he refers to objectively as if it has a separate existence from his own. The phrase 'in this rough rynd embard' expresses the painfulness of Fradubio's situation in terms of physical imprisonment within the tree, even though logically both the phrases 'this rough rynd' and 'My tender sides' refer to Fradubio's own body. The distinction he draws between them is actually non-existent; Fradubio's metamorphosis has clearly not changed his psychological identity, and in his own mind he therefore tries to disassociate himself from his new physical existence. Ironically, Fradubio's desire to express his distinct internal being becomes more apparent as his concern for his own personal distress turns into an expression of his fears for Redcrosse's safety. The intensity of his warning, with its alliterative and tautological insistence on the need to 'fly far hence away, for feare', which then reminds him of his own 'deare loue' and fills him with tender remorse for the condition he has brought her to, expresses the confused but undeniably human feelings within him.

Fradubio's outbursts contain more than just an expression of complex emotions constituting a real human identity. His language is imbued with a series of Christian symbols which universalize the whole tenor of his discourse. Fradubio 'or man, or tree' (I. ii. 34), however, must not be reductively interpreted. Much like the Tree of Charity in Passus XVIII of *Piers Plowman*, Fradubio embodies the entire history and duality of Christian man, simultaneously linked to both Adam and Christ, Man's fall and redemption, or as Langland neatly sums it up:

> And as Adam and alle thorugh a tree deyden,
> Adam and alle thorugh a tree shal turne to lyve.
>
> (XVIII. 359–60)[20]

J. Nohrnberg explains the nature of Fradubio's symbolic kinship with Adam:

> Fradubio is clearly Adam's ironic aspect. As a bleeding tree who was once a man, he conforms to a type known to folklore,

namely the soul cut off in the midst of life – and thus cut off unjustly – whose existence is continued thereafter in the compensatory form of vegetation.... Adam is properly included in this company because he is cut off from that paradise containing the tree of life (the eternal life that was intended for him), and because his life is extended, not in himself, but in his 'stock.'... Adam is probably a tree for Spenser, as Nelson has shown, because at his fall he hid himself *in medio ligni paradisi* (literally, 'in the middle of the tree of paradise'), where according to Revelation the tree of life ought to have been.[21]

The link between Fradubio and Adam, developed throughout the episode, is strongly emphasized in the conclusion to the scene, ironically, just as Redcrosse is attempting to disassociate himself from Fradubio:

> When all this speech the liuing tree had spent,
> The bleeding bough did thrust into the ground,
> That from the bloud he might be innocent,
> And with fresh clay did close the wooden wound.
>
> (I. ii. 44)

The allusions to the red clay from which man was created and the dust to which he is destined to return, reveal the impossibility of Redcrosse attaining innocence from the stain of inherited sin. His literal actions completely ignore the symbolic nature of his guilt, which cannot be healed until he recognizes its presence and meaning. In attempting to disassociate himself from Fradubio, Redcrosse is not just shutting himself off from his spiritual past but also from his spiritual future. For Fradubio, strongly associated with Adamic man, will only be delivered from his state of limbo when 'bathed in a liuing well' (I. ii. 43). Fradubio awaits the redemption of the second Adam whose own blood will be his healing balm. The 'living tree' is thus also a prefiguration of the cross of Christ's crucifixion, whose 'wooden wound' was necessitated by Adam's fall. And yet, the nature of Fradubio's 'wooden wound' should not be entirely foreign to Redcrosse; the armour he wears bears reminders of linguistically and symbolically similar injuries:

> Wherein old dints of deepe wounds did remaine,
> The cruell markes of many' a bloudy fielde;
> Yet armes till that time did he neuer wield.
>
> (I. i. 1)

In the poem's opening stanza, attention was drawn to the element of human suffering implicit in the phrase 'old dints of deepe wounds' which forces recognition of the 'old dints' in terms of bodily injuries by harnessing a noun referring to the armour ('dints') to one referring to the body inside ('wounds') in a single verbal formula. The further revelation in the line 'Yet armes till that time did he neuer wield' then shifts the perspective of the description away from the particular and present, placing it within the wider context of the continued Christian struggle against the forces of evil. Redcrosse's armour carries in its description precisely the same linguistic device as Fradubio's 'wooden wound', emphasizing the suffering that must be undergone by Christian man in this life, and reflecting the suffering Christ underwent on the cross.

Fradubio's essential humanity, although disguised by his physical metamorphosis, cannot be completely hidden. Duessa and the forces of evil, in attempting to distort appearances and seeking to hide literal truths, paradoxically reveal metaphoric ones. Fradubio, typically, exposes Duessa's ultimate impotence even though he and Redcrosse remain unable to penetrate her latest disguise, despite the fact that all she has really changed is her name. The final ironies of Duessa's deceitful nature are brought out in Spenser's concluding description of her fainting fit:

> Then turning to his Lady, dead with feare her found.
>
> Her seeming dead he found with feigned feare,
> As all vnweeting of that well she knew.
>
> (I. ii. 44–5)

The final line of the forty-fourth stanza ostensibly provides a reliable description of the condition Redcrosse finds Duessa in when he turns to look at her. When we first read the stanza, because we initially observe events from Redcrosse's point of view, we too see Duessa lying 'dead with feare'. The first line of the next stanza, however, by repeating the second half of the preceding line but inserting the adverb 'seeming' and the adjective 'feigned', subtly shifts our perspective on the preceding narrative action. What is now seen is the deliberate deception of Duessa's behaviour which still remains hidden from Redcrosse, who fails to penetrate the surface reality of the narrative in which he is participating.

Yet, in a spiritual sense, Duessa's feigned death is her very real and eternal death. What 'well she knew' is, after all, nothing other than the truth of Fradubio's story, whose metaphoric meaning confirms Duessa's ultimate spiritual mortification. Although the actual unclothing of Duessa must wait until later, no magic ring is required to help characters see her real nature, as it was for Ruggiero in order to perceive Alcina's deformity in *Orlando Furioso*. Spenser's magic is not to be associated with charmed objects that must be specially introduced into his narrative. Spenser's magic is ever present, embedded within the narrative's metaphoric correspondences. To see them is to open the world to moral and spiritual enlightenment; not to see them is to live in a world devoid of spiritual values, to replace hope with despair and to overlook the living for the dead.

NOT SEEING IS NOT BELIEVING

> Thou damned wight,
> The author of this fact, we here behold,
> What iustice can but iudge against thee right,
> With thine owne bloud to price his bloud, here shed in sight?

(I. ix. 37)

With these words Redcrosse angrily accuses and condemns Despair for the 'piteous spectacle' (I. ix. 37) of Sir Terwin, who lies at his feet, his 'luke-warme blood' (I. ix. 36) still welling from the mortal wound in which a 'rustie knife' (I. ix. 36) remains embedded. Were evidence required, Sir Terwin is the dying proof that words lead directly to actions: that what is said and written changes what men do. Despair, 'The author of this fact', thus validates a major premise of the traditional grounds for the defence of poetry (that poetry can teach men how to act), while in the same breath, corrupting its intended purpose. When in the prefatory letter to Sir Walter Raleigh, Spenser states his intention 'to fashion a gentleman or noble person in vertuous and gentle discipline',[22] it is in the firm belief that poetry can produce noble and virtuous acts in men. Despair, with is store of doctrinal perversions and metaphoric suppressions, threatens to invert the entire poetic enterprise as he distorts God's word to destroy His creation. Of all the deceitful enemies Redcrosse encounters in the Book of Holiness, Despair is the most pernicious. Arguing with an apparent logic, supported by a rhetorical trick 'as simple as it is bold',[23] he aims to undermine Christian faith in God's mercy and by representing justice 'as constituting the whole relation of God to human conduct',[24] to lead men into a state of hopelessness resulting in the damnable act of suicide.

The rhetorical volley Despair fires at God's canon against self-slaughter, thus endangers the status of poetry as severely as it does the life of Redcrosse. For while Sidney and other poets reiterated the argument that it was unreasonable to blame poetry for the work of bad poets, their defence was still powerless to protect the individual or the state from their abusive practices. Out of such fears concerning the subversive and harmful powers of poetry, Plato (with extensive influence on Renaissance discussions of the issue) banished poets from his republic altogether. In the context of contemporary attacks upon poetry, Redcrosse's encounter with Despair attests to the honesty of Spenser's commitment to his art, developing a belief in the ultimate good of poetry only after exhibiting its contrary power, in the wrong hands, to corrupt.[25] The crucial word here is belief, for it is with a view to establishing a direct link between the grounds of Christian faith in the good of God and the reader's faith in the good of metaphoric language that Spenser presents the discourse of Despair.

A sequence of words and phrases associating Despair with the figure of the false poet runs through the whole episode. Even before Redcrosse's reference to him as 'author', Sir Treuisan's description of Despair's 'subtill tongue' which 'like dropping honny, mealt'th / Into the hart' (I. ix. 31), associates the rhetoric with which Despair disguises his foul purposes with the sweet, melodious voice of poetry. Redcrosse wishes to pit himself against 'that treachours art' (I. ix. 32), where the pun could hardly be more explicit. Later, once the main spiritual debate is concluded (where direct allusions to poetry are necessarily less prominent), Spenser is careful to reintroduce a vocabulary which reaffirms the previous association between Despair and poet. Despair's arguments begin to take a hold on Redcrosse, 'As he were charmed with inchaunted rimes' (I. ix. 48) and Una coming to his aid warns him not to 'let vaine words bewitch thy manly hart' (I. ix. 53). Her final dismissal of the doctrine of Despair invokes a faith in the 'greater grace' of God and envisages its victory in terms of a metaphor that has obvious literary connotations:

> The which doth quench the brond of hellish smart,
> And that accurst hand-writing doth deface.
>
> (I. ix. 53)

Despair is presented as the author of false doctrine, the perverter of true faith. His corrupt text must be rewritten and reinterpreted if the full import of Christian metaphor is to be kept alive.

Redcrosse, who has previously failed to read through the deceptive wiles of far less cunning adversaries, not surprisingly proves particularly susceptible to the debative skills of this most eloquent of false poets. Yet, Despair is not entirely responsible for the error into which Redcrosse falls, anymore than he can directly be accused of murdering Sir Terwin, as Redcrosse blusteringly tries to assert. For, as Despair truthfully, if scurrilously, answers:

> None else to death this man despayring driue,
> But his owne guiltie mind deseruing death.
>
> (I. ix. 38)

Despair acts on the minds of the guilty and his only weapons are 'wounding words' (I. ix. 29). Culpability for the self-destructive acts he persuades others to commit, is consequently difficult to prove. The body of Sir Terwin which Redcrosse takes as 'approuing trew / The wofull tale that *Treuisan* had told' (I. ix. 37) is merely circumstantial evidence of which Despair washes his hands. Treuisan's 'wofull tale', while implicating Despair, itself states clearly that Sir Terwin's death wound was undoubtedly self-inflicted:

> That wofull louer, loathing lenger light,
> A wide way made to let forth liuing breath.
>
> (I. ix. 30)

Despair, like all Redcrosse's other allegorical enemies, externalizes an inner mental and spiritual conflict or psychomachia.[26] The active, physical sense in which Sir Treuisan talks of Despair:

> He pluckt from vs all hope of due reliefe,
> That earst vs held in loue of lingring life,
>
> (I. ix. 29)

implies an action on the part of Despair which is physically impossible; hope cannot literally be stolen or possessed like treasure. The physicality of Spenser's language must not be allowed to hide the real nature of Despair; he is the enemy within, dramatizing the spiritual decline taking place inside the mind of the guilty and faithless Christian. His 'charmed speeches' (I. ix. 30) work rapidly on Redcrosse, who has yet to develop a firm belief in the strength of Christian metaphors to reveal the true meaning and function of scriptural texts and the foreshadowing in the Old Testament's Law of the New Testament's Covenant of Grace which replaces justice with mercy.

Redcrosse's failure to recognize the significance of Christian symbols is a potentially fatal flaw which could undermine the protection of his armour and shield:

> But on his brest a bloudie Crosse he bore,
>   The deare remembrance of his dying Lord,
>   For whose sweete sake that glorious badge he wore,
>   And dead as liuing euer him ador'd:
> Vpon his shield the like was also scor'd.
>
> (I. i. 2)

The image of Christ's sacrifice is carried on Redcrosse's breast, but has yet to be accepted within it. Not until the external symbols are internalized through the process of interpretation, will their memory carry with it the faith that comes from true understanding.

When Redcrosse confronts Despair, it is still with the desire to test his hardiness: 'To proue his puissance in battell braue / Vpon his foe' (I. i. 3). Nine cantos into the first book he has yet 'his new force to learne' (I. i. 3): a force which should come from 'The deare remembrance of his dying Lord' and the hope of new life that was bought with His death. Redcrosse has reached a dangerous impasse; his incomplete spiritual education leaves him blind to the significance of the Christian symbols and metaphors in which he must place his trust. He cannot believe because he does not see, and he cannot see because he does not believe; blindness and faithlessness are here inseparable.

Learning to read the Christian metaphors correctly demands an act of faith in metaphor itself, a belief in the power of the language of metaphor to reveal spiritual truths. F.E. Sparshott has pointed out an important similarity between religious and metaphoric faith:

> In a poet's imaginary garden the toads are real, and so are the eyes and the gazelles. Spender sees the gazelle and knows it for his eye, not by a masterly feat of investigative ingenuity like that by which Sherlock Holmes identifies the man with the twisted lip as the missing financier, but by an act of faith like that of the Christian who knows that his Redeemer lives.[27]

Unlike Spender, Spenser associates literary faith in metaphor with Christian faith in divine grace directly. In Book I of *The Faerie Queene*, Christian faith is not just a metaphor for metaphor, it is the primary subject, although paradoxically, one whose mystery and complexity can only possibly be encompassed by a language richly imbued with metaphor. Christian faith in redemption and literary faith in metaphor are here mutually inclusive.

Redcrosse's susceptibility to the discourse of Despair must be viewed as the result of his lack of faith in metaphor as much as his lack of faith in God's grace. Spenser draws attention to the duality of his faithlessness through the exchange of gifts which takes place between Arthur and Redcrosse just before his encounter with Despair:

> Prince *Arthur* gaue a boxe of Diamond sure,
>   Embowd with gold and gorgeous ornament,
> Wherein were closd few drops of liquor pure,

Of wondrous worth, and vertue excellent,
That any wound could heale incontinent:
Which to requite, the *Redcrosse* knight him gaue
A booke, wherein his Saueours testament
Was writ with golden letters rich and braue;
A worke of wondrous grace, and able soules to saue.

(I. ix. 19)

The two gifts, both symbolizing divine grace offered to man through Jesus Christ, provide a physical and a textual representation of that message. Arthur's 'boxe of Diamond sure' actually contains drops of divine grace, but the 'booke, wherein his Saueours testament / Was writ', is obviously the New Testament, the scriptural text telling of the same gift of divine grace. It is a 'worke of wondrous grace' where the word 'grace' punningly implies both skilful craftsmanship and salvific power. Redcrosse and Arthur thus swop gifts symbolizing precisely the same thing, but differing in the nature of their symbolism. Divine grace is simultaneously to be seen as a literal gift freely given, and as a symbolic gift metaphorically represented. True Christian faith comes from accepting the gift in both its literal and metaphoric sense: faith as an act of metaphor as well as metaphor as an act of faith.

Redcrosse has yet to develop a true faith in either God or metaphor. Time after time, his impetuous actions confront him with dangers he is spiritually and metaphorically unprepared for. No opportunity is missed to display the nature and extent of his blindness in this episode, where even his initial interception of Sir Treuisan carries ironic overtones: 'The *Redcrosse* knight toward him crossed fast' (I. ix. 23). Instead of riding straight across to confront danger, Redcrosse should perhaps first have 'crossed fast', in other words, made the sign of the cross as protection against the enemy he is about to confront. Forgetful of his reliance upon the symbolism scored on his shield and armour, and expressed in his own name, Redcrosse shows, even before arriving at the Cave of Despair, the faithlessness that will allow the 'villein' to wrest from him all hope of salvation.

Redcrosse's initial challenge to Despair (quoted at the opening of this section) opens the debate as Despair means it to go on. What Redcrosse emphasizes is a point of law and the judgement and punishment that must follow. His statement encodes both the Old Testament – eye for an eye – code of revenge and the Covenant of Law's keynote of justice. Without faith in the New Testament's Covenant of Grace, which Redcrosse's words recall in their parodic allusion to Christ's salvific blood, he will be left wide-open to Despair's perversion of Christian doctrine, with its emphasis on God's justice rather than His mercy.[28]

Despair's entire discourse simply extends Redcrosse's own concept of justice from a secular into a divine context. If Redcrosse demands justice and revenge, Despair will let him have it with a vengeance, persuading him to attempt suicide with a language all the more potent, because it resembles so closely Redcrosse's own. The legalistic terms Redcrosse had employed are redoubled against him in Despair's climactic sequence of rhetorical questions depicting God's judgement of the erring knight's catalogue of sins:

> Is not he iust, that all this doth behold
>   From highest heauen, and beares an equall eye?
>   Shall he thy sins vp in his knowledge fold,
>   And guiltie be of thine impietie?
>   Is not his law, Let euery sinner die:
>   Die shall all flesh?
>
> (I. ix. 47)

'Sometimes the devil doth preach.'[29] This 'man of hell, that cals himselfe *Despaire*' (I. ix. 28), when it serves his purpose, can always find a biblical text to support him. In this case, Despair glosses Ezekiel 18:4 'the soule that sinneth, it shal dye'. His speeches constitute a patchwork of citations including 'commonplaces of Stoic philosophy used in the Christian "art of dying" tradition',[30] intermixed with incomplete biblical texts. Perversion and suppression are the hallmarks of Despair's rhetoric, expressed at its most eloquent with a natural appeal to his victim's particular weaknesses.

Despair is not only furnished with a detailed knowledge of Redcrosse's past history: his imprisonment by Orgoglio and betrayal of Una, but is also possessed of a vocabulary designed to lure Redcrosse away from his purpose:

> Who trauels by the wearie wandring way,
>   To come vnto his wished home in haste,
>   And meetes a flood, that doth his passage stay,
>   Is not great grace to helpe him ouer past,
>   Or free his feet, that in the myre sticke fast?
>   Most enuious man, that grieues at neighbours good,
>   And fond, that ioyest in the woe thou hast,
>   Why wilt not let him passe, that long hath stood
> Vpon the banke, yet wilt thy selfe not passe the flood?
>
> (I. ix. 39)

This is more than the start of an appeal to sloth, although it is that too. It is a carefully phrased description of the desire to reach a goal, to complete a journey or quest which is naturally strongly felt by Redcrosse. The 'wearie wandring way' of his own narrative quest is pitted with obstacles and hazards which stand in the way of the immediate completion of his adventure. Despair's ensuing description of death as a state of 'eternall rest' (I. ix. 40), which men crave but fear to entertain, is not dissimilar in intention from Cleopatra's attempt to reduce the fear of pain associated with suicide in her image of a 'lover's pinch, / Which hurts, and is desir'd' (V. ii. 294–5):

> Is not short paine well borne, that brings long ease,
> And layes the soule to sleepe in quiet graue?
>   Sleepe after toyle, port after stormie seas,
> Ease after warre, death after life does greatly please.
>
> (I. ix. 40)

Despair's images of active strife, followed by deserved rest, are designed to appeal to Redcrosse's concept of the epic, and to present death as the natural conclusion to the heroic life. What Despair ignores is the fundamental difference between death and suicide within the Christian heroic code, where taking one's life 'after the high Roman fashion' or any other fashion is not even to be contemplated. Struggle, toil and sin are all necessary and inevitable parts of the Christian's life, which far from negating the Covenant of Grace, as Despair implies, are designed to teach its truth in so far as salvation cannot be achieved through man's own efforts on earth, but only with the help of divine grace. Could Redcrosse awaken his faith in the spiritual nature of his quest, he would perceive the futility of the action Despair is drawing him towards, expressed in the very words Despair uses to distort the Christian message. Douglas Brooks-Davies explains the relevant Christian connotations of passing over the river bank:

> Suppressed here is the salvific significance of the water of baptism (death leading to life): e.g., Romans 6:3–4: 'Knowe ye not, that all we which have bene baptized into Jesus Christ, have bene baptized into his death? We are buryed then with him by baptisme into his death, that like as Christ was raised up from the dead by the glorie of the Father, so we also shulde walke in newnes of life'. The passing over the river bank to death alludes ironically to the crossing of the Jordan into the Promised Land, a traditional figure for baptism.[31]

Redcrosse's stock response of the sentinel remaining at his post (a commonplace of the suicide debate), in emphasizing duty, fails to supply the missing concept of mercy without which man can never fulfil his Christian destiny. It is in response to this unconvincing retreat into metaphor that Despair launches his most vicious perversion of all, combining an attack on Christian free will with a denial of the reader's autonomous right to interpret the text:

> Is not his deed, what euer thing is donne,
>   In heauen and earth? did not he all create
> To die againe? all ends that was begonne.
>   Their times in his eternall booke of fate
>   Are written sure, and haue their certaine date.
>   Who then can striue with strong necessitie,
>   That holds the world in his still chaunging state,
>   Or shunne the death ordaynd by destinie?
> When houre of death is come, let none aske whence, nor why.
>
> (I. ix. 42)

Despair here presents his own version of the metaphor of the Book of the World: God's universe as a written text. The metaphor, rich in its implications for Christianity, in its present context in

The Faerie Queene is ideally suited to Spenser's further examination of the relationship between literary and Christian faith. Despair's presentation of the metaphor denotes the relationship between the author and his work: God and His universe. In doing so, he refers to Redcrosse only in his role as character, and denies him the status of reader or interpreter of his own narrative. Theologically, Despair strives to emphasize 'fate', 'necessitie' and 'destinie', reducing individual existence to the blind fulfilment of a preordained plan. The denial of Christian free will metaphorically translates back into the constriction of the reader's participation in the text through interpretation. Spenser's metaphor thus seeks to contradict the authorial tyranny Despair tries to impose, in much the same way that the submerged Christian metaphors ironically undercut Despair's earlier suppression of baptismal imagery. Here, however, instead of responding to hidden Christian significations, the reader must bring the metaphor of the Book of the World textually back to life, by paradoxically reading it literally again as a distortion of the relationships between author, text and reader.

Despair's fatalism preaches hermeneutic paralysis: a textual determinacy, leaving no room for an active reader within the author's dictatorship. The tension between the determinate and the indeterminate concept of the text is here energized by the ambiguity of the fluctuating concept contained in the phrase 'still chaunging state'. Potential interpretations of the word 'state' are endlessly expansive, from concrete concepts of individual, nation, world and universe on the one hand, to more abstract concepts concerning the nature and ordering of reality on the other. 'Still' can either mean at rest or motionless, or alternatively always, ever or now as before. In conjunction with the rest of the phrase it is impossible to decide on a single, clear meaning; either a state perpetually changing is implied, or else a state, that although altering in some respects, remains essentially the same. What matters is not the privileging of one interpretation over the other, as Despair wishes, but the conflict of interpretations, the ambiguity of indeterminacy creating a tension out of the very phrase Despair uses to deny the existence of such interpretational gaps. Spenser's text thrives on the same desire Roland Barthes speaks of 'to live to the full the contradiction of my time, which may well make sarcasm the condition of truth.'[32] For much as Barthes's analysis of the *readerly* nature of *Sarassine* in *S/Z* ends up revealing its *writerly* qualities, so Despair too finds his words constantly, as if in refutation of Humpty Dumpty, not meaning what he chooses them to mean.

The undermining of Despair's reductive readings is necessary if the Christian is to regain faith in God's justice and mercy and if the reader is to develop a positive understanding of the nature of the text of *The Faerie Queene*. At stake here is Spenser's whole poetic enterprise. Despair, in tempting Redcrosse to commit suicide, is metaphorically drawing readers towards a similarly self-destructive act: persuading them to deny their role as co-creator of the text, just as Redcrosse denies himself control over his own life. Despair, as false poet, is still unable to inflict the actual death wound on the reader, just as he is limited to proffering Redcrosse the instruments of his death: 'swords, ropes, poison, fire' (I. ix. 50). The precise nature of the reader's death is alluded to in Despair's reference to the unquestioning attitude with which it must be accepted: 'When houre of death is come, let none aske whence, nor why' (I. ix. 42).

Blind, unquestioning, passive reading is what deprives the reader of real existence. No wonder the whole of Despair's argument is punctuated with rhetorical questions. He would create automatons, going through the motions of reading as they consume the words on the page without thought. The earlier appeal to rest was also an appeal to intellectual inactivity, a refusal to question the status and authority of the text. It is not so surprising, therefore, that Despair's references to the sinful path of the Christian straying ever further from God are reminiscent of the opening language describing 'the wandring wood' (I. i. 13). Just as there, loss of direction was associated with interpretational confusion, so here, Despair's words carry with them the same implication of the deepening frustration of the ever increasing hermeneutic crisis confronting the wayward reader:

> For he, that once hath missed the right way,
> The further he doth goe, the further he doth stray.

(I. ix. 43)

But readers' lives are entirely in their own hands. Despair is ultimately impotent unless readers participate wilfully in the transaction of their own textual elimination. Like Redcrosse, who can be saved by the simple insertion of mercy into Despair's damnable script, readers resurrect themselves by asserting faith in the activity of reading itself. For, as Una's final words imply, Despair's authorial despotism can be swiftly defaced. Christian faith in God's grace, literary faith in the metaphoricity of language will exorcize Despair as both spiritual and textual demon. The false text he inscribes must be actively opposed by a reading that constitutes its own rewriting of the text and one that, in a profound sense, also becomes the 'righting' of the poem.

The reader's assertion of identity and faith in his or her textual independence naturally has far reaching implications for the autocratic author. These are metaphorically hinted at by Spenser's concluding portrayal of Despair's suicidal enactment of his eternal destiny:

> Which when the carle beheld, and saw his guest
> Would safe depart, for all his subtill sleight,
> He chose an halter from among the rest,
> And with it hung himselfe, vnbid vnblest.
> But death he could not worke himselfe thereby;
> For thousand times he so himselfe had drest,
> Yet nathelesse it could not doe him die,
> Till he should die his last, that is eternally.
>
> (I. ix. 54)

The reader's escape from authorial bondage brings about the destruction of an entire textual system that requires the symbolic execution of the authoritarian author. Spenser's defence of the reader's critical revolution thus ends with an image of the author's inevitable and masochistic self-obliteration that must accompany the achievement of the reader's hermeneutic liberation. Despair's repeated attempts at suicide point to the same conclusion Roland Barthes reaches in his essay entitled 'The Death of the Author'. Spenser's image is a prefiguration of Barthes's realization that the participation of the reader in the life of the text signals the death of the old concept of author:

Thus is revealed the total existence of writing: a text is made of multiple writings, drawn from many cultures and entering into mutual relations of dialogue, parody, contestation, but there is one place where this multiplicity is focused and that place is the reader, not, as was hitherto said, the author. The reader is the space on which all the quotations that make up a writing are inscribed without any of them being lost; a text's unity lies not in its origin but in its destination.... Classic criticism has never paid any attention to the reader; for it, the writer is the only person in literature. We are now beginning to let ourselves be fooled no longer by the arrogant antiphrastical recriminations of good society in favour of the very thing it sets aside, ignores, smothers, or destroys; we know that to give writing its future, it is necessary to overthrow the myth: the birth of the reader must be at the cost of the death of the Author.[33]

Despair's defeat marks the rejection of a closed system of textual denotation. It is a defeat, however, which can never be absolute. The reader's new freedoms must be defended against the reconstitution of oppressive literary structures and the rebirth of the Author. The reader's struggle, like the Christian's, demands vigilance and fortitude to stand up to the assaults of heretical detractors. Brachiano's statement about the devil in *The White Devil* holds just as true for the false poet – 'He's a rare linguist.'[34] Spenser never tires of confronting the linguistic manoeuvres of potential adversaries in *The Faerie Queene*. The poem continually addresses self-referential questions of form and intention in defence of the aspirations of a sincere spiritual and literary faith in metaphor.

BLINDNESS AND INSIGHT

The interpretation of the Despair episode put forward in the last section might appear to raise serious theological objections if the conclusions about the relationships between author, text and reader are applied to a religious context via the metaphor of the Book of the World. Barthes's essay 'The Death of the Author' includes the following passage:

> In precisely this way literature (it would be better from now on to say *writing*), by refusing to assign a 'secret', an ultimate meaning, to the text (and to the world as text), liberates what may be called an anti-theological activity, an activity that is truly revolutionary since to refuse to fix meaning is, in the end, to refuse God and his hypostases – reason, science, law.[35]

Barthes can readily broach deicide, Spenser obviously could not. How then is Barthes's movement towards the negation of God to be levelled with Spenser's intended affirmation of religious faith, when both apparently reach the same conclusions about the roles of author, reader and text and apply them to the same theological metaphor? Is this not proof of what Spenser's detractors see as the inevitable danger of poetry – its inability to control the metaphors which bring it to life?

The answer to these objections lies in a fundamental difference between Spenser's and Barthes's presentation of the correspondences between textual relationships and their theological counterparts. Barthes's analysis, having reached conclusions about the nature of the text, then introduces the 'world as text' metaphor and derives an anti-theological argument almost in passing. Spenser, however, has Despair introduce the metaphor of the Book of the World into a context that is simultaneously theological and textual, with the express purpose of distorting Christian doctrine. Relationships between the textual and the theological fields of discourse are consequently rather more complicated for Spenser than they are for Barthes. Barthes's primary interest is always overtly and unashamedly textual and only fleetingly theological, when he translates his textual theory wholesale onto the theological metaphor. Spenser, working in the opposite direction, derives his textual theory from the theological metaphor, but then chooses not to map it directly back. The reason for Spenser's reticence is not a fear of anti-theological conclusions inherent in his literary theory, but an awareness that two very different mappings are possible, one of which Despair emphasized in his original presentation of the metaphor, the other equivalent to the one Barthes emphasizes in his essay. Spelled out, these are: (i) God: Man = Author: Character; and (ii) God: World: Man = Author: Text: Reader. In isolation, either system of mappings could be used to develop an anti-theological position. Spenser's presentation of the second system of correspondences, however, is introduced to complicate rather than to contradict Despair's interpretation of the metaphor, purely in terms of the first system. It means that by the end of the debate with Despair, no wholesale mapping between the fields of discourse of theology and literature is possible. For Spenser, the completely different textual roles of character and reader are both theologically performed by man. It is not a matter of choosing either one or the other, as it is for Despair and Barthes; Spenser's faith relies crucially on the coexistence of man's double role in God's universe. It also means that Spenser is able to expound a literary theory emphasizing the reader's autonomy from the author, while at the same time expressing his belief in an omniscient and omnipotent God.

The opening stanza of the tenth canto is perhaps designed to ensure that no misconceptions concerning Spenser's theological doctrine are derived from his figurative discussion of literary theory in the ninth canto:

> What man is he, that boasts of fleshly might,
>   And vaine assurance of mortality,
>   Which all so soone, as it doth come to fight,
>   Against spirituall foes, yeelds by and by,
>   Or from the field most cowardly doth fly?
>   Ne let the man ascribe it to his skill,
>   That thorough grace hath gained victory.
>   If any strength we haue, it is to ill,
>   But all the good is Gods, both power and eke will.
>
> (I. x. 1)

Paul J. Alpers has referred to this stanza as 'a drastic account of human frailty: more than any other in Book I it invites the term "Calvinist."'[36] Certainly, it is a forthright declaration of man's spiritual fallibility and total dependence on the grace of God, in stark contrast to the newly found independence of the liberated reader. Misinterpretation of Spenser's comparison between spiritual faith and literary faith is clearly not to be brooked. Only when he has established his doctrinal position with a clarity virtually unparalleled elsewhere in *The Faerie Queene*, is Spenser willing to proceed with his dual analysis of spiritual and literary education.

Redcrosse's regeneration as a Christian and as a reader reaches its climax when he is led by Contemplation to:

> see the way,
> That neuer yet was seene of Faeries sonne,
> That neuer leads the traueiler astray,

> But after labours long, and sad delay,
> Brings them to ioyous rest and endlesse blis.
>
> (I. x. 52)

The same metaphor of the traveller's journey which Spenser has used throughout Book I to explore the reader's interpretational progress reappears in Contemplation's promise of divine and hermeneutic illumination. Yet, even here, what is offered is not the possession of ultimate meaning, but knowledge of the way to achieve it without falling into the confusion and despair of irremediable interpretational loss. Contemplation's description of eternal rest, unlike Despair's, offers bliss not as an immediately attainable goal, but as a potentially realizable condition. Instead of Despair's image of sudden relief from toil and hardship, inviting a Lady Macbeth-like perception of 'the future in the instant', that overlooks means for ends and the natural development that leads towards fruition, Contemplation stresses the temporality of 'labours long' (I. x. 52). This 'sad delay' (I. x. 52), as Contemplation terms it, is sad because it enforces man's inevitable separation from his desired ends, whether his spiritual entry into 'The new Hierusalem' (I. x. 57) or his hermeneutic attainment of ultimate truths. The reader, like the Christian, cannot separate the ends from the means, the meaning from the text and the process of reading it. When it comes to reading, the means not only justify the end, they are the end; the medium is the message.

When Redcrosse arrives at the House of Holiness, he has lost faith in the medium and lost sight of the message. Punning on the meaning of 'errant' and maintaining the metaphor of the wayward traveller, Caelia jokes about the habitual loss of direction common to both 'errant knight' and reader alike:

> Strange thing it is an errant knight to see
> Here in this place, or any other wight,
> That hither turnes his steps. So few there bee,
> That chose the narrow path, or seeke the right:
> All keepe the broad high way, and take delight
> With many rather for to go astray.
>
> (I. x. 10)

The return to 'the narrow path' and the arduous struggle of perceptive, alert reading demands the re-education of the wayward reader that is to be metaphorically described through Redcrosse's spiritual schooling. Una asks Fidelia:

> To haue her knight into her schoolehouse plaste,
>   That of her heauenly learning he might taste,
>   And heare the wisedome of her words diuine.
> She graunted, and that knight so much agraste,
>   That she him taught celestiall discipline,
> And opened his dull eyes, that light mote in them shine.
>
> (I. x. 18)

Fidelia's teachings are described in terms that express both their form and content. The phrases 'heauenly learning', 'words diuine' and 'celestiall discipline' all employ adjectives that apply equally well to the literal subject of her lessons as to the manner of their expression. Faith is best taught when its tutor can both teach and delight, especially when the text is not immediately penetrable, but like Fidelia's, requires initiation into its mysteries:

> And that her sacred Booke, with bloud ywrit,
>   That none could read, except she did them teach,
>   She vnto him disclosed euery whit,
>   And heauenly documents thereout did preach,
>   That weaker wit of man could neuer reach,
> Of God, of grace, of iustice, of free will,
>   That wonder was to heare her goodly speach:
>   For she was able, with her words to kill,
> And raise againe to life the hart, that she did thrill.
>
> (I. x. 19)

Fidelia is the House of Holiness's first presentation of the true poet, introduced to counteract the poem's earlier false poets Archimago and Despair. A. Leigh DeNeef has commented on the similarity between Fidelia's 'sacred Booke' and the 'Magick bookes' from which Archimago 'seekes out mighty charmes, to trouble sleepy mindes' (I. i. 36).[37] The difference is that Fidelia aims to influence the alert, perceptive mind, to open Redcrosse's 'dull eyes' while Archimago sets to work on the dulled senses, intending to keep Redcrosse's eyes firmly and perpetually closed. These are the conflicting poetic intentions Spenser's narrative dramatizes throughout Book I.

Redcrosse, Spenser's surrogate reader, must now be initiated into the art of reading the enigmatic or metaphoric text. Fidelia offers no easy interpretations; she refuses to use language reductively, to simplify, where simplication amounts to perversion or distortion. Her words are just as powerful as Archimago's or Despair's and the last two lines of the stanza declare their miraculous powers, which, as in the next stanza, express both the literal meaning of their spiritual power and the metaphoric sense of their literary effect on the reader:

> And when she list poure out her larger spright,
> She would commaund the hastie Sunne to stay,
> Or backward turne his course from heauens hight;
> Sometimes great hostes of men she could dismay,
> Dry-shod to passe, she parts the flouds in tway;
> And eke huge mountaines from their natiue seat
> She would commaund, themselues to beare away,
> And throw in raging sea with roaring threat.
> Almightie God her gaue such powre, and puissance great.
>
> (I. x. 20)

Once more, Spenser strives to associate religious and metaphoric faith. The powers which Fidelia commands are all celebrated acts of faith in the Bible.[38] Faith, the faith which moves mountains, relies upon the reader's faith in their representation in the biblical text, or Spenser's poem. Spiritual faith cannot be divorced from literary faith and the power of language to figure forth spiritual truths in the speaking pictures of poetry.

The precise nature of the literary faith Spenser hopes to foster in his readers becomes more explicit with the introduction of the second figure of the true poet dwelling at the House of Holiness:

> His name was heauenly *Contemplation*;
> Of God and goodnesse was his meditation.
>
> (I. x. 46)

Spenser here uses a typographical trick to distinguish this representation of Contemplation from a purely religious contemplative. The word 'heauenly' functions purely as an adjective for, unlike the word 'Contemplation', it is not capitalized. Spenser, it would appear, is reflecting the new humanist conception of the *vita speculativa* in its secular, rather than its purely sacred context, in the way Klibansky describes:

> In the same manner, the life of the classical philosopher whom the Renaissance humanist strove to imitate, lay not between 'vita activa' and 'vita voluptuaria' but beyond either of them. To a certain extent it lay beyond good and evil, very differently from the God-directed course of medieval theologians and mystics, and we can understand how the Renaissance, in order to separate the rediscovered way of life of the classical 'philosophus' from that of the medieval 'religiosus', abandoned the traditional expression 'vita contemplativa' (which had grown with the centuries to mean purely and simply 'contemplatio Dei') and coined a new term which, looking back across the Middle Ages, reasserted the ancient notion of self-sufficient thought and research – 'vita speculativa sive studiosa', in contrast to 'vita contemplativa sive monastica.'[39]

Spenser's Contemplation is a fusion of both concepts of the *vita speculativa*, combining in a single personage the potential for both spiritual and philosophical insight. Contemplation thus represents the final stage of Spenser's development of the analogy between literary and religious faith. In him, Spenser can unite poetic vision and a faith in the literary means of achieving it with spiritual vision and the mystical process of revelation.

Once Spenser's primarily Neoplatonic portrayal of the contemplative under the influence of melancholic Saturn is understood, it goes some way to explaining the unexpected and perplexing reactions of Redcrosse to Fidelia's teaching. For, far from drawing closer to an acceptance of his sins, Redcrosse falls into a condition very like that which Despair had tried to work in him:

> The faithfull knight now grew in litle space,
> By hearing her, and by her sisters lore,
> To such perfection of all heauenly grace,
> That wretched world he gan for to abhore,

> And mortall life gan loath, as thing forlore,
> Greeu'd with remembrance of his wicked wayes,
> And prickt with anguish of his sinnes so sore,
> That he desirde to end his wretched dayes:
> So much the dart of sinfull guilt the soule dismayes.
>
> (I. x. 21)

Even Una is confused by this unexpected reaction in her 'faithfull knight' as he gains 'perfection of all heauenly grace':

> In this distressed doubtfull agonie,
> When him his dearest *Vna* did behold,
> Disdeining life, desiring leaue to die,
> She found her selfe assayld with great perplexitie.
>
> (I. x. 22)

The contradictory reactions of Redcrosse to his spiritual initiation are linked to the conflicting moods of the Saturnine melancholic:

> The birth of this new humanist awareness took place, therefore, in an atmosphere of intellectual contradiction. As he took up his position, the self-sufficient 'homo literatus' saw himself torn between the extremes of self-affirmation, sometimes rising to hubris, and self-doubt, sometimes sinking to despair; and the experience of this dualism roused him to discover the new intellectual pattern, which was a reflection of this tragic and heroic disunity – the intellectual pattern of 'modern genius.'[40]

Redcrosse must, therefore, experience a form of despair that is the concomitant of contemplative vision, and should not be confused with the purely destructive doctrine of Despair in the ninth canto, which is conceived merely as evil and not as a positive intellectual force. Redcrosse's sufferings represent both the process of Christian repentance, on the one hand, and a movement towards literary insight, on the other. The image of disease Spenser uses to describe the healing of the 'soule-diseased knight' (I. x. 24), portrays his sufferings in a manner much resembling later portraits of the angst-ridden poet/philosopher of which Dürer's *Melancholia I* is an early and celebrated example.

A paradox is thus placed at the centre of Spenser's dual analysis of poetry and religion. Religious faith, like poetic faith, can only exist alongside self-doubt. Without doubt, there is no faith; faith is rooted in the knowledge of its own uncertainty. *Homo religiosus* can only attain revelation by first experiencing the doubt of his own salvation; *homo literatus* can only achieve textual insight while contemplating the extent of his hermeneutic loss. Spenser's awareness of the close proximity of faith and doubt, blindness and insight in both spiritual and literary contexts is inherent in his choice and presentation of Contemplation as Book I's final tutelary figure:

> Great grace that old man to him giuen had;
> For God he often saw from heauens hight,
> All were his earthly eyen both blunt and bad,
> And through great age had lost their kindly sight,
> Yet wondrous quick and persant was his spright,
> As Eagles eye, that can behold the Sunne.
>
> (I. x. 47)

There is more to Contemplation than meets the eye. In the tradition of the blind seer, he draws attention to the commonplace notion that spiritual understanding is not dependent upon sense perception. But, having established Contemplation's spiritual as opposed to his visual perception, Spenser then introduces the final image of an eagle looking at the sun. This somewhat mysterious image by comparing spiritual insight to the ability to gaze into the centre of a blinding light points towards a further paradox in Spenser's treatment of spiritual and literary faith. While spiritual insight may be hindered by visual perception, ultimately, it is only by contemplating the source and extent of its own blindness that true insight can be gained. This, or something akin to this, is suggested by Paul de Man with reference to what he terms the 'crisis of criticism' in the introduction to his book *Blindness and Insight: Essays in the Rhetoric of Contemporary Criticism*, from which the title of this section is derived:

> In the same manner that the poetic lyric originates in moments of tranquillity, in the absence of actual emotions, and then proceeds to invent fictional emotions to create the illusion of

Metaphor as an Act of Faith 71

recollection, the work of fiction invents fictional subjects to create the illusion of the reality of others. But the fiction is not myth, for it knows and names itself as fiction. It is not a demystification, it is demystified from the start. When modern critics think they are demystifying literature, they are in fact being demystified by it; but since this necessarily occurs in the form of a crisis, they are blind to what takes place within themselves. At the moment that they claim to do away with literature, literature is everywhere; what they call anthropology, linguistics, psychoanalysis is nothing but literature reappearing, like the Hydra's head, in the very spot where it had supposedly been suppressed. The human mind will go through amazing feats of distortion to avoid facing 'the nothingness of human matters.'[41]

This is why Paul de Man argues 'that all true criticism occurs in the mode of crisis', questioning itself, seeking what it can only find when it contemplates the centre of its own delusions and discovers, instead of the absence of something, the presence of nothingness.[42]

In *The Faerie Queene*, the crisis of criticism – the fear of perpetual hermeneutic loss – is located in the structure of metaphor. As many modern theorists point out (especially those like Max Black and Lakoff and Johnson, who claim most about the conceptual and creative function of metaphor),[43] metaphor is structured in such a way that it can never be static or complete:

> The very systematicity that allows us to comprehend one aspect of a concept in terms of another . . . will necessarily hide other aspects of the concept. In allowing us to focus on one aspect of a concept . . . a metaphorical concept can keep us from focusing on other aspects of the concept that are inconsistent with that metaphor. . . . It is important to see that the metaphorical structuring involved here is partial, not total. If it were total, one concept would actually *be* the other, not merely be understood in terms of it.[44]

Metaphor is a structure of incompletion, a means of revelation that can never reveal all at once. The very source of its mysterious educative and heuristic powers stems from its structural blind spots, that can be contemplated and explored, but never removed without obliterating metaphor itself. When Redcrosse returns from the Mount of Contemplation, a mountain Spenser carefully associates with both spiritual and poetic revelation, his discoveries about his identity and his position within the divine plan leave him dazzled and momentarily blinded:

> This said, adowne he looked to the ground,
> To haue returnd, but dazed were his eyne,
> Through passing brightnesse, which did quite confound
> His feeble sence, and too exceeding shyne.
>
> (I. x. 67)

Redcrosse, whose desire for self-knowledge mirrors the reader's desire for knowledge of the text, here reflects the sense of blindness that must always accompany metaphoric insight. It is a blindness that, as a structured component of the insight, must be rigorously and perpetually contemplated if self-mystification is to be avoided.

The text of *The Faerie Queene*, by repeatedly addressing itself to the problem of the authority and purpose of its own metaphors, opens up the same cycle of questions in relation to the literary text which Paul de Man associates with the crisis in criticism:

> We can speak of crisis when a 'separation' takes place, by self-reflection, between what, in literature, is in conformity with the original intent and what has irrevocably fallen away from this source. Our question in relation to contemporary criticism then becomes: Is criticism indeed engaged in scrutinizing itself to the point of reflecting on its own origin? Is it asking whether it is necessary for the act of criticism to take place?[45]

Should the literary text too define itself in terms of origins rather than destinations? Is Spenser's serpentine narrative in the process of swallowing its own tale? In *The Sense of an Ending*, Frank Kermode writes of the association between fictional narratives and human lives:

> Men, like poets, rush 'into the middest,' *in medias res*, when they are born; they also die *in mediis rebus*, and to make sense of their span they need fictive concords with origins and ends,

Metaphor as an Act of Faith

such as give meaning to lives and to poems. The End they imagine will reflect their irreducibly intermediary preoccupations. They fear it, and as far as we can see have always done so; the End is a figure for their own deaths. (So, perhaps, are all ends in fiction).[46]

Men may fear death as children fear to go into the dark, because of the unknown, a fear of what might be, but perhaps worse still is the fear of the what might not be, 'the nothingness of human matters.'[47] And just as fearful as this empty sense of an ending is the absence of a beginning. Beginnings provide a cause that suggests causality and progression towards an effect. Find the beginning and one may well find the end and, in so doing make sense of the intermediate by creating what Frank Kermode refers to as 'almost another way of describing what we call "form"':

> 'An inter-connexion of parts all mutually implied'; a duration (rather than a space) organizing the moment in terms of the end, giving meaning to the interval between *tick* and *tock* because we humanly do not want it to be an indeterminate interval between the *tick* of birth and the *tock* of death.[48]

Frank Kermode privileges the end because his study has a vested interest in concepts of closure. But, clearly, the *tock* would remain formless without the *tick*; an end implies a beginning and a beginning implies an end. They are mutually interdependent; you can't have one without the other. The search for an order to the apparent chaos of existence can consequently take one of two directions, and there is no reason not to assume, like Abel Tillfauges at the opening of Michel Tournier's novel *The Erl-King*, that the beginning, as preceding the end, should be given priority:

> And I do believe I issued from the mists of time. I've always been shocked at the frivolous way people agonize about what's going to happen to them after they die and don't give a damn about what happened to them before they were born. The heretofore is just as important as the hereafter, especially as it probably holds the key to it.[49]

Religion has always known this. The human need for beginnings is just as strong as its desire for endings. It is not just the promise of a hereafter that makes religion so reassuring, it is also the firm commitment to an origin, enshrined in the various creation myths. The ideal beginning, like Christianity's, finds in its origin the source of its conclusion. Genesis generates the entire biblical narrative, envisaging Paradise regained in Paradise lost, the Resurrection in the Fall – 'an inter-connexion of parts all mutually implied'. Take away the beginning, replace creationism with evolution and things fall apart, the centre cannot hold. The certainty of contained duration is replaced by the confusion of unending sequence. Unable to begin at the beginning, the moment of origin must be sought in reflection on the process it must have once engendered.

The historian, the archaeologist, the palaeontologist: men at the forefront of this quest to rediscover the past by reclaiming it from the mists of time know only too well that the history of the world, like that of the individual's conception of the self in William Golding's novel *Free Fall*, is a frustrating battle against permanent loss. The individual originates in the individual's own consciousness, but only at the point when his memory has retained the past. He can never fully know, therefore, those parts of his own life which have been wiped from the tablet of his memory. The historiographic disciplines, likewise, can only construct a concept of origin out of those fragments of the past which come to light, never knowing what has been irremediably lost. To perpetuate the search, the belief in the ultimate attainment of the origin must be maintained, like the fragmented body of Osiris, to be gradually reclaimed by a process of progressive retrieval, ending with the eventual reconstruction of the complete original. That it is a myth does not matter, the original must be believed in, if it is to be sought at all. Sir Walter Raleigh knew this and acknowledged in *The History of the World* that the question of origin is not ultimately answered by the biblical creation myth:

> And therefore (saith *Mirandula*) wee ought to loue God *Ex fide* and *ex effectibus*, (that is) both perswaded by his word; and by the effects of the worlds creation... For he of whome there is no higher cause, cannot bee knowne by any knowledge of cause or beginning, (saith *Montanus*) but either by the obseruing and conferring of things, which he hath, or doth create and gouerne, or else by the word of God himselfe.[50]

Perhaps this is why *The Faerie Queene* begins and ends *in medias res*. In the prefatory letter to Sir Walter Raleigh, Spenser suggests a beginning and an end for the poem, that in both cases would be set in the court of the Faerie Queene, but which are only ever conceived outside the text of the poem itself. The origin and destination of the poem are thus singularly located and only to be discovered in the contemplation of the narrative process, by examining the text of the poem and not 'by any knowledge of cause or beginning'. Presumably, the irony of the address would not have been lost on Raleigh.

The Faerie Queene's endemic self-referentiality can now be better understood. It results from the recognition that only by rigorous self-scrutiny can text and reader develop an awareness of the dynamic interplay of textual relations which define the literary process that has consumed its own origin and destiny. Metaphor, as the structuring principle of *The Faerie Queene*, must ultimately be trusted '*Ex fide*, and *ex effectibus*'. That is why Book I associates metaphor directly with religious faith. This chapter, having examined metaphor as an act of faith, must now give way to an examination of its effects in a less specifically Christian environment. The next chapter will explore the processes of metaphoric discourse in the hope of minimizing blindness and maximizing insight.

2
Metaphor as a Process of Change

METAPHOR, METAMORPHOSIS AND EMBLEM

Patricia Parker has shown how, in certain texts, what she terms 'metaphoric plots' develop, in which the rhetorical language used to discuss metaphor gives rise to distinctive narrative scenarios.[1] The most prominent metaphors embedded in rhetorical definitions of metaphor generate narratives of rivalry, usurpation and deception, in which the impostor, usurper or deceiver enacts the figurative's attempt to displace literal words from their 'proper' place.

The Faerie Queene contains numerous episodes which appear to read as perfect examples of such 'metaphoric plots'. The deceptions and displacements of Archimago and Duessa in Book I immediately come to mind; their very names link them to the image-making and duplicity rhetorically associated with metaphor. Thus, reading in a translative sense: Truth (Una/the one) is replaced by Falsehood (Duessa/duality) after Hypocrisy (Archimago/the archetypal image-maker) has separated Truth from Holiness (Redcrosse/wholeness). The figurative abuse which produces the mystification of literal language is the 'metaphoric plot' enacted by Una's wanderings in the wilderness. But this is neither the whole story, nor is it an entirely accurate account of the opening of Book I. What it overlooks is the 'hermeneutic plot': the interpretational nature of Redcrosse's quest which the last chapter examined.

The Faerie Queene complicates the 'metaphoric plot' by emphasizing the tension between literal and metaphoric discourse in the act of reading and interpreting. The text is finally written only when it is read. Textual 'truth' relies upon the reader and the process of decoding just as much, if not more than, the writer and the process of encoding; Redcrosse, the text's own surrogate reader, performs this 'hermeneutic plot'. He sets off with Una by his side, but unable to read the symbolic nature of his world has still to learn to understand her. There is clearly no point in having literal truth if you cannot understand it: possession may be nine-tenths of the law, but in the textual case it is worthless. The only grounds for possession there are interpretational; right reading is not proved by mere appropriation of the facts. From the start, the interpretational problem is stressed in the paradoxical nature of Una herself. If literal truth is present, it cannot be clearly seen, but remains hidden beneath a black stole. Book I is devoted to realizing the means by which a metaphoric reading can gradually lead towards a descriptive comprehension of the literal, showing how metaphors reveal truths. Archimago and Duessa are image-makers, but false ones, who attempt to reduce metaphor to a shabby imitation of the literal.

This violent displacement of the literal by the figurative in *The Faerie Queene* is just as much an abuse of the figurative as it is of the literal. In the hands of the poem's detractors, metaphor is turned into a nominative parody of the literal, instead of its predicative redescription. The 'metaphoric plot' of *The Faerie Queene* assumes a symbiotic relationship between the figurative and literal. The real battle is not between figurative and literal uses of words, but between alternative uses of figurative language. False metaphor is reductive and like the metaphor of Patricia Parker's 'metaphoric plot' is seen to imitate the literal in order to usurp its position. But true metaphor is expansive, striving to explain an otherwise illusive and incomprehensible literal world by offering alternative ways of interpreting it. Thus, metaphor is paradoxically transformed from the enemy of the literal into its redeemer, offering the only means of developing a deeper understanding of it. The figurative can explore and potentially explain the literal without trying to replace it. In emphasizing the importance of metaphor as an heuristic device assisting the hermeneutic process, Spenser displaces the usual opposition between literal and figurative discourse that pervades the pages of traditional rhetorics. Metaphor is only false when it pretends to be what it is not, when it sports the clothing of the literal. Archimago and Duessa perform precisely this metaphoric abuse, pretending to be figures they are not, practising the art of false nomination. Their defeat, however, cannot be achieved by literal discourse or predicative metaphor without the mediation of the reader's interpretation. Literal truth is revealed at the same moment metaphoric abuse is exposed – when Redcrosse has learnt to resist the temptation to read metaphor nominatively and gained insight into its predicative function.

In avoiding the metaphoric reductiveness of Despair and following the teachings of Contemplation, Redcrosse attained the metaphoric knowledge that enabled him to complete his quest. His final battle with the dragon – a mythical creature that had taken on a pseudo-literalness of its own through its representation in medieval and Renaissance bestiaries – provides a fitting climax. The 'dreadfull Dragon' (I. xi. 4), as figurative abuse, cannot be physically overcome by literal weapons: 'That nought mote perce, ne might his corse be harmd / With dint of sword, nor push of pointed speare' (I. xi. 9). Like the dragoness Errour, of Redcrosse's first encounter, this monster too possesses a 'huge long tayle wound vp in hundred foldes' (I. xi. 11) and a frightful, destructive mouth. Redcrosse's victory can only be achieved with the assistance of the restorative waters flowing from both *'The well of life'* (I. xi. 29) and *'The tree of life'* (I. xi. 46). His symbolic redemption allows him to overcome the distorting forces of false figuration, with the final defeat of the dragon enacting the symbolic overthrow of deformed figurative abuse at its very source:

> The weapon bright
> Taking aduantage of his open iaw,
> Ran through his mouth with so importune might,
> That deepe emperst his darksome hollow maw,
> And back retyrd, his life bloud forth with all did draw.
>
> (I. xi. 53)

His figurative foe defeated, pierced through the mouth and revealed for what it is,[2] Una can emerge from beneath her veil, figuratively understood:

> So faire and fresh, as freshest flowre in May;
> For she had layd her mournefull stole aside,
> And widow-like sad wimple throwne away,
> Wherewith her heauenly beautie she did hide,
> Whiles on her wearie iourney she did ride;

Metaphor as a Process of Change

> And on her now a garment she did weare,
> All lilly white, withoutten spot, or pride,
> That seemd like silke and siluer wouen neare,
> But neither silke nor siluer therein did appeare.
>
> The blazing brightnesse of her beauties beame,
> And glorious light of her sunshyny face
> To tell, were as to striue against the streame.
> My ragged rimes are all too rude and bace,
> Her heauenly lineaments for to enchace.
>
> (I. xii. 22–3)

The unveiling of truth is achieved by proper metaphoric reading – or is it? This passage, like the arrival of Archimago bearing Duessa's false letters that follows it, is provocative rather than conclusive. Una might have 'layd her mournefull stole aside' and 'sad wimple throwne away' but how much more clearly is she seen? The description of her is highly figurative; if this is the unveiling of literal truth, it is only achieved in terms of the metaphoric. The literal sounding 'So faire and fresh' is immediately consumed after the caesura by the translation of the terms into the context of a figurative phrase 'as freshest flowre in May'. The same is true of the garment she wears. The colour is figuratively and symbolically described as 'lilly white, withoutten spot, or pride', while the material, although 'like silke and siluer wouen neare', has neither silk nor silver in it. Una's dress, like Una herself, is strangely seen and not seen. The description of her face, hidden by its own brightness is reminiscent of both Redcrosse's vision from the Mount of Contemplation and Spenser's reference to the nature of his own poetic composition in the fifth stanza of the Proem to Book II:

> The which O pardon me thus to enfold
> In couert vele, and wrap in shadowes light,
> That feeble eyes your glory may behold,
> Which else could not endure those beames bright,
> But would be dazled with exceeding light.
>
> (II. Proem. 5)

The sun, the 'blazing brightnesse' that dazzles those who look at or into it, recurs as an image for truth throughout *The Faerie Queene*, with poetry as the veil or shadow that enables it to be known at all. In *The Faerie Queene*, truth, literal truth, consequently has a tendency to disappear at the moment of its own revelation. What is left behind is a figurative representation, 'her sunshyny face', which the poet's 'ragged rimes' must strive 'to enchace' as best they can.

The self-referential commentary on the limitations of poetic images appears here, as elsewhere, just as the poem approaches a moment of insight and potential closure. *The Faerie Queene* thus locates the limit of metaphor; it is doomed to see and not to see, to understand and not to understand, for the structural reason F.E. Sparshott describes:

> There is a sense in which every metaphor does call a thing what it is not, or say that it does what it does not do, or imply that it is like what it is not like.[3]

Metaphor functions via this trick or negative capability, perceiving things as they are not, to discover things about how they are. For, like the man with the blue guitar in Wallace Stevens's poem of that title, the poet can never sing 'Of things exactly as they are' because 'Things as they are / Are changed upon the blue guitar'[4] of metaphor. The predicative process of metaphor cannot attain the final nominative act, naming the subject it describes as itself. The moment something is called by its own name, metaphor is eliminated. Metaphor is not when things are or are thought to be as they are. It can begin to define its world; it can know when something is not what it claims to be, just as Archimago and Duessa are finally recognized as impostors. But metaphor can never know or refer to the literal for what it is. The limit of metaphor is identity; it thrives on otherness and must, consequently, contemplate its own blindness and loss at the moment of its greatest insight – in the perception of 'the similarity of dissimilars'. Its goal is not, therefore, to name or supplant the literal, but to explore and explain it. Metaphor strives after neither identity nor irreconcilability but to evoke a tension somewhere between the two in an awareness of the system of correspondences and relationships that sustains it.

The 'metaphoric plot' of Book I thus proffers a view of metaphor that has rather more in common with recent interaction theories than the substitution theory of traditional rhetorical definitions of metaphor. Metaphor, as interaction, goes beyond mere lexical deviance; rather than an act of false nomination, metaphor is seen as a process of predication that leads directly to semantic innovation in the manner Paul Ricoeur describes:

> In other words, metaphorical meaning does not merely consist of a semantic clash but of the *new* predicative meaning which emerges from the collapse of the literal meaning, that is, from the collapse of the meaning which obtains if we rely only on the common or usual lexical values of our words.[5]

This relation between the literal deviance of metaphor at the lexical level and its new figurative acceptability at a contextual level pinpoints the crucial development involved in the metaphoric process.

Metamorphosis, as a prominent and recurrent process in *The Faerie Queene*, presents itself as a highly plausible 'metaphoric plot' exploring the workings of the metaphoric process within the text. The words metaphor and metamorphosis are etymologically linked, an association brought out by the definitions in Thomas Elyot's *Dictionary 1538*, where the words appear consecutively:

> Metamorphosis, eos, a transformation or chaungynge of fygure.
>
> Metaphora, a translation of wordes frome their propre sygnifycation.[6]

The use of the phrase 'a chaungynge of fygure' is presumably no more than a coincidence, drawing attention to the metaphoric use of the word 'fygure' when it is applied to linguistic tropes. Nevertheless, it does point to a potentially fruitful relation between the two words. Metamorphosis constitutes the action or process of change of form, substance or state; but metaphor also involves a process of change in the alteration of the meaning of words within the figure or trope itself. In *The Faerie Queene*, narratives of metamorphosis might reasonably be expected to act as a means of literalizing, in the form of a physical transformation, the figurative translation that is performed during the metaphoric process. The collapse of the original form would correspond to the initial moment of lexical deviation of metaphor, while the shaping and emergence of a new form would correspond to the metaphoric tension that creates a new contextual meaning and semantic disclosure. Metamorphosis, in capturing this movement from an inconsistent statement for a literal interpretation to a meaningful statement for a figurative interpretation, could thus enact, in its own magical transformation, the mysterious secret of the 'metaphoric twist'.[7]

There is no finer or more extensive example of metamorphosis in The Faerie Queene with which to investigate this hypothesis than the transformation of the miserly old cuckold Malbecco into the monster Gealosie. Although the metamorphosis is confined to the final seven stanzas of the tenth canto of Book III, the two preceding cantos establish the narrative environment out of which the metamorphosis eventually emerges. What Malbecco becomes is dependent upon what he was; his final metamorphosis is to be seen as the extension of his archetypal narrative character. The squire's opening description of Malbecco introduces several traits that will feature prominently when the metamorphosis takes place:

> But he is old, and withered like hay,
>   Vnfit faire Ladies seruice to supply;
>   The priuie guilt whereof makes him alway
>   Suspect her truth, and keepe continuall spy
>   Vpon her with his other blincked eye;
>   Ne suffreth he resort of liuing wight
>   Approch to her, ne keepe her company.

(III. ix. 5)

Malbecco's 'gealous feares' (III. ix. 4) that cause him to closet his wife away create for him, out of his own castle, a prison environment apart from society. Right from the start, Malbecco hideously distorts the world he lives in.

The final grotesque distortion his own body undergoes is, in this respect, the inevitable transformation of a man's moral and psychological degeneration into its own allegorical representation, that is not unlike the view Golding holds of the purpose of metamorphosis in the Preface to his translation of Ovid's *Metamorphosis*:

So was *Elpenor* and his mates transformed intoo swyne,
For following of theyr filthie lust in women and in wyne.
Not that they lost theyr manly shape as too the outward showe:
But for that in their brutish brestes most beastly lustes did growe.[8]

Golding talks of metamorphosis as a representation of a moral state rather than a change in physical form. It is a man's spiritual condition that precedes and dictates the depiction of his outward shape which, as Golding is at pains to point out, is not necessarily to be thought of as a physical change at all. Metamorphosis is here conceived of primarily as a means of applying an appropriate image or symbol to a man's moral or psychological condition. Metamorphosis creates moral emblems.

That Spenser sometimes used metamorphosis in an overtly emblematic manner is apparent from the concluding stanzas of the Bower of Bliss episode. The Palmer replies to Guyon's question: 'what meant those beastes, which there did ly' (II. xii. 84), the phrasing of which presupposes their symbolic interpretation:

> These seeming beasts are men indeed,
> Whom this Enchauntresse hath transformed thus,
> Whylome her louers, which her lusts did feed,
> Now turned into figures hideous,
> According to their mindes like monstruous.
>
> (II. xii. 85)

The use of metamorphosis to translate a state of mental depravity into a picture of physical monstrosity clearly has a direct but limited application. In the end, it is probably more similar to the denomination associated with dead metaphor or cliché than the predication of new emerging meaning of fresh metaphor. When a sententious passage requires moral reinforcement, such metamorphic exemplars are ideal. The presence of Grill at the end of Book II provides the perfect emblem to plant in the mind of the reader, serving much the function of an epigrammatic maxim:

> But one aboue the rest in speciall,
> That had an hog beene late, hight *Grille* by name,

> Repined greatly, and did him miscall,
> That had from hoggish forme him brought to naturall.
>
> Said *Guyon*, See the mind of beastly man,
> That hath so soone forgot the excellence
> Of his creation, when he life began,
> That now he chooseth, with vile difference,
> To be a beast, and lacke intelligence.
> To whom the Palmer thus, The donghill kind
> Delights in filth and foule incontinence:
> Let *Grill* be *Grill*, and haue his hoggish mind.
>
> (II. xii. 86–7)

'Let *Grill* be *Grill*'. Nomination has taken place, and with it Grill's nature is defined once and for all. No metamorphosis can change him, no metaphor can be applied within this closed moral context. His outward shape is now irrelevant; he may look like a man, but it is his 'hoggish mind' that now identifies him. Metamorphosis, in this passage, is not required to act dynamically or alter perceptions but rather to strengthen established moral attitudes. The literary tradition from which the character of Grill is drawn leaves no room for doubt. Grill is a swine, an established literary figure,[9] an ideal moral coda acting in much the fashion of a dead metaphor.

Malbecco's metamorphosis must clearly do much more than show a man becoming the emblem of his own passion, if it is to be seen as a metaphor for the dynamic process of predicative metaphor. Emblems function mainly visually and seek to fix meaning in static images. Metaphor, however, as something that happens to words, is a verbal phenomenon that actively seeks to undermine static conceptualization. Emblem and metaphor, the visual and the verbal are not naturally compatible. The truly metaphoric text must resist the pictorial stability of the emblematic, if it is to maintain the investigative restlessness of its own metaphoricity.

The first hint that Malbecco's passion could lead to a hideous physical transformation begins by articulating something of this opposition between the emblematic and metaphoric, the visual and verbal potentialities of metamorphosis:

> Which when *Malbecco* saw, out of his bush
> Vpon his hands and feete he crept full light,

> And like a Gote emongst the Gotes did rush,
> That through the helpe of his faire hornes on hight,
> And misty dampe of misconceiuing night,
> And eke through likenesse of his gotish beard,
> He did the better counterfeite aright.
>
> (III. x. 47)

Spenser's commentators have, in the past, had trouble with Malbecco's horns. Jortin commented:

> He gives Malbecco a pair of real horns because he was a cuckold, which is descending very low.[10]

And in a similar vein, Warton objected:

> Malbecco's similitude is made out by his horns, which he wears as a cuckold; a fiction, the meanness of which nothing but the beautiful transformation, at the end of the canto, could have made amends for.[11]

Jortin and Warton are in full agreement: Malbecco's horns, as the figurative attributes of a cuckold, are not real horns and have no right to be there as part of his attempt to look like a goat. They assume, of course, that Malbecco's enactment of the etymological derivation of his own name (Mal: male; becco: buckgoat, then virtually a synonym for cuckold)[12] is to be considered in literal and primarily visual terms. Thus, while Malbecco can quite feasibly get down on all fours with his beard, in the circumstances, being seen to look like a goat's, the horns, having no counterpart in Malbecco's physical behaviour or appearance, should not participate in the description.

In recognizing the inconsistency, Jortin and Warton completely miss the point. The horns are not a mean fiction, they are an inspired invention, drawing attention to the fundamental difference between description as visual representation and as verbal event. At the verbal level, Malbecco's horns can remain purely figurative; they break no linguistic rules and there is no problem. It is only if they are assumed to be literally and pictorially present that the passage breaks down because there are plainly no real horns to be seen. In exposing the conflict between the visual and verbal aspects of a text, the passage exhibits the natural opposition between the figurative playfulness of metaphor and the literal morality of emblem. It is not an opposition that is accidentally evoked, as Jortin and Warton presume. It is wittily and deliberately fostered to frustrate the literal minded reader's desire for textual conformity. The joke becomes more obvious if one considers the line in which Spenser refers to the assistance Malbecco's deception receives from the 'misty dampe of misconceiuing night'. Malbecco's horns can hardly become less conspicuous if they were never present in the first place. They must either be accepted verbally or not at all. Just like metaphor itself, they challenge the reason, demanding the rejection of the comfortable but confined limits of the literal for the volatile and unlimited potential of the metaphoric.

When Malbecco's metamorphosis proper begins in the fifty-fourth stanza, it is as an extension of this initial investigation of the relationship between the visual and the verbal, the emblematic and metaphoric aspects of the text. It is set in motion by a sequence of events which, in fulfilling Malbecco's worst fears, threaten to remove the causes of his jealousy. Dictionary definitions of the state of jealousy, whether with regard to material possessions or love, stress it as a state of anxiety arising from the apprehension of suspected or imagined loss, as the *OED* makes clear:

> Troubled by the belief, suspicion, or fear that the good which one desires to gain or keep for oneself has been or may be diverted to another; resentful towards another on account of known or suspected rivalry (*OED*, 4).

Malbecco no longer distrusts his wife or suspects a rival. If a man ever needed his suspicions proved, then Hellenore's antics with the satyrs provide incontrovertible ocular and aural proof:

> At night, when all they went to sleepe, he vewd,
> Whereas his louely wife emongst them lay,
> Embraced of a *Satyre* rough and rude,
> Who all the night did minde his ioyous play:
> Nine times he heard him come aloft ere day.
>
> (III. x. 48)

Malbecco, having witnessed the grotesque display of his wife's unfaithfulness, then returns to find that his other love, his gold, has been stolen from its hiding place too. The sudden realization of all his 'gealous feares' (I. ix. 4) confronts Malbecco with the reality he had previously only projected, thereby destroying the anxiety on which his passion fed. A narrative impasse has been created, and Malbecco's narrative must be permanently arrested, if he is to be remembered as a representation of jealousy.

The metamorphosis of Malbecco into Gealosie is paradoxically designed to terminate the narrative of the jealous man by turning him into the emblem of his own passion. The impression of a process of change taking place is largely illusory. There is nothing here of the metaphoric tension involved in coming to terms with a radically new way of perceiving things as they are, by thinking of them as they are not. Malbecco is not seen afresh, he is simply mapped onto a traditional system of received commonplaces. He undergoes no real alteration in acquiring the external features and attributes that allow his character to be replaced by its own personification. What Malbecco flees in his wild fury is the termination of his narrative existence, the mortification of his character that its emblematization will bring about:

> High ouer hilles and ouer dales he fled,
> As if the wind him on his winges had borne,
> Ne banck nor bush could stay him, when he sped
> His nimble feet, as treading still on thorne:
> Griefe, and despight, and gealosie, and scorne
> Did all the way him follow hard behind,
> And he himselfe himselfe loath'd so forlorne,
> So shamefully forlorne of womankind;
> That as a Snake, still lurked in his wounded mind.
>
> (III. x. 55)

Malbecco carries within himself the fear he is running away from. His actions are entirely self-defeating, just as shortly they are to become self-destructive. The episode is imbued with a sense of frustration and pointlessness encapsulated in the extensive use of oxymoron. Malbecco's own hatred is directed inwards against himself, while the impression of rapid flight and desperate action is negated by its self-evident futility. Malbecco has nowhere to go, having already become what he must now be the emblem of; there is no escape. In the extraordinary pursuit of Malbecco by his own feelings, what we witness is the flight of a character from his textual destiny as a personification. 'Griefe, and despight, and gealosie, and scorne' are simultaneously internal and external to Malbecco, ambiguously inviting the reader to assume they are personifications, while lacking the capitalization that would make them undeniably so. Malbecco is poised on the verge of personification, still clinging to a semblance of his previous narrative identity. The conventional iconic attributes of jealousy – the horns and the snake – now participate in the description, but in the form of similes they have not yet achieved the full independence of true emblem. While they remain similes, they succumb to the semantic inconclusiveness of metaphor, still functioning as verbal structures that cannot easily be conceived as visual images.

Metaphor and emblem stand in direct opposition at this point in Malbecco's metamorphosis. The emblematic features strive to create a fixed representation of a character's passion that can take his place; metaphor resists the finality of such an emblem in an attempt to perpetuate the exploratory analysis of jealousy. This crucial difference between the substitution of emblem and the interaction of metaphor again surfaces in the next stage of Malbecco's metamorphosis, after he has thrown himself from the 'rockie hill' (III. x. 56):

> From thence he threw himselfe dispiteously,
> All desperate of his fore-damned spright,
> That seem'd no helpe for him was left in liuing sight.
>
> But through long anguish, and selfe-murdring thought
> He was so wasted and forpined quight,
> That all his substance was consum'd to nought,
> And nothing left, but like an aery Spright,
> That on the rockes he fell so flit and light,
> That he thereby receiu'd no hurt at all,
> But chaunced on a craggy cliff to light;
> Whence he with crooked clawes so long did crall,
> That at the last he found a caue with entrance small.

(III. x. 56–7)

Malbecco's metamorphosis hangs between the semantic inventiveness of metaphor and the reassuring definitiveness of emblem. Malbecco's leap from the cliff top glimpses the cognitive crisis that is undergone during the metaphoric process, a moment when things are and are not. Metaphor demands a dangerous leap in the dark, a confrontation with semantic disorientation before a new perception of reality can be achieved, as Paul Ricoeur explains:

> To summarize, poetic language is no less *about* reality than any other use of language but refers to it by the means of a complex strategy which implies, as an essential component, a suspension and seemingly an abolition of the ordinary reference attached to descriptive language. This suspension, however, is only the negative condition of a second-order reference, of an indirect reference built on the ruins of the direct reference.[13]

To abandon the known for the as yet unknown, the world of literal concepts for a world of figurative conceptions, involves a pseudo-suicidal 'selfe-murdring thought' – a glance at death – out of which a faith in the metaphoric act develops. Only if the leap is taken, or is willing to be taken, can metaphoric faith be born; just as for Gloucester in *King Lear*, it is only after Edgar convinces him he has fallen from Dover Cliff that he can accept the miracle of divine redemption. Once more, the link between the metaphoric act and an act of faith surfaces; the 'metaphoric twist' is a metaphoric miracle. The ability to metaphorize well is not just a gift of genius as Aristotle thought it, it is also an act of bravery that pushes the metaphorizer to the brink of insanity. The maker of metaphor relies as heavily on his ability to survive the collapse of a known order as on his perception of a new order. William Blake, whose own visionary writings had him frequently branded a madman, knew only too well the dangers involved in questioning the accepted structures of perceived reality. He describes in his own idiosyncratic way, both the fear and eventual euphoria experienced by the metaphoric 'seer' in *The Marriage of Heaven and Hell*, when the terrifying approach of a leviathan suddenly vanishes and the narrator finds himself in a pastoral setting, listening to a harper whose aphoristic theme is:

> 'The man who never alters his opinion is like standing water, and breeds reptiles of the mind.'[14]

But Malbecco's metamorphosis is not of this order. He is 'consum'd to nought' to make way for the monstrous personification that is to replace him. The appearance of his 'crooked clawes' starts because they are metaphorically conceived, introducing a sudden semantic clash that demands figurative reinterpretation. Malbecco, as a man, does not possess claws; the lexical deviation must be accommodated in an alternative, figurative context where Malbecco is a monster. The metamorphosis of Malbecco thus testifies to the power and vitality of metaphor even as it plots the elimination of the semantic tension it generates. When the completed emblematic figure of jealousy finally obliterates the memory of Malbecco the man, it denies its own origin in the metaphoric process that generated it. Emblem cannot exist like metaphor in the midst of contextual fluctuation; it demands the stability of signifier and signified, a closed denotative system of symbols. The emblematic cannot stand in the textual lacunae that the dynamic process of metaphoric redefinition creates. It must wait until metaphor is dead, and then, like Errour's unnatural brood, feed on the remains of its progenitor.

The next stanza reveals how the monstrous figure which Malbecco is turning into, is related to the character the narrative first presented. Malbecco is not two different figures at the beginning and end of his metamorphosis, as the finished emblem would have us believe; he is the same character throughout, displayed, at the end, as a version of what he always was. The paranoid environment Malbecco now inhabits is merely a figurative extension of his former world, the grotesque fulfilment of his masochistic passion:

> Into the same he creepes, and thenceforth there
> Resolu'd to build his balefull mansion,
> In drery darkenesse, and continuall feare
> Of that rockes fall, which euer and anon
> Threates with huge ruine him to fall vpon,
> That he dare neuer sleepe, but that one eye
> Still ope he keepes for that occasion;
> Ne euer rests he in tranquillity,
> The roring billowes beat his bowre so boystrously.
>
> (III. x. 58)

Malbecco has turned into a new figure that is really the external representation of the deformity that was within him. The description, therefore, highlights one of the most prominent features of Malbecco's earlier existence and transforms it into a central image defining the environment of the monster he has become. In Malbecco's case, keeping an eye on his wife (his one eye) was ever a traumatic experience. The seasoned seducer Paridell never misses an opportunity to seat himself on Malbecco's blind side: 'But his blind eye, that syded *Paridell*, / All his demeasnure from his sight did hyde' (III. ix. 27). Malbecco's original physical deformity now becomes a fearful image of impending doom, with his one eye perpetually open, fixed on the rock that threatens to fall and ruin him.

The anxiety of jealousy has been reconstructed and frozen in an image of perpetual dread. The 'balefull mansion' can now be recognized as an intensified version of the castle he inhabited before. Malbecco never used to be at ease, always fearful of new guests. Now, his tranquillity is disturbed by the 'roring billowes' which buffet his cave. The process of metamorphosis struggles to maintain this interaction of images that metaphor demands before the new, autonomous form of the established emblem disassociates itself completely from the tension of metaphor. The struggle between the descriptive understanding of metaphor and the moral definition sought by emblem comes to a head in the next stanza where disease takes the place of monstrosity as the underlying metaphor.

In his analysis of the iconography of the passage, Paul J. Alpers argues that the fifty-ninth stanza 'as it proceeds... moves from a physiological to a moral account of Malbecco's condition.'[15] This movement marks an abandonment of the searching inventiveness of active metaphor for the safe morality of emblem. The monster that has emerged is only truly monstrous in its attempts to deny the narrative history of the individual it grew out of and the metaphoric process that engendered it. For jealousy is not monstrous in itself; it is only monstrous as the human reality it manifests itself as. In *Othello*, it is not Iago's description of a 'green-eyed monster' that turns jealousy into a terrifying spectacle. It is the human reality of a man's happiness and nobility monstrously destroyed by his own passion that creates the sense of tragedy. The monstrousness of jealousy becomes oddly less monstrous if it becomes divorced from human lives. Othello wakes from his passion and examines his crime as a man, but Malbecco, at the end, forgets his human individuality completely. The emblem of jealousy is neither so affecting nor so profoundly disturbing as its living counterpart.

It is in the last stanza that the completed emblem can transfix the soul of Malbecco with the final anti-metaphoric act of nomination:

> Yet can he neuer dye, but dying liues,
> And doth himselfe with sorrow new sustaine,
> That death and life attonce vnto him giues.
> And painefull pleasure turnes to pleasing paine.
> There dwels he euer, miserable swaine,
> Hatefull both to him selfe, and euery wight;
> Where he through priuy griefe, and horrour vaine,
> Is woxen so deform'd, that he has quight
> Forgot he was a man, and *Gealosie* is hight.
>
> (III. x. 60)

Nomination arrests the investigative metaphoric process. When the final line of the stanza names Malbecco as Gealosie, his character becomes lexically and emblematically fixed. Nomination constitutes the death of metaphor, the establishment of a literal lexical context for words. Malbecco is called Gealosie and must forget the process that has allowed him to be so called. His metamorphosis has turned out to be nothing more than an external version of the sort of moral emblem Grill represents.

At the end, Malbecco is dehumanized and becomes a mere personification. The whole pattern of Spenserian allegory is reversed. Instead of initiating a narrative, metaphorically exploring an abstract concept, Malbecco's metamorphosis depicts the gradual loss of individual characterization and the reduction of a man into a word. The metamorphosis of Malbecco moves from one fixed state to another, and cannot remain as sheer process – a conflict between alternative states – in the manner of metaphor. His metamorphosis as an act of nomination stands opposed to the predicative structure of metaphor.

The final stanza encapsulates this deactivation of the metaphoric process and the final identification of the completed emblem. The interaction that generates the tension of metaphoric insight has been replaced by the self-negation of oxymoron. It is a state of living death in which 'painefull pleasure' turns into 'pleasing paine' in a final parody of dynamic metaphoric interaction. There is no verbal tension here, no semantic clash, merely a verbal inversion that points out its own pointlessness. Malbecco has been turned into the very concept his narrative was apparently designed to analyse. Metaphor cannot coexist with emblem, for where metaphor actively strives to create a clash of images, emblem, in contradistinction, seeks to replace one image with another to establish a complete and self-contained iconographic representation.

CONCEIVING METAPHORS OF LOVE

Metamorphosis as it is used in the Malbecco episode works against the dynamic spirit of metaphor because it focuses on the product of change. Like the transformation scene in Rouben Mamoulian's 1931 production of *Dr Jekyll and Mr Hyde*, Malbecco is described before and after his metamorphosis, implying a transformation has taken place, without actually showing the process at work. In Malbecco's case, this is not due to technical limitations but because his metamorphosis is illusory; his character is not altered in substance but only in name. He starts the narrative as Malbecco and finishes it as Gealosie, but to all intents and purposes he is still the same character. All the features which defined him as a traditional fabliau figure in the castle are present in the final emblematic description of him in the cave. Malbecco, having been turned from a stock character into an iconographic representation, has become what Angus Fletcher has termed an *idée fixe*[16] with all the obsessional qualities the psychological term implies.

This closing down of meaning within a system of rigidly defined symbols denies the exploratory function metaphor is granted elsewhere in *The Faerie Queene*. Metamorphosis, as such, is functioning definitively in much the same manner ascribed to metaphor under the various substitution theories, where any change that takes place via the metaphoric act is described at a purely lexical level, as false nomination. A different narrative model from metamorphosis needs to be found for the process of predication functioning at a semantic level and generating new images and ideas in the manner of metaphor in Book I.

The metaphor of conception, if only because of the ambiguity inherent in the term itself, makes a useful starting point. Jay L. Halio has found it an interesting metaphor with which to explore Elizabethan theories of the imagination and to establish:

> sufficient evidence that the imagination was not in their view merely a reproductive faculty of the intellect, but was frequently, and even essentially, creative.[17]

Imagination, as the faculty assigned to the poet in the Elizabethan age, was thus virtually synonymous with poetic creation. The natural transfer of the metaphor of conception from imagination in general, to poetry in particular, appears frequently in Elizabethan poetry as in the opening sonnet of *Astrophil and Stella*, where Sidney presents the sonneteer: 'Thus great with child to speake, and helplesse in my throwes'. It is on the basis of this underlying metaphoric concordance between physical and mental conception that I intend to examine firstly, the conception of Amoret and Belphoebe and secondly, Spenser's description of the creative process at work in the Garden of Adonis.

Amoret and Belphoebe stand within the narrative of the sixth canto as images of love and chastity. In the most obvious sense, therefore, they are allegorical figures representing the abstract concepts they are to enact. Spenser's treatment of the parthenogenesis of the twins, however, boldly inverts the normal allegorical pattern, so that instead of defining the concepts the figures stand for, Spenser explores the processes which generate such figures in the first place. In other words, the literal description of the conception of the figurative characters is being used metaphorically to examine the poet's own conception of allegorical narrative. When the story of the conception and birth of Amoret and Belphoebe is extended into the further presentation of the Garden of Adonis, what is being described is the whole literary process by which the creation of allegorical characters generates an entire allegorical environment through which they can be metaphorically understood.

The stanzas which tell how Chrysogone bathes in water and flowers on a warm sunny day, before falling asleep and being impregnated by the sun, evoke a narrative environment that is reminiscent of the opening of a particular genre of allegorical writing: the dream vision:

Metaphor as a Process of Change

> It was vpon a Sommers shynie day,
> When *Titan* faire his beames did display,
> In a fresh fountaine, farre from all mens vew,
> She bath'd her brest, the boyling heat t' allay;
> She bath'd with roses red, and violets blew,
> And all the sweetest flowres, that in the forrest grew.
>
> Till faint through irkesome wearinesse, adowne
> Vpon the grassie ground her selfe she layd
> To sleepe, the whiles a gentle slombring swowne
> Vpon her fell all naked bare displayd;
> The sunne-beames bright vpon her body playd,
> Being through former bathing mollifide,
> And pierst into her wombe, where they embayd
> With so sweet sence and secret power vnspide,
> That in her pregnant flesh they shortly fructifide.
>
> (III. vi. 6–7)

Similar features appear in the openings of all the following dream visions: *Piers Plowman*, *The Romaunt of the Rose*, *The Legend of Good Women* and *The Parliament of Fowles*. The description of Chrysogone's conception, by mirroring the depiction of the origin of allegorical visions, strengthens the association of poetic invention and natural conception, already inherent in the metaphor. The miraculous process described in the seventh stanza, however, involves an inversion of the natural order of conception. Chrysogone's flesh is described as 'pregnant' before the 'sunne-beames' have 'fructifide'. Their effect, therefore, is to bring to fruition something which already exists but lacks substance. In terms of human fertilization, this is quite the wrong way round; the flesh is not pregnant prior to conception but becomes so afterwards. In terms of the conception of an idea or image, however, the description is quite logical. Sidney's explanation of how a poet produces an image will help in this context. The terms Sidney uses are the 'idea', the 'foreconceit' and the 'conceit' and the creative act consists of a process of representation that requires that an ideal image (the idea) is first conceived by a writer as an image in his mind (the foreconceit) which he must then present as an image in the poem (the conceit). The final poetic image thus stands as a representation at the end of a creative process that is designed to bring to fruition an ideal that pre-exists the poem but which lacks substance. This order of events is precisely that which Spenser's description portrays; the miraculous conception that brings about the creation of Belphoebe and Amoret is the inspirational act of the poet (the play of the 'sunne-beames') that brings to life a pre-existing concept by giving it substance within the body of the poem.

In the next stanza, Spenser draws on the belief that strange creatures were born out of the action of the sun on the sediment left after the Nile's seasonal flooding, as a metaphor for the mysterious process of conception he has described:

> Miraculous may seeme to him, that reades
>   So straunge ensample of conception;
> But reason teacheth that the fruitfull seades
> Of all things liuing, through impression
> Of the sunbeames in moyst complexion,
>   Doe life conceiue and quickned are by kynd:
> So after *Nilus* invndation,
>   Infinite shapes of creatures men do fynd,
> Informed in the mud, on which the Sunne hath shynd.

(III. vi. 8)

It was an interest in the creatures formed after the inundation of the Nile, of course, which led to Mark Antony's attack on the descriptive inadequacies of non-metaphoric language.[18] Here, Spenser offers the reader a miraculous example of creation as a double metaphor, both for the conception of the twins in Chrysogone's womb and for the genesis of allegorical figures. Thus, the metaphor of conception, as normally employed by Elizabethan writers, has been given a clever twist. Conception, far from being represented as a natural process, is itself conceived in a miraculous manner that partly mystifies the enigma of metaphor as it professes to clarify it. What metaphor is seen to produce is new forms from existing matter: 'Infinite shapes of creatures men do fynd, / Informed in the mud, on which the Sunne hath shynd.'

Metaphor is like a generative force that has the power to transform matter by 'informing' new 'shapes' in lifeless material. The 1596 printing of these lines, where the word 'creatures' is in its singular form, makes the effect of metaphor even more apparent.

For metaphor does not produce infinite new creatures but infinite versions of the same creature, which 'Doe life conceiue and quickned are by kynd', or the act of metaphoric comparison. The creation of new life and the authorial generation of new metaphors are thus brought together in Spenser's miraculous metaphor of conception:

> Great father he of generation
> Is rightly cald, th'author of life and light;
> And his faire sister for creation
> Ministreth matter fit, which tempred right
> With heate and humour, breedes the liuing wight.
>
> (III. vi. 9)

The introduction of the term 'author' at this crucial moment in the text (just as it did in the Despair episode) ensures the metaphoric equation between God and writer.[19] Bringing literature to life is a matter of conceiving metaphoric associations that will ensure both a fresh and virtuous moral vision. Poetic composition is, therefore, inspirational but it must also be virtuous. The passage describing Belphoebe's conception, birth and upbringing, stresses the purity of the whole procedure which takes place while 'all the *Graces* rockt her cradle' (III. vi. 2):

> Her berth was of the wombe of Morning dew,
> And her conception of the ioyous Prime,
> And all her whole creation did her shew
> Pure and vnspotted from all loathly crime,
> That is ingenerate in fleshly slime.
> So was this virgin borne, so was she bred,
> So was she trayned vp from time to time,
> In all chast vertue, and true bounti-hed
> Till to her dew perfection she was ripened.
>
> (III. vi. 3)

Spenser's emphasis on the immaculate nature of Belphoebe's creation is thus linked via the metaphor of conception to the defence of poetry that surfaces throughout *The Faerie Queene*. The phrase 'all her whole creation', which ambiguously refers to both the act of creation and the figure created, emphasizes the control the poet should maintain over the figures he produces, from their conception to their fruition. If he neglects this responsibility, then he opens himself up to the charge of carelessness and potentially corruption.

The defence of poetry centres on this crucial issue – the poet's conscious control over his writing – and his capacity to maintain that control throughout the entire creative process. But while the passage is aware of the potential dangers, it celebrates the ideal poetic product in the form of the figure of Belphoebe. Poetry can never afford to become complacent about the forces that threaten to subvert it, but it should not forget that the source of its great power lies in its capacity to produce an endless number of figures that are 'Pure and vnspotted from all loathly crime, / That is ingenerate in fleshly slime.' Poets, because they are not tied to the actual but can work with the possible and the ideal, are able to keep their writing untainted by the immorality of the fallen world. But to do so, the poet must maintain rigorous control over the figures he creates, not just at their inception but throughout their poetic life. At the end of the stanza, Spenser therefore introduces the new metaphor of cultivation to describe the continued growth of Belphoebe's character.

This is typical of the metaphoric transformations that propel the narrative of *The Faerie Queene* and which are particularly prevalent in this canto. Spenser is able to shift quite naturally from a language associated with human birth to a language appropriate to the growth of plants. Thus, where he wishes to talk about the origin of Belphoebe, Spenser employs the terms 'berth', 'wombe', 'conception', 'creation', 'ingenerate', 'fleshly' and 'bred'. But as he moves on to consider her development, he follows the word 'bred' with 'trayned vp' and the final word of the stanza 'ripened'. Without drawing attention to the fact, Spenser has simply changed metaphor to find an appropriate means of expressing the development of his thought. There is nothing odd or inconsistent about this stanza which, after all, reads perfectly naturally. All Spenser has done is to adopt one metaphor in place of another, where the meaning he wished to convey was best served by transplanting the language of horticulture into a passage initially based on the language of conception.

Spenser's poetry demands an acceptance of this sort of metaphoric shift and many apparent inconsistencies melt away once the development of his poetry is plotted as a metaphoric exploration rather than a narrative sequence. Nowhere is this more apparent than in the Garden of Adonis where the logic of the episode defies linear progression. The sixth canto does not develop as a sequential narrative, it occupies an exploratory space for which the garden is itself an appropriate image (a plot of land, not a narrative plot).[20] As such, the garden is a self-contained image which the poet can cultivate at will to produce a fuller understanding by planting in it the images which best explore his subject. Once the organizing principle behind the Garden of Adonis is accepted as metaphoric and spatial rather than narrative and linear, the structure cannot only be more clearly perceived but is seen to proceed in a perfectly logical manner.

In order to understand this metaphoric structure, it is important to be quite clear about the positioning of the Garden of Adonis, not only within the sixth canto, but within Book III as a whole. If Book III is nominally about chastity, by the sixth canto it has become evident that chastity is not to be contemplated in isolation but in contrast to its counterpart love, to which it is for Britomart a response in any case as Harry Berger Jr has noted:

> Chastity is the response to love, and Britomart must learn not to suppress the force that impels her, but to accept it, suffer it, understand it, build up a habit of will which enables her to direct this energy to a higher goal in the enduring love of human persons.[21]

Chastity must not allow itself to become sterile any more than love should let itself become uncontrolled and wanton. Chastity and love must learn to control each other, thus tempering their own destructive extremes. Book III has plotted a pantheon of frustrated relationships where the paths of numerous men and women cross in a seemingly endless portrayal of thwarted love.

The figure of Florimell, who appears recurrently in Book III perhaps best embodies the concept of barren chastity. In the Argument to the first canto, Spenser punningly alludes to the nature of Florimell's chastity when he writes *'faire Florimell is chaced'*. Florimell maintains her chastity by running away from every man she ever meets. Ironically, it is only when she is being chased that she enacts her own concept of being chaste. The result is a perverse need to inspire men to pursue her in order to prove to herself that she is resisting their pursuit. Florimell consequently flees from all male characters quite indiscriminately and without knowledge of their motives for following her. In her eyes, Guyon and Arthur appear to be as much a threat as the 'griesly Foster' (III. i. 17), for Florimell is ultimately fleeing her own self-conception. Spenser alludes to this when he says she is 'selfe pursewd' (III. i. 18) by her equation of the state of chastity with the narrative experience of being chased.

Unless chastity can be wedded to love, it inevitably ends up as a parody of love generating not pleasure but its surrogate pain. Book III is filled with descriptions of figures suffering the torments of frustrated love, which in the extreme cases of Timias and Marinell lead them to the verge of death. The most grotesque disfigurements of love are thus Malbecco who can no longer distinguish pleasure from pain and Busyrane who sadistically derives pleasure from pain. The two figures represent the ultimate degradation of chastity divorced from love, as jealousy and courtly love, which both derive their existence from a separation from their professed desire. Busyrane, as the embodiment of an entire tradition of such false conceptions of love, is the ultimate challenge to chastity whom Britomart must defeat as the culmination of her quest in Book III. The figure she releases is Amoret, the child born to Chrysogone and taken by Venus to the Garden of Adonis, 'To be vpbrought in goodly womanhed' (III. vi. 28). The end of Book III thus envisages the freeing of fertile love from a sterile perversion of chastity. Returning to the sixth canto, however, it is with similar effects to Busyrane's that Venus's wayward son, Cupid, torments his victims. In the court, cities and the country everyone complains:

> how with his empoysned shot
> Their wofull harts he wounded had whyleare,
> And so had left them languishing twixt hope and feare.

(III. vi. 13)

Protean Cupid is a wanton or thoughtless form of love which can no more give rise to pleasure than sterile chastity. True love, as a force for moral good and civil order, requires the marriage of profusion and restraint: a productive but controlled love that can alone produce real pleasure.

The narrative of Venus's search for Cupid and her subsequent meeting and discussion with Diana are no more digressions from the main subject of the sixth canto than the Garden of Adonis is a digression from the rest of Book III. The whole of the sixth canto is not an escape from, but a metaphoric exploration of, the central theme of Book III: the nature of chastity and its relevance to the generative forces of love which, for Spenser, are themselves an image of poetic creativity.

Interestingly then, when we first meet Venus and Diana they are not behaving quite as distinctly as we might expect. Venus, as already mentioned, is trying to restrain the activities of her wanton son, while Diana, relaxing after the chase, is anything but an image of stark chastity, as Spenser's sensuous description makes abundantly clear:

> She hauing hong vpon a bough on high
> Her bow and painted quiuer, had vnlaste
> Her siluer buskins from her nimble thigh,
> And her lancke loynes vngirt, and brests vnbraste.
>
> (III. vi. 18)

No sooner has she been 'so loose surprized' (III. vi. 19) than Diana immediately tries to reassert her chaste image. But both she and Venus, in the ensuing dialogue, are forced to recognize that they are not nearly so different as they would like to think. They may constitute different images of love, but in so doing they merely reflect an order set down by the heavens, which acknowledges the need for both the worlds these goddesses govern: 'We both are bound to follow heauens beheasts, / And tend our charges with obeisance meeke' (III. vi. 22).

It is at this point in the narrative that the twins Belphoebe and Amoret are discovered, and lest it should be forgotten, the nature of their conception and birth is emphasized:

> Vnwares she them conceiu'd, vnwares she bore:
> She bore withouten paine, that she conceiued
> Withouten pleasure.
>
> (III. vi. 27)

Chrysogone's pregnancy can now be seen in terms of the polarities of love. 'Vnwares she them conceiu'd', without responsibility for her progeny and, as such, is an example of natural procreation, uncontrolled generation that is productive but entirely devoid of love. This is the opposite of sterile chastity which negates love by denying the generative force altogether and explains why Chrysogone experienced neither pleasure nor pain. Pain is the product of frustration, while pleasure is the child of controlled generation. The birth of Amoret and Belphoebe thus presents an initial image of natural generation that stands opposed to the restraint of thwarted desire so prevalent in Book III. But Chrysogone's experience is far from the solution to the problem, for her entire pregnancy is an example of unconscious love that knows nothing of either desire or restraint, despite generating figures who ostensibly portray aspects of these qualities. It is the purpose of the sixth canto to present a series of motifs in an attempt to harmonize the conflicting images of love. But the birth of the twins is also an image of poetic creation through the metaphor of conception. The unifying vision of the forces of love enacts the controlled generation of metaphor as a productive act, that gives rise to opposed potentials that can only be fruitfully harnessed, not by negation or suppression, but by their controlled employment.

In the Garden of Adonis, the metaphor of human conception is replaced by that of natural creation. It is a garden from which nature's adornments 'Are fetcht' (III. vi. 30). This phrase emphasizes the selectivity of the process that brings things to life. The garden as: 'the first seminarie / Of all things, that are borne to liue and die, / According to their kindes' (III. vi. 30) is an infinite source of potential realities which, as Spenser implies, cannot therefore be described exhaustively:

> Long worke it were,
> Here to account the endlesse progenie
> Of all the weedes, that bud and blossome there;
> But so much as doth need, must needs be counted here.
>
> (III. vi. 30)

The circumlocutory nature of this sentence humorously alludes to the incompatibility of terms of necessity and enumeration within the context of metaphoric exploration. Underlying the thirtieth stanza, therefore, is the metaphor of clothing and adornment, itself a common metaphor for the rhetorical application of figurative language.[22] The garden is the provider of the clothes or 'weedes' through which nature is outwardly perceived.

This same metaphor becomes more explicit in the thirty-second and third stanzas:

> He letteth in, he letteth out to wend,
>   All that to come into the world desire;
>   A thousand thousand naked babes attend
>   About him day and night, which doe require,
>   That he with fleshly weedes would them attire:
>   Such as him list, such as eternall fate
>   Ordained hath, he clothes with sinfull mire,
>   And sendeth forth to liue in mortall state,
> Till they againe returne backe by the hinder gate.
>
> After that they againe returned beene,
>   They in that Gardin planted be againe;
>   And grow afresh, as they had neuer seene
>   Fleshly corruption, nor mortall paine.
>   Some thousand yeares so doen they there remaine;
>   And then of him are clad with other hew,
>   Or sent into the chaungefull world againe,
>   Till thither they returne, where first they grew:
> So like a wheele around they runne from old to new.
>
> (III. vi. 32–3)

Harry Berger Jr writes that: 'The very difficulty of visualizing this garden with any precision suggests that the images symbolize mystical objects.'[23] So long as one seeks objects beneath the description they will necessarily prove illusory as Berger discovers: 'Precisely what object is to be identified beneath the changing terms of *flower, thing, weed, men, babe*?'[24] However, if the passage is viewed as the simultaneous description and enactment of the process of metaphor, then the shifting terms merely simulate the protean nature of metaphoric discourse. Spenser's description of the poet's own creative act must represent the different stages involved in that process. This can only be achieved if the terms of the metaphors selected are freely interchangeable, so that instead of a set of fixed terms, the description involves shifts from one metaphor to another as required. Thus, when Spenser explores the relationship between the Sidneyan concepts of 'the idea' and 'the foreconceit', he adopts the metaphor of the first seminary, but when he moves on to deal with the progression from 'the foreconceit' to 'the conceit', he switches to the metaphor of clothing naked babes. The logic of Spenser's metaphors is not dictated by internal consistency but by descriptive applicability. The metaphoric description of the generation of a poetic narrative is here seen to imply a process of degeneration from the initial and perfect 'idea' to the reality of the poet's embodiment of it in his own poem. This inevitable degeneration cannot be avoided since it is inherent in the creative process, as Spenser's language of sin and mortality makes plain. But, while the poet's own poetic figuring forth of the 'idea' is to a greater or lesser extent a corruption of it, it does not actually alter the original from which it derives its existence, but rather will return to it to be replenished, even reformed in the future.

In the thirty-fourth and thirty-fifth stanzas, far from literalizing the garden metaphor as Harry Berger Jr implies, Spenser reinforces its metaphoric nature:

> Ne needs there Gardiner to set, or sow,
>   To plant or prune: for of their owne accord
>   All things, as they created were, doe grow,
>   And yet remember well the mightie word,
>   Which first was spoken by th'Almightie lord,
>   That bad them to increase and multiply:
>   Ne doe they need with water of the ford,
>   Or of the clouds to moysten their roots dry;
> For in themselues eternall moisture they imply.
>
> Infinite shapes of creatures there are bred,
>   And vncouth formes, which none yet euer knew,
>   And euery sort is in a sundry bed
>   Set by it selfe, and ranckt in comely rew:
>   Some fit for reasonable soules t'indew,
>   Some made for beasts, some made for birds to weare,
>   And all the fruitfull spawne of fishes hew
>   In endlesse rancks along enraunged were,
> That seem'd the *Ocean* could not containe them there.
>
>   (III. vi. 34–5)

The terms which Berger lists as: 'setting, sowing, planting, pruning, water of the ford, dry roots, beds, rows, and ranks'[25] are not all treated as literally present in the garden. In fact, the thirty-fourth stanza specifically denies the relevance of the terms of cultivation in this particular garden where things grow naturally as the fulfilment of their original creation. The garden metaphor is only realized in the thirty-fifth stanza where it is not terms of actions but of organization which are developed to reinforce the concept of order governing the infinite variety of the forms generated in the garden. Spenser's description of ideal creativity presents the act of natural generation as self-governed and productive of natural order. The underlying tension between these naturally opposed forces, far from being denied, is highlighted at the end of the thirty-fifth stanza where the profusion threatens to spill over the structure containing it.

This image of natural generation as controlled abundance encapsulates the conflict that is present in metaphor as a force generating endless changes of form. In striving to produce orderly description, metaphor must exist on the verge of disorderly degeneration. These metaphoric potentialities do not exist separately, they are two sides of the same coin and together produce an uneasy equilibrium. The metaphoric ideal sees in its continual alterations the means of defining its subject and, in this sense, of becoming more truly itself with each successive change. This transforms metaphor into a means of progressing through the Neoplatonic hierarchies towards the perfection of ideas, even though its progress can never hope to complete the journey through the countless layerings that separate created forms from ultimate being. This Plotinian vision of a Platonically structured universe can certainly be located in the description of the Garden of Adonis. Alongside perfectibility, however, exists an awareness of the other side of creative change which, from a different perspective, sees only mortal decay. The Garden of Adonis, in a sequence of shifting metaphoric descriptions evokes at a variety of levels the tension that is present in the creative acts of nature and metaphor.

The organization of the whole is of necessity fluid, because the subject it seeks to describe is a protean process that can only be approached through a series of overlapping metaphors which develop out of each other in much the way Judith C. Ramsay describes:

Spenser does not want us to forget that the various versions of the creation myth can co-exist in the human understanding; intellectually we may separate them as he is doing if we are philosophers but, if we are not, then our apprehension of these truths will overlap just as his images overlap. It is as if he were pulling out the sections of a collapsible telescope; all the sections may be contained within the last one just as our world carries within it the idea of the other levels of creation but, when the telescope is extended, we see how much more complex it is than we imagined.[26]

This telescopic effect becomes increasingly noticeable as the description of the Garden of Adonis progresses. The search for internal consistency has, in the past, led to a critical debate which in seeking to explain the passage philosophically, through references to its possible sources, encountered problems of logic which seem less pressing when the episode is experienced metaphorically as poetry.[27]

Spenser's technique here is a more condensed version of the procedure employed throughout *The Faerie Queene* and which governs the structure of allegorical narratives generally.[28] One metaphor or mythic narrative replaces another the moment it is deemed to improve the perception of the allegory's subject. The logic of the Garden of Adonis is metaphoric and exploratory rather than philosophical and explanatory. What takes place is a shifting of metaphoric perspectives, where the Garden of Adonis is not a fixed geographical place but an expansive metaphoric space. The displacement of one metaphor by another, which has already been seen in individual stanzas, is a principle which governs the structure of the whole passage. The Garden of Adonis enacts in its own development the creative process it sets out to describe. In this respect, Spenser is adopting the version of the Garden of Adonis described in Plato's *Phaedrus*. The garden in this tradition, as was suggested in the Introduction, is not just a *locus amoenus* but an environment in which metaphors of growth and cultivation are specifically used to reflect on the nature of writing.

Throughout the sixth canto, therefore, the primary subject never changes, though the metaphoric vehicle for its description goes through a series of transformations. The sun that brought about the birth of the twins at the beginning is the same force we see embodied in Adonis at the end. The sun is described as 'Great father he of generation' (III. vi. 9) and Adonis as 'the Father of all formes' (III. vi. 47). These two figures are one figure: the force that generates the creative process, whether in poetry or nature.

The Garden of Adonis in displaying different perspectives of the same creative process must strive to find an ever more unified vision of the opposed forces that coexist within it. At first, the emphasis falls on the cyclical nature of creation in which created form changes but substance remains permanent:

> All things from thence doe their first being fetch,
>   And borrow matter, whereof they are made,
>   Which when as forme and feature it does ketch,
>   Becomes a bodie, and doth then inuade
>   The state of life, out of the griesly shade.
>   That substance is eterne, and bideth so,
>   Ne when the life decayes, and forme does fade,
>   Doth it consume, and into nothing go,
> But chaunged is, and often altred to and fro.
>
> The substance is not chaunged, nor altered,
>   But th'only forme and outward fashion;
>   For euery substance is conditioned
>   To change her hew, and sundry formes to don,
>   Meet for her temper and complexion:
>   For formes are variable and decay,
>   By course of kind, and by occasion;
>   And that faire flowre of beautie fades away,
> As doth the lilly fresh before the sunny ray.
>
> (III. vi. 37–8)

These stanzas discuss the creation of living substance from formless matter or chaos. It is because Spenser views the process in abstract terms that he is able to focus positively on the constancy of substance which underlies the variable forms which bring it to life. There is no sense here of the loss of individual forms this process involves, for they are not realized in terms of their material existence, either visually or emotionally. Lines which in a different context might readily contribute to a lament about the decay of the world are here consumed in sentences which negate the destructiveness of death and decay. What fades and dies is 'But th'only forme and outward fashion' which is dismissed as secondary in its alterations to the larger cycle of permanence that is expressed through the continual changes of its external appearance. The theory of constancy through change, described in this abstract fashion, allows the positive, regenerative force of creation to surface most strongly. But an abstract perspective is not complete in itself and in the last two lines of the thirty-eighth stanza the way is prepared for a more material vision of the cycle of change that is to follow in the next stanza.

The specific image of the lily, as a symbol of purity, acts as a sudden reminder of the sorrowful loss involved in the alteration of form. This loss may be necessary but from a perspective within rather than without the world of forms, is pitiless and brutal. The force that here destroys the lily is the sun, which is also associated in the Garden of Adonis with the generation of life. The image thus encapsulates the duality that is present throughout the garden where life and death, creation and destruction have been written into the structure of the material universe. The transitional image of the fading lily introduces the sense of pity and sorrow which enters the Garden of Adonis when the material loss of forms is contemplated instead of the abstract process expressed through their alteration:

> Great enimy to it, and to all the rest,
>   That in the *Gardin* of *Adonis* springs,
>   Is wicked *Time*, who with his scyth addrest,
>   Does mow the flowring herbes and goodly things,
>   And all their glory to the ground downe flings,
>   Where they doe wither, and are fowly mard:
>   He flyes about, and with his flaggy wings
>   Beates downe both leaues and buds without regard,
> Ne euer pittie may relent his malice hard.
>
> (III. vi. 39)

The material world is governed by time, which ruthlessly, and apparently arbitrarily, lays waste the beautiful forms of creation. Yet, the destructive process cannot be redressed since it is itself part of a universal law that paradoxically implies fruition through decay: 'For all that liues, is subiect to that law: / All things decay in time, and to their end do draw' (III. vi. 40). The lines typify the paradoxical nature of the Garden of Adonis as a paradise in which the universal law of permanence and the earthly experience of mutability are fused.[29] The phrase 'to their end do draw' implies in one breath both death and spiritual fulfilment – the very progress towards perfection which the forms live out through their continual cycle of growth and decay. This is a world in which the apparently opposed forces of nature are harmonized: 'There is continuall spring, and haruest there / Continuall, both meeting at one time' (III. vi. 42). In this meeting of spring and autumn, unified in a complementary partnership, is a perspective of creation that hangs between the temporal experience of the fallen world as disorder and decay, and the ultimate vision of universal order as a permanence beyond time. The cycle of the year is arrested and the linearity of temporal progression suspended as apparently opposed forces within nature become integrated in the spatial environment of the Garden of Adonis.

The metaphor of the garden, or earthly paradise, has been extended as far as is possible and must itself gradually fade and be replaced by a further mythical representation of the same paradox of creation. The 'stately Mount' situated 'Right in the middest of that Paradise' (III. vi. 43) is a grove constructed naturally at this point in the poem to house the mythical forms of Venus and Adonis. Around their grove grow the metamorphosed flowers of other mythical lovers, in a description that foreshadows the means by which the forces of disorder can be contained:

> Sad *Amaranthus*, made a flowre but late,
> Sad *Amaranthus*, in whose purple gore
> Me seemes I see *Amintas* wretched fate,
> To whom sweet Poets verse hath giuen endlesse date.

(III. vi. 45)

Here the symbolic flower Amaranthus (which means unfading) becomes an image of the eternal life that can be bestowed through the perpetuation of poetic images. Amintas, who has traditionally been taken to refer to Philip Sidney, is endlessly revived and revised through verse in a process which the poet's own recognition of the symbolic association repeats. The poet's faith in the perpetuation of form amounts to a faith in the poetic language of allegorical myth. The first glimpse of the restorative powers of symbolic imagery ushers into the Garden of Adonis a final unifying mythological vision of Venus enjoying 'Her deare *Adonis* ioyous company' (III. vi. 46):

> And sooth it seemes they say: for he may not
>   For euer die, and euer buried bee
>   In balefull night, where all things are forgot;
>   All be he subiect to mortalitie,
>   Yet is eterne in mutabilitie,
>   And by succession made perpetuall,
>   Transformed oft, and chaunged diuerslie:
>   For him the Father of all formes they call;
> Therefore needs mote he liue, that liuing giues to all.
>
> (III. vi. 47)

The 'Father of all formes' is finally perceived as a figure which combines the forces of creation and destruction in a single state of dynamic stasis. The image of Adonis encompasses the paradoxical impulses that also coexist in the changing figure of metaphor and which the Garden of Adonis has presented in its own succession of metaphoric representations. The entire episode consists of a succession of metaphors describing the same process; the metaphors change but the subject remains the same: by 'succession made perpetuall'.

The contradictory figure at the centre of the Garden of Adonis, in expressing the principle of permanence through change underlying natural creation, thus encapsulates the paradox of metaphoric creation too, which discovers its permanent state to be a state of permanent change. Metaphor, like Adonis, discovers life in death to become 'eterne in mutabilitie'.

MIMETIC METAPHOR

Metaphor in *The Faerie Queene* exists in a perpetual state of tension, a dynamic conflict which governs the metaphoric structures of the poem and brings to the fore questions concerning the authority and status of metaphor. The metaphors of conception and horticulture contained in the Garden of Adonis, as embedded metaphors exploring the origin and nature of the metaphoric process, are in this respect typical. The whole episode grows out of a structure of tensions: creation and destruction, order and chaos, cultivation and wildness, the transient and the eternal, the mutable and the permanent. Metaphor by its very nature is condemned to seek stasis in the midst of flux. Its predicative function involves it in a process of definition that can never be definitive. The moment metaphor begins to replace the predicative with the nominative it sets in motion the process of its own decline, as in the Malbecco episode.

Ostensibly, therefore, metaphor desires the perfect description of its subject and yet to achieve such a state is to destroy itself. In its quest for identity through difference, metaphor cannot afford to create complete synonymity. It can approach its subject time and time again, but is never able to see it in the flesh. Metaphor can tentatively dream of a time and a place where it can live in harmony with the object of its predicative desire, but even then it is constantly reminded of the prospect of its loss. This is the vision of Venus and Adonis planted at the centre of the Garden of Adonis: the lovers parted by death, reunited eternally in an ecstasy of pleasure. Yet, even here, in the metaphoric paradise are the reminders of the real world in which metaphor actually dwells. The 'wilde Bore' (III. vi. 48) has had to be imprisoned while Adonis must be hidden 'from the world, and from the skill / Of *Stygian* Gods' (III. vi. 46) who would demolish this fragile state of imagined bliss. The metaphoric dream, the perfect coupling in which two become one can never be realized though it is constantly yearned for. It is an ideal state of permanent union unobtainable in the mutable world of metaphor, and unsustainable in the narrative of *The Faerie Queene*.

This may constitute one of the main reasons for Spenser's decision to replace the stanzas which originally concluded Book III in the first edition of *The Faerie Queene* with a new ending in the 1596 Quarto. The union of Scudamour and Amoret introduces into the poem an image of complete fulfilment in the lovers' embrace that then gives way to a startling metaphor:

>   Lightly he clipt her twixt his armes twaine,
>   And streightly did embrace her body bright,
>   Her body, late the prison of sad paine,
>   Now the sweet lodge of loue and deare delight:
>   But she faire Lady ouercommen quight

> Of huge affection, did in pleasure melt,
> And in sweete rauishment pourd out her spright:
> No word they spake, nor earthly thing they felt,
> But like two senceles stocks in long embracement dwelt.
>
> Had ye them seene, ye would haue surely thought,
> That they had beene that faire *Hermaphrodite*,
> Which that rich *Romane* of white marble wrought,
> And in his costly Bath causd to bee site:
> So seemd those two, as growne together quite,
> That *Britomart* halfe enuying their blesse,
> Was much empassiond in her gentle sprite,
> And to her selfe oft wisht like happinesse,
> In vaine she wisht, that fate n'ould let her yet possesse.
>
> (1590 Edition, III. xii. 45–6)

The description of the passionate union of Scudamour and Amoret becomes increasingly sensuous and erotic as Amoret allows herself to be overcome by pleasure.[30] At the height of the experience the two figures are speechless and become strangely dehumanized: 'No word they spake, nor earthly thing they felt, / But like two senceles stocks in long embracement dwelt.' Nowhere in *The Faerie Queene* does the etymological link between the copula involved in metaphoric union and the copulation of sexual union surface more explicitly or climactically.[31] What happens in the consummation of the longed for marriage of separate beings is ecstatic but beyond words and human experience.

It is as if this experience, in fulfilling their deepest desire, also robs Scudamour and Amoret of the very individuality that is part of their humanity. Until the last two lines of the stanza, their actions and feelings had been separately narrated, but now the third person singular is replaced with the third person plural; their experience is jointly described. The simile which is introduced to illustrate this experience captures in the image of 'two senceles stocks' the ambiguity of the lovers' being. The comparison implies, firstly, that they are still two separate beings and yet the image of branchless tree trunks, in emphasizing the way they are entwined in each others' arms, further suggests a process of engrafting that is also associated with the word stock. They are two becoming one and in that process, which began in the extreme of pleasure, they lose all feeling and become like 'senceles' dead wood. Something seems to be lost in this metamorphosis of the lovers which is perhaps explained when a third meaning of the word 'stock' is taken into account. One meaning for stock (particularly current in Spenser's day) was its contemptuous reference to religious icons.[32] The idolatry of the Papists was the ultimate example of a false image actually being worshipped in place of the living God. The comparison of the two lovers to an icon thus links the definition of Amoret through total union with the being whose quest it was to seek and define her, with the desire of false metaphor to become one with the object of its description. Idolatry and metaphoric abuse are human weaknesses that must be resisted if truth and genuine metaphor are to survive.

The metaphor which appears in the following stanza develops the image of the metaphoric desire that cannot be achieved. The image of the hermaphrodite is associated elsewhere in *The Faerie Queene* with Venus (IV. x. 41) and Nature (VII. vii. 5), as what Roche terms 'images of the *natura unialis*, the ultimate unity that underlies all being'.[33] This ultimate unity, however, cannot be experienced as part of earthly experience. The copula of the metaphoric act and the copulation of the sexual act are the nearest mortals can come to experiencing the bliss of the ultimate unity which lies beyond human experience. Spenser offers an image that in presenting the perfect earthly coupling, never once forgets the imperfections of that mortal union. For, Scudamour and Amoret are not one but only ever 'seemd those two, as growne together quite'.

Spenser's evocation of the figure of the 'faire *Hermaphrodite*' as a metaphor for the lovers' long embrace is even more cunningly constructed. Here, the comparison is only suggested as a conditional tense: what the reader 'would haue surely thought'. This conditional comparison, however, is not to an original figure but only to a statue of it. The final irony of the devices employed to distance the lovers from the object of comparison is that the specific statue to which Spenser apparently alludes has not been successfully identified.[34] It is as if the quest to unite in a single figure, whether through love or metaphor, two distinct beings is an impossible dream. Nonetheless, it is a dream that in attempting its fulfilment endangers the true quest of metaphor to explore its subject. The false metaphoric act thus offers a promise of final union that is all the more dangerous because at first sight it seems so complete. The false metaphoric ending to Book III must consequently be replaced with an alternative ending that cannot offer completion but the continuation of the predicative quest. In this version the union of Scudamour and Amoret is postponed, never to be witnessed in the text of the poem as it stands.

Metaphor must learn to be content with its differences from its subject and what these reveal about the identity of that subject. A predicative mode of discourse must satisfy metaphor which, at its furthest reaches, may glimpse through revelation the identity of the subject it seeks but with which it cannot be identical. Metaphor must not aspire to replace its subject altogether by literally becoming the thing it exists to divine. This is the ultimate temptation metaphor must at all costs resist.

The Faerie Queene's narratives of disguise, falsehood and usurpation plot out this ultimate abuse of the power of metaphoricity. The narrative of False Florimell, interwoven through Books III, IV and V of the poem, depicts the story of a figure designed to stand in the place of the original from which it was copied. The Mutabilitie Cantos, generally positioned at the end of the poem, also provide in the figure of Mutabilitie herself a figure of change aspiring to usurp control of the entire universe. These two narratives offer metaphoric plots in which the potential dangers of metaphoric abuse are worked out, freeing metaphor to function productively as a force of predicative exploration. These then constitute key passages in the metaphoric debate as it is presented in *The Faerie Queene*. Only if metaphor can be shown to be neither good nor bad in itself, but dependent upon the way in which it is utilized, will its true nature be known. Metaphor is a potential form without substance until it is realized in the metaphoric utterance. Metaphor, like writing itself, to which its defence is so closely aligned, shifts the blame away from the medium and onto the message. Where falsehood is perpetrated through metaphor, then metaphor is more abused than abusing. It is at this point in the metaphoric debate that the essential duality of metaphor becomes apparent. An examination of precisely what is at stake when metaphor strives to deny its heuristic function will be undertaken in the final chapter with reference to the Mutabilitie Cantos, in which the question of the rule of metaphor in *The Faerie Queene* culminates. For now, however, it will be helpful to define a more straightforward example of the form and purpose of metaphoric abuse.

The narrative of the creation of False Florimell in the seventh and eighth cantos of Book III follows on directly from the Garden of Adonis and precedes the narrative of Malbecco's metamorphosis. The origin of false metaphor is placed immediately after the description of the creation of true metaphor to help clarify the distinction. It is also placed just before the depiction of the perverse degeneration of metaphor into a monstrous emblem.

Right from the start, the purpose for creating the simulacrum is made plain. After Florimell has escaped from the witch and her son, the witch sends a beast to follow and destroy her. When the beast returns 'Tyde with her broken girdle' (III. viii. 2), the witch and her son mistakenly assume Florimell to be dead. The son falls into a rage at the loss and threatens to kill his mother. To pacify this rage the witch decides to make 'Another *Florimell*' (III. viii. 5) to replace the original in his eyes. False Florimell is conceived because the real Florimell is believed to be irretrievably lost. The fake is created as a surrogate for its lost original but actually attempts to stand in its place. This is the classic case of false metaphor: used not to define its subject but to replace it. Motivated by the belief that the original cannot be rediscovered, it gives up the metaphoric quest of predication and attempts to invert the metaphoric function into its nominative contrary by pretending to be the figure it should know it is not. The temptation to end metaphor's heuristic quest by setting up a false idol or icon to fill the lacunae that coexist alongside metaphoric predication is strong but must be resisted by the true metaphorizer. The description of how *'The Witch creates a snowy Lady, / like to Florimell'* (III. viii. Argument), is a fascinating example of the literalization of the metaphoric process.

The witch calls her sprights, 'The maisters of her art' (III. viii. 4), around her and then:

> By their aduise, and her owne wicked wit,
>   She there deuiz'd a wondrous worke to frame,
> Whose like on earth was neuer framed yit,
>   That euen Nature selfe enuide the same,
>   And grudg'd to see the counterfet should shame
> The thing it selfe. In hand she boldly tooke

> To make another like the former Dame,
> Another *Florimell*, in shape and looke
> So liuely and so like, that many it mistooke.
>
> (III. viii. 5)

The witch's art is an art of evil precisely because it is generated by her 'owne wicked wit'. The art of metaphor is not in itself wicked, it is the intention with which it is employed that defines its moral status. The work she frames is therefore wondrous but still a work, a contrived replica and not the thing itself. The witch's mimetic art functions primarily visually and at this level is envied even by 'Nature selfe' in case 'the counterfet should shame' her own creation. The reference to 'Nature selfe' at this point in the description and to the underlying threat the witch's imitative art constitutes to the Creator of original form is an indication of what is at stake when Mutabilitie's case is heard and judged by Nature in the Mutabilitie Cantos. The moment the metaphorizer seeks to supplant the thing itself with its metaphoric description, then an act of falsehood has been committed and instead of revealing truths, metaphor has attempted to perpetrate a lie by hiding the truth.

The false metaphoric construct, however, is not perceived to be less attractive in itself so long as its form is divorced from the intentions of its maker. Only at the point when false metaphor is revealed alongside the actual object it seeks to mimic and usurp will the emptiness of its claims become obvious. The deceptive power of such metaphor is consequently reinforced by the unexpected grammar of the second half of the stanza's last line: 'So liuely and so like, that many it mistooke.' The previous two and a half lines have dealt entirely with the witch's bold enterprise of making another Florimell, placing the emphasis on the intention prior to its actualization, which is then described in the following four stanzas. But while the witch's purpose in forming her creation is to deceive people, nobody can be fooled by it until after its completion. The phrase 'that many it mistooke', by placing the verb firmly in the past tense instead of the future or conditional tense that is logically to be expected, proclaims the success of the enterprise as a narrative event prior to its narration. False metaphor is employed in the full knowledge that it will work, precisely because it only differs from genuine metaphor in intention: its desire to be 'like' its original and not to accept its differences from it. This is why the word 'like' is repeated in the last three lines. At the point where metaphor rejects its identity through dissimilarity and voices its similarity to the thing it describes, it effectively begins to function as simile through the comparison of likes. False metaphor consists of the comparative intent of simile adopting the direct voice of metaphor.

What we see when the witch actually makes 'The substance' of this *'snowy Lady, / like to Florimell'* is an unusual literalization of poetic imagery presented as an alchemical process. The phrase *'a snowy Lady'* is a common metaphor in love poetry, implying the woman's complexion has qualities associated with the whiteness of snow.[35] In this metaphor, whiteness stands symbolically for purity and chastity, while the coldness of snow may allude to the lady's 'iciness': her indifference to the lover's passionate advances. The witch in making a woman in the image of Florimell, with whom to bewitch the eyes and hearts of men, takes hold of this metaphor and begins literally to mould the body out of snow:

> The substance, whereof she the bodie made,
> Was purest snow in massie mould congeald.
>
> (III. viii. 6)

The witch then continues the process of chemical composition:

> The same she tempred with fine Mercury,
> And virgin wex, that neuer yet was seald,
> And mingled them with perfect vermily,
> That like a liuely sanguine it seem'd to the eye.
>
> (III. viii. 6)

This mixture of elements at first sounds original and pure. Spenser's description is in fact detailing the process used in the production of red wax for sealing letters. Vermilion pigment was mixed with clear wax to produce the ('sanguine') blood-red colour of sealing wax. Right away, it is clear that the *'snowy Lady'* is not to be snowy in appearance after all. The snow is being mixed to produce a sanguine complexion (sanguine, as one of the four humours, was associated with boldness, success and amorousness).

This '*snowy Lady*', far from being cold, is to be an extremely warm-blooded creation. The symbolic coldness and purity that could have been associated with False Florimell have melted away, to such an extent that in the second line which refers to 'virgin wex, that neuer yet was seald', there is the suggestion that it is only virgin because never before sealed and that now, not only has it been sealed, but will shortly be unsealed. Even the word 'wex' punningly draws out the sense in which wax is essentially malleable and inconstant. The witch is creating a lady out of snow, literally a '*snowy Lady*', but one who is nothing like the '*snowy Lady*' of poetic convention. This is why in the last line of the stanza the emphasis again falls on the words 'like' and 'seem'd', for False Florimell, as a false metaphor, is trapped in the act of seeming – the as of simile.

The next stanza takes this literalization of the conventional images of love poetry further, drawing attention to the process ever more overtly:

> In stead of eyes two burning lampes she set
> In siluer sockets, shyning like the skyes,
> And a quicke mouing Spirit did arret
> To stirre and roll them, like a womans eyes;
> In stead of yellow lockes she did deuise,
> With golden wyre to weaue her curled head;
> Yet golden wyre was not so yellow thrise
> As *Florimells* faire haire: and in the stead
> Of life, she put a Spright to rule the carkasse dead.

(III. viii. 7)

The images of burning lamps for eyes and golden wire for hair are part of the love sonneteer's stock in trade.[36] The entire stanza mimics the style and tone of the sonnet tradition which had become so conventionalized that it was in danger of losing sight of the metaphoricity of its own images. The witch as an abuser of metaphor is able to draw on these most commonplace images and make her dame out of their literal equivalents. The irony is that once the metaphoric origin of these images has been lost, due to their conventionalization, then female beauty begins to be measured in terms of its likeness to the artificial and crafted objects which were first employed to describe the incomparable perfection of true female beauty. The artificially constructed False Florimell is literally more beautiful than her counterpart. This is the perverse inversion of truth false metaphor seeks: the replacement of the real with its metaphoric predicative in an act of false nomination, where the image takes on a pseudo-literalness prior to adopting the role of the thing itself.

In making the process of False Florimell's construction a literalization of the metaphoric, a narrative example of the abuse of metaphor is provided which also amounts to a condemnation of poetry that divorces itself from the exploratory mode of the metaphoric in the name of convention. It is this perversion of metaphor which must be defined rigorously prior to redressing its wrong doings. The last three lines of the stanza, however, explain both how and why the abuse of metaphor must be resisted. Reference is suddenly made to '*Florimells* faire haire'. Later on in the narrative of False Florimell, this occurrence would not necessarily indicate whether it was the original or imitation Florimell who was being referred to. The epithet 'false' is rarely used, as the witch's Florimell is increasingly mistaken for her original namesake. The confusion concerning her identity grows within the narrative itself, the reader thus experiencing a nominative uneasiness, as the characters do, in deciding which Florimell is being talked about. Here, however, False Florimell has yet to develop her full potential as a counterfeit and the reference to Florimell is indeed to Florimell herself. The 'golden wyre' used to weave False Florimell's hair 'was not so yellow thrise / As *Florimells* faire haire'. To free the nature of the real from its metaphoric impersonation, the difference between the two must be evoked. Hair made from 'golden wyre' is not the same as Florimell's hair which is in fact not 'golden' but 'yellow'. Yellow may be less costly than gold, but the natural yellow colour of Florimell's hair, which cannot be surpassed by a metallic fabrication, is clearly of greater worth.

In stating the obvious, Spenser is not only distinguishing between the two Florimells, he is rescuing an image from becoming conventionalized. It is at the moment when an image is no longer seen as an image but as somehow real, or worse, better than the real, that it loses all its powers of predication and suffers its metaphoric death. This, after all, is precisely what a dead metaphor is: an embedded metaphor that through conventional use in language has ceased to function as a metaphor any more and has become accepted in a nominative role. The witch's creation is effectively a dead metaphor, generated unnaturally by literalizing conventional metaphors to death so that it can have a lively appearance but no life: 'and in the stead / Of life, she put a Spright to rule the carkasse dead.' Here is a perfect description of dead metaphor: the dominion over a lifeless carcass. False Florimell's entire narrative is the story of the attempted imposition of the impulse leading towards dead metaphor in the place of living descriptive metaphor.

Once the spirit of false metaphor has been installed it immediately begins to employ its skills of resemblance:

> A wicked Spright yfraught with fawning guile,
> And faire resemblance aboue all the rest,
> Which with the Prince of Darknesse fell somewhile,
> From heauens blisse and euerlasting rest;
> Him needed not instruct, which way were best
> Himselfe to fashion likest *Florimell*,
> Ne how to speake, ne how to vse his gest,
> For he in counterfeisance did excell,
> And all the wyles of wemens wits knew passing well.
>
> (III. viii. 8)

The kinship of false metaphor with the 'Prince of Darknesse' as forces of evil is not just because both are rooted in deceit. There is another more fundamental reason alluded to in the passage. False metaphors function through deception and guile but, as the narrative of False Florimell makes plain, are generated by the intention of replacing an original. The primary motive of false metaphor, the cause that brings it into existence, is the desire to usurp. In wishing to unseat its own original, false metaphor perpetually repeats the error that led to Satan's fall from heaven. The nature of his original sin is illustrated clearly in the Bible, for it is as a result of his pride that Satan challenges God and is cast down to Hell. Only after that does he adopt guile and deceit when he journeys to Paradise to tempt Eve and cause the Fall of Man. Satan is motivated by pride but employs deception in the eternal war against Heaven. Spenser, by referring to the fall of Satan in establishing the spright's mastery of 'fawning guile, / And faire resemblance', confirms the origin and nature of metaphoric abuse as a repetition of Satanic pride. It is no accident, therefore, that False Florimell should be linked to Braggadocchio in the next stage of her narrative development and later choose him from all other knights to be her champion.

The witch completes her work by actually dressing her creation in clothes which Florimell had left behind:

> That who so then her saw, would surely say,
> It was her selfe, whom it did imitate,
> Or fairer then her selfe, if ought algate
> Might fairer be.
>
> (III. viii. 9)

The grammatical structure of the second line quoted above reinforces the difficulty of distinguishing the abuser from the abused. Logically, we know 'her selfe' refers to Florimell and 'it' to her impersonation. Yet, the certainty of logic is brought into question the moment a second reading is made to establish or confirm interpretation. The moment an impostor has sown the seeds of any doubt, it has started to achieve its goal and, in the absence of the 'thing it selfe', may even appear to outshine it.

False Florimell is now finished and yet her creator cannot control her future. Once an act of metaphoric abuse has taken place, even if the purpose of the originator was limited in scope, its potential for evil is dictated by its innate desire to live the independent existence of that which it imitates. False metaphor will seek the final act of usurpation. In her very first act of imitation, when she appears before the witch's son, the description of their embrace mimics the union of Scudamour and Amoret originally placed at the end of Book III:

> Tho fast her clipping twixt his armes twaine,
>   Extremely ioyed in so happie sight,
>   And soone forgot his former sickly paine;
>   But she, the more to seeme such as she hight,
>   Coyly rebutted his embracement light.
>
> (III. viii. 10)

False Florimell, as a parody of true metaphor, immediately copies the very act of union of which metaphor can dream but which must be withheld if the metaphoric is to maintain its predicative function. False Florimell, as this passage makes clear, exists to perpetrate an act of false nomination, so that everything she does is designed to verify the name she has assumed: 'the more to seeme such as she hight'. The metaphoric dream of nominative union that false metaphor seeks to make a reality was identified as potentially idolatrous in the case of Scudamour and Amoret. In the deliberate fraudulence of False Florimell there can be no doubt and in the very next stanza she is specifically referred to as an 'Idole faire' (III. viii. 11). The betrayal of metaphor is a betrayal of truth and is to be associated directly with the iconic defamation of God through idolatry.

False Florimell requires a more fitting companion than the witch's son if she is to further the worship of her figure. The narrative coupling of this idol with 'Proud *Braggadocchio*' (III. viii. 11), the knight of vain boastfulness, is the inevitable and perfect development, since he will proclaim her worth in suitably unsuitable vaunts at every opportunity. After her creation, False Florimell appears twice more in The Faerie Queene: in the fifth canto of Book IV and the third canto of Book V. On both occasions her real nature is contested publicly.

The first test follows a tournament held for love of Florimell, where the victor is to claim the girdle of Florimell and the woman deemed to be most worthy of its possession. Britomart, as the Knight of Chastity, wins the girdle but the question of who should wear it has still to be decided. After all the other women have appeared two still remain: Britomart's Amoret and Blandamour's False Florimell:

> At last the most redoubted *Britonesse*,
>   Her louely *Amoret* did open shew;
>   Whose face discouered, plainely did expresse
>   The heauenly pourtraict of bright Angels hew.
>   Well weened all, which her that time did vew,
>   That she should surely beare the bell away,
>   Till *Blandamour*, who thought he had the trew
>   And very *Florimell*, did her display:
> The sight of whom once seene did all the rest dismay.
>
> For all afore that seemed fayre and bright,
>   Now base and contemptible did appeare,
>   Compar'd to her, that shone as Phebes light,
>   Amongst the lesser starres in euening cleare.

> All that her saw with wonder rauisht weare,
> And weend no mortall creature she should bee,
> But some celestiall shape, that flesh did beare:
> Yet all were glad there *Florimell* to see;
> Yet thought that *Florimell* was not so faire as shee.
>
> (IV. v. 13–14)

Amoret, the figure of chaste love, is deemed the victor until the appearance of the false figure of Florimell. She has now established herself quite independently of her slain creator and has begun to be accepted as 'the trew / And very *Florimell*'. In the absence of the real Florimell the impostor is believed to outshine all other figures of purity. Her audience, ravished by her beauty, makes the mistake, already hinted at during her fashioning, of valuing the artificial above the genuine and accepting an image instead of the 'thing it selfe'.

To define the nature of this misconception, which false metaphor must accomplish if it is to maintain its grip on reality, an explanatory stanza follows in the form of an extended simile:

> As guilefull Goldsmith that by secret skill,
>   With golden foyle doth finely ouer spred
>   Some baser metall, which commend he will
>   Vnto the vulgar for good gold insted,
>   He much more goodly glosse thereon doth shed,
>   To hide his falshood, then if it were trew:
>   So hard, this Idole was to be ared,
>   That *Florimell* her selfe in all mens vew
> She seem'd to passe: so forged things do fairest shew.
>
> (IV. v. 15)

The simile, in employing the image of a forger of gold, draws attention to the difference between surface appearance and inner worth. The judgement of false metaphor cannot simply be in material terms, it must also encompass moral values. False Florimell will always appear to be beautiful because of the effort lavished on the details of her material existence. In order to disguise what is not genuine it is necessary to pay more attention to its external features than is the case with an original and solid item. The fake may be betrayed inwardly by its faultless external appearance. The image thus emphasizes two aspects which together explain the frequent success of 'forged things': firstly, the secret skill with which they are fashioned with the intention of deceiving and secondly, the difficulty of judging them correctly. The phrase Spenser uses to link the comparison to forgery back to the figure of False Florimell ensures the comment on the status of metaphor is not missed: 'So hard, this Idole was to be ared'. False Florimell is an idol, a false image or icon, but her interpretation depends on the ability of those who come into contact with her to interpret her correctly. Right reading is the problem here, since it is not always possible to protect even the virtuous reader from rash judgements.

The fake Florimell is therefore declared the paragon of beauty in the very next stanza. The golden belt of Florimell is awarded to her but when placed round her waist is 'disclos'd'. The real disclosure, punningly alluded to by the unfastening of the girdle, is not recognized by those present, who persist in their desire to claim False Florimell for themselves. Blinded by the outward splendour, they are incapable of seeing through the false image before them, even when prompted by the magical intervention of the girdle. False metaphor triumphs in the absence of its real counterpart, which it must now seek to confront directly.

The final confrontation between the true and false Florimell takes place after a tournament celebrating the marriage of Florimell and Marinell, held to maintain the excellence of Florimell. When the tournament finishes, Braggadocchio is wrongly believed to have won the day. Florimell thanks him for defending her honour but he rudely proclaims his own 'snowy *Florimele*' (V. iii. 17) to be her superior and unveils her before the assembled audience:

> Whom when discouered they had throughly eide,
> With great amazement they were stupefide;
> And said, that surely *Florimell* it was,
> Or if it were not *Florimell* so tride,
> That *Florimell* her selfe she then did pas.
> So feeble skill of perfect things the vulgar has.
>
> (V. iii. 17)

The final line which passes judgement on those who misjudge cannot disguise the fact that the difficulty of distinguishing the true from the false is a problem that will never really go away.

Metaphor as a Process of Change

Marinell himself is 'dismayd' and incapable of distinguishing the impostor from his own bride:

> He long astonisht stood, ne ought he sayd,
> Ne ought he did, but with fast fixed eies
> He gazed still vpon that snowy mayd;
> Whom euer as he did the more auize,
> The more to be true *Florimell* he did surmize.
>
> (V. iii. 18)

It requires the intervention of Sir Artegall, the Knight of Justice, to establish the status of the two Florimells. Yet, even he does not at first speak with total conviction, as the bracketed phrase inserted in his speech indicates:

> As for this Ladie, which he sheweth here,
> Is not (I wager) *Florimell* at all;
> But some fayre Franion, fit for such a fere,
> That by misfortune in his hand did fall.
>
> (V. iii. 22)

Artegall does not state a fact; he 'wagers' an opinion. The basis of his opinion, however, is not an intuitive ability to recognize False Florimell as an impostor, but a view that as the companion of Braggadocchio, she is unlikely to be of real worth. Artegall therefore withholds final judgement until the two Florimells can be tried by direct comparison:

> Then did he set her by that snowy one,
>   Like the true saint beside the image set,
>   Of both their beauties to make paragone,
>   And triall, whether should the honor get.
>   Streight way so soone as both together met,
>   Th'enchaunted Damzell vanisht into nought:
>   Her snowy substance melted as with heat,
>   Ne of that goodly hew remayned ought,
> But th'emptie girdle, which about her wast was wrought.
>
> (V. iii. 24)

There can, of course, be no trial between the false image and the reality it seeks to mimic. The moment metaphor abandons the basis of its comparative existence and tries to suppress the differences that distinguish it from its subject, it denies the very qualities that give vitality to its existence. Metaphor is not mimetic, it is descriptive, and False Florimell has always been an empty shadow because she has sought to become what she can never be. The moment she confronts the being she has so long imitated, the emptiness of her vain attempt is apparent and she melts into nothing. Her entire body vanishes and all that remains is the belt belonging to Florimell which she was awarded earlier in the narrative. The belt which would not stay round her of its own accord but which having been awarded she has 'wrought' to her figure survives as a reminder that false metaphor can be invested with the qualities of the real by those who are deceived by it. False metaphor cannot destroy the original; it can only deny or deride it. Florimell was shamed by the boastful words of Braggadocchio against her but is restored to her rightful position the moment that her false image dares to stand by her. There is not even any need to pass sentence on False Florimell, her form is unsustainable in the presence of her own original.

The message that has been present beneath the entire narrative of False Florimell is strongly introduced at the moment of her dissolution in the simile in the second line of the stanza: 'Like the true saint beside the image set'. Florimell has been threatened by a false image that in seeking to stand in her place has attempted to turn itself into an iconic representation. The parallel with idolatry and the perversion of true faith reveals how metaphoric abuse in *The Faerie Queene* always entails a joint threat to the poet's Christian and linguistic belief in the language of metaphor.

3
Metaphor as an Act of Idolatry

ALLEGORY AND IDOLATRY

The narrative of False Florimell draws attention to the potentially idolatrous nature of metaphor and, in so doing, introduces a particularly insidious threat for Spenser's poetics. The alignment of Christian faith with a belief in the veracity of poetic discourse certainly constitutes a powerful metaphor in the armoury of the defence of poetry. By the same token, however, this Christian metaphor exposes metaphor itself to the risk of virulent attack should its linguistic figures become associated in any way with the idolatrous abuse of images. What is at stake if metaphor is unable to defend itself against the charge of idolatry within *The Faerie Queene* is the destruction of the poem's own allegorical project of educating the Christian reader.

It would seem that figurative language in the service of divine truth has a natural defence against the charge of idolatry since it can point to Scripture as an incontrovertible source sanctioning its use. The authors of the sacred texts not only provide examples of all the rhetorical tropes but, as no less an authority than Augustine agrees, also give 'the names of some of them, like *allegoria, aenigma, parabola*'.[1] Nevertheless, the abundance of these figures in the Bible is not a justification of their use *per se* in poetry. The interpretation of figurative expressions in Scripture is fraught with problems, not least of which is knowing whether to interpret them literally or figuratively in the first place. Augustine testifies to this primary exegetical dilemma, warning against unnecessary figurative reading and suggesting that where a single passage gives rise to more than one meaning, different interpretations are not harmful as long as they are congruous with truth expressed elsewhere in Holy Scripture:

For he who examines the divine eloquence, desiring to discover the intention of the author through whom the Holy Spirit created the Scripture, whether he attains this end or finds another meaning in the words not contrary to right faith, is free from blame if he has evidence from some other place in the divine books. For the author himself may have seen the same meaning in the words we seek to understand. And certainly the Spirit of God, who worked through that author, undoubtedly foresaw that this meaning would occur to the reader or listener.

(*On Christian Doctrine*, III. 27. 38)

For Augustine, the examination of passages made obscure by the presence of figurative words should wherever possible be supported by testimonies from other places in Scripture. This then ensures the sanctity of figurative interpretation which is safeguarded by the authority of the Spirit of God as the true author of the Holy Text.

The Bible therefore allows freedom of figurative exegesis so long as the resultant readings are internally referenced. When this is not possible, the only recourse is to the interpreter's own reason to make the meaning clearer. Augustine views this practice with suspicion calling it 'a dangerous pursuit' (*On Christian Doctrine*, III. 28. 39) since, lacking the authority of God, it is in danger of being motivated by the worldly concerns of humanity. And if the Bible cannot, in all cases, secure itself against the misinterpretation of its figurative expressions, then the tropes of poetry are even more vulnerable. The ideal of a poetic theology protecting divine knowledge beneath the enigmatic veil of allegory is unable to hide from its mundane origins.[2] Lacking the divine authority of Scripture, it is impossible for the language of allegory to be endorsed without reservation. The allegorist must acknowledge the dangers of the medium and the possibility that instead of leading to divine revelation, his own figurative discourse could replace the love of God with an inordinate enjoyment of its own metaphors.

It is precisely because Spenser's defence of his poetry is so firmly rooted in its professed ability to figure forth spiritual truth, that the poem continually confronts and guards itself against the possibility of its own metaphors becoming an idolatrous parody of that truth. Spenser must prove at all times that the metaphors he adopts are only a figurative means of exploring their subject and are not, and never can be, an independent alternative to it. Metaphor cannot afford to forget for one moment that it exists as a means of understanding, not as an end in itself. The threat posed by the corrupting influence of figures seeking to turn metaphor into a perversion of its proper heuristic function consequently translates naturally into the theological metaphor of idolatry.

It is not surprising, therefore, that idolatry as a metaphor for the misuse of metaphor should have started to surface in episodes where the poem reflects on the status of its own figurative language. In a number of significant ways, Spenser's false poets, his abusers of metaphor, are also figures of idolatry. Archimago, Duessa and the creator of the False Florimell, as magicians and witches, embody the superstitious magic Protestants like Bishop Bale associated with the Catholic ritual of 'masses and other sorcerous witchcrafts' which for Bishop Hooper were 'nothing better to be esteemed than the verses of the sorcerer or enchanter'.[3] These associations with the invective of Protestant attacks on the Roman Mass are important and have received detailed attention particularly in relation to Book I,[4] but they do not in themselves explain why idolatry should constitute quite such a potent threat to the poem's faith in the fidelity of its own allegory. There is a much more fundamental reason why metaphor, or extended metaphor in the form of allegory, can be seen as potentially idolatrous. A passage from C.S. Lewis's *The Allegory of Love*, in which he considers the basis of a comparison between allegory and Catholicism, provides a helpful starting point:

> It would appear that all allegories whatever are likely to seem Catholic to the general reader, and this phenomenon is worth investigation.... Do Protestant allegorists continue as in a dream to use imagery so likely to mislead their readers without noticing the danger or without better motive than laziness for incurring it? By no means. The truth is not that allegory is Catholic, but that Catholicism is allegorical. Allegory consists in giving an imagined body to the immaterial; but if, in each case, Catholicism claims already to have given it a material body, then the allegorist's symbol will naturally resemble that material body.... In the world of matter, Catholics and Protestants disagree as to the kind and degree of incarnation or embodiment which we can safely try to give to the spiritual; but in the

world of imagination, where allegory exists, unlimited embodiment is equally approved by both.[5]

Lewis is determined to free Protestant allegories from the misconception that they are in any way Catholic simply because they contain embodiments of abstractions which show similarities to those of the Catholic Church. In liberating allegory from such a superficial confusion with Catholicism, Lewis unwittingly exposes it to a more serious and insidious charge. The real question is not whether allegory is Catholic, or Catholicism allegorical, but whether both, because of the nature of allegory itself, are in peril of falling into idolatry. As Lewis rightly points out, what makes Catholicism allegorical is its desire to embody the immaterial in the first place. The crucial difference, as far as Lewis is concerned, is that whereas Catholicism is willing to embody the immaterial in the material world, allegory functions only in 'the world of imagination', where he claims all embodiment can be approved.

Lewis's confidence in the sanctity of the human imagination was by no means shared by all Protestants in the late sixteenth century. For many, the whole question of the origin of idolatry had become a vexed problem involving philosophical and aesthetic questions about the nature of human perception and the processes involved in the construction of mental images. Increasingly, idolatry was associated in theological discourse with the inner world of the imagination, and the mental images it produced. Bishop Hooper gives a sense of the suspicion with which Protestant theologians of the time viewed such images both in terms of the faculty which created them and the process which represented them:

> The mind of man, when it is not illuminated with the Spirit of God, nor governed by the scripture, it imagineth and feigneth God to be like unto the imagination and conceit of his mind, and not as the scripture teacheth. When this vanity or fond imagination is conceived in the mind, there followeth a further success of the ill. He purposeth to express by some figure or image God in the same form and similitude that his imagination hath first printed in his mind; so that the mind conceiveth the idol, and afterward the hand worketh and representeth the same unto the senses.[6]

The terms Hooper employs reveal just how easily the language of theological recrimination directed against idolatry can implicate allegory. Once the mind of man is perceived, to use Calvin's phrase, as a 'factory of idols', then there is no real difference between physical figures in the form of paintings or statues and figures of speech in the form of metaphors, since both are understood to involve the incarnation of the immaterial. From this perspective, not only is the poet's imagination suspect in the first place but, in figuring forth his conceptions of the invisible in the form of specific metaphors, he increases the probability that his sign will be mistaken for the thing it signifies and become manifestly idolatrous. And even if the poet recognizes the essential difference between his figurative image and its abstract subject, how can he ensure that the reader will do the same? In using metaphor to embody the immaterial, he inevitably runs the risk that it will end up supplanting its original subject altogether.

This fear of taking the sign for the thing signified was at the heart of Protestant discussions of idolatry throughout the Elizabethan period, whether in relation to the figurative nature of the sacrament or the actual adoration of images. The essence of the problem derived from the necessary relation of the figurative to the prototype it seeks to illuminate, as Bishop Jewel recognized in quoting Chrysostom on the subject: '"The figure may not be far off from the truth; otherwise it were no figure: neither may it be even, and one with the truth; otherwise it would be the truth itself" and so no figure.'[7] Chrysostom's statement could almost have been written as a summation of the relation of metaphor to the truth it seeks to embody in *The Faerie Queene*. It also underlines the reason why it is so easy for metaphor to be abused and, like the idolatrous image, to forget its actual relation to the truth it seeks to delineate, in a misguided attempt to turn itself into a literal version of that truth. This is why the metaphor of idolatry is detectable each time the poem reflects on its own allegorical procedures and the dangers they entail. The narrative of False Florimell is simply the most overt example of the idolatrous characteristics of false metaphor examined so far, since it combines the attempt to usurp the place of an original, associated with figures like Archimago and Duessa, with the literalizing of metaphoric discourse generated by Despair or, in a different way, by the iconic metamorphosis of Malbecco.[8]

The Bower of Bliss episode from the last canto of Book II offers an ideal opportunity for the further exploration of metaphor's idolatrous potentialities. The Bower has traditionally been seen as something of a *locus classicus* for discussions of Spenserian poetics. A romantic view links the Bower, as a place of sensual pleasure, with Spenser's temptation to abandon the poem's moral purpose for the sensuous delights of its own imagery, until this literary decadence is puritanically repressed in the final stanzas.[9] More recently, readings of the Bower have started to reinterpret its destruction within the framework of Elizabethan political discourses including, in Stephen Greenblatt's study, 'the European response to the native cultures of the New World, the English colonial struggle in Ireland, and the Reformation attack on images'.[10] That the Bower of Bliss can accommodate such different analogies at the same time is not so surprising given the Renaissance view of gardens as places inciting actions of particular kinds. Of the two analogies which concern this discussion, poetry (along with philosophy and love) was one of the three sorts of activity finding its proper place in gardens in the tradition of the *loci amoeni* of Plato;[11] idolatry and iconoclasm, on the other hand, as Kenneth Gross points out, are often associated in the Bible with 'the tearing down of groves and "high places," natural or cultivated sites'.[12] The embedding of analogies with idolatry and iconoclasm within an episode of self-referential reflection on poetic pleasure makes the Bower of Bliss a natural site for a discussion of the idolatrous potential of the very metaphors on which allegory relies to authenticate its poetic voice.

At the threshold of the Bower of Bliss is a personage whose elliptical description includes repeated phrases reminiscent of the language used in rhetorical definitions of allegory. In particular Puttenham's reference to '*Allegoria*, or Figure of False Semblant'[13] has an affinity with the presentation of the Bower's false Genius. In each of the three stanzas which refer to him directly, a similarity with Puttenham's description of allegory can be found: firstly, in his 'semblaunce pleasing, more then naturall' (II. xii. 46), then, in his 'guilefull semblaunts' (II. xii. 48), and finally, in 'his staffe, with which he charmed semblants sly' (II. xii. 49). These verbal correspondences with Puttenham's terms for allegory invite further investigation, especially as this 'figure of false semblant' has proved to be particularly problematic for critics who have sought to fix his literary lineage.[14] Not only is he never named directly, but a considerable proportion of his description is in the indirect form of an extended negative comparison:

> They in that place him *Genius* did call:
>   Not that celestiall powre, to whom the care
>   Of life, and generation of all
>   That liues, pertaines in charge particulare,
>   Who wondrous things concerning our welfare,
>   And straunge phantomes doth let vs oft forsee,
>   And oft of secret ill bids vs beware:
>   That is our Selfe, whom though we do not see,
> Yet each doth in him selfe it well perceiue to bee.
>
> Therefore a God him sage Antiquity
>   Did wisely make, and good *Agdistes* call:
>   But this same was to that quite contrary,
>   The foe of life, that good enuyes to all,
>   That secretly doth vs procure to fall,
>   Through guilefull semblaunts, which he makes vs see.
>
>   (II. xii. 47–8)

This evil genius, it would appear, must be carefully distinguished from his contrary, the 'good *Agdistes*', for whom he is apparently so easily mistaken. In the very attempt at defining the differences between the two geniuses, the passage ironically ends up alluding to the difficulty of telling them apart: a problem the syntax of the stanzas actually enacts in the dynamics of the reading process. The opening line leaves the reader waiting for a unit of meaning that will complete its description of the individual called Genius by the inhabitants of the Bower. The introduction of the comparison with his contrary, announced with the words 'Not that', postpones the completion of the initial clause for ten lines spreading across into a new stanza and a new sentence. Logically, the clause beginning 'Not that' announces the return to the main subject with the words 'But this'; yet, it is hardly surprising, given the delay and the convoluted development of ideas, that the reader is tempted to try to link earlier lines referring to Agdistes back to the Genius of the Bower. This is particularly likely to occur at the start of the forty-eighth stanza and even though any misreadings can be corrected retrospectively, their effect is to reveal just how easily the distinction between the two figures can become blurred. Far from reinforcing their separate identities, the poem manages to display how a figure of 'False Semblant', like the Bower's porter, can undermine the identity of the prototype it impersonates at the very moment when that prototype is called forth to expose the impostor.

The ironies of this passage continue to multiply the more its structure is explored. After all, it is the description of Agdistes which is interpolated into a passage concerned with the entrance to the Bower of Bliss. In this sense it is Agdistes, the 'celestiall powre', who ends up behaving in the very manner of the deceitful interloper he was brought in to unmask. Once more, the boundaries between truth and falsehood seem perilously insecure. Even the processes by which the true and false geniuses influence the human mind are, on closer inspection, not very easy to tell apart. The Genius of the Bower employs 'guilefull semblaunts, which he makes vs see', while Agdistes with his 'straunge phantomes doth let vs oft forsee'. What distinguishes them is not the mode of representation, since it is not clear how 'guilefull semblaunts' differ from 'straunge phantomes'. The type of image they bring into the mind is essentially the same; it is the purpose of the depiction of an image and the freedom given to the individual with respect to perceiving it in the first place which makes for the only real difference. When we remember that for Puttenham allegory was categorized as one of the 'figures altering and affecting the mynde by alteration of sence or intendements in whole clauses or speaches',[15] a further link is created between these figures of mental orientation and the figure of allegory, or 'False Semblant'. Unfortunately, it is a link which associates allegory just as readily with the guiding spirit of a malevolent poetic environment as it does with a benevolent one.

The entrance to the Bower of Bliss initiates the debate about the ambiguous nature of allegory that is continued throughout the rest of the canto. The potential for good or evil of figurative modes of discourse ensures that the metaphors of poetry must be scrutinized to determine their real intentions. The problem here is primarily one of differentiation which, as this threshold Genius reveals, is not easy to perform when the false metaphors can so successfully masquerade as their legitimate counterparts. It is this question concerning the use and abuse of figurative images which finds in idolatry or, perhaps, in idolatry's own resistance to an agreed definition, such an appropriate metaphor for metaphoric misuse.

The Bower's porter is therefore to be associated with the

extended metaphoric discourse of allegory but also with the latent idolatry false metaphor always entails:

> With diuerse flowres he daintily was deckt,
>   And strowed round about, and by his side
>   A mighty Mazer bowle of wine was set,
>   As if it had to him bene sacrifide;
>   Wherewith all new-come guests he gratifide:
>   So did he eke Sir *Guyon* passing by:
>   But he his idle curtesie defide,
>   And ouerthrew his bowle disdainfully;
> And broke his staffe, with which he charmed semblants sly.
>
> (II. xii. 49)

The depiction of 'Pleasures porter' (II. xii. 48) here continues the verbal echoes with the flowers of rhetorical figuration. His floral ornamentation is, in this context, suggestive in itself,[16] as is the final reference to his 'semblants sly.' In his role as a simulacrum, formed in the specious likeness of the antique god Agdistes, the Bower's false Genius is literally an idol. The 'mighty Mazer bowle of wine' set alongside him, while a potent symbol of Bacchic intemperance, is also, as the reference to its sacrificial appearance emphasizes, suggestive of idolatrous worship. When Guyon passes him by and defies his 'idle curtesie', he refuses an offer that is idle in the sense that it is both futile and a temptation to drunken idleness. What Guyon also refuses, if the latent pun is brought into play, is an idol offering that would lead him to perform an act of idolatry in drinking from the cup of a false god.[17] The appearance of this pun at the gateway to the Bower of Bliss is no accident; it introduces an aspect of the idolatrous nature of the Bower of Bliss central to its entire depiction.

Idleness, while a potent source of evil in *The Faerie Queene* in its own right, is frequently linked to the intemperance of concupiscence. The most notable scenes of idleness involve a call to ease but an ease which brings with it the desire for sexual indulgence in environments displaying many of the salient features of the Bower of Bliss. When Redcrosse is surprised and defeated by Orgoglio, it is not just the waters of the slothful fountain which weaken his 'manly forces' (I. vii. 6) but his sexual advances to Duessa 'Pourd out in loosnesse' (I. vii. 7) which leave him incapacitated. The shady glade with its sweet bird song and bubbling fountain is like a miniature version of Acrasia's bower, with Redcrosse lying 'Disarmed all of yron-coted Plate' (I. vii. 2), a prefigurement of the dishonourable luxuriousness of Verdant. Phaedria and her island in the aptly named 'Idle lake' foreshadow Acrasia's intermingling of idleness, idolatry and sexual intemperance even more strongly. Her invitation to Cymocles and Guyon to 'Refuse such fruitlesse toile, and present pleasures chuse' (II. vi. 17) constitutes essentially the same attempt to lead the Knight of Temperance, through idleness *'into loose desire'* (II. vi. Argument) that will be made again, only with more sophistication, in the Bower of Bliss.

As a figure of 'guilefull semblaunts', the Bower's gatekeeper initiates the presentation of the intemperate metaphoric text as an environment inviting the idolatry of idle concupiscence. That Acrasia's domain should present such a strong link between sexual intemperance and idolatry is hardly surprising given the traditional pairing of idolatry and adultery and the Old Testament's insistent condemnation of idol-worship as spiritual whoredom.[18] The treatise 'Against Peril of Idolatry' in *The Second Book of Homilies* of 1562 repeated the terms of the ancient injunction referring to the 'spiritual wickednesse of an idol's enticing' as 'like the flatteries of a wanton harlot' and 'a gilt or painted idol, or image' as 'a strumpet with a painted face'.[19] The rhetorical question in which this passage culminates could not be more specific in its conclusion: *'Be not men and women prone to spiritual fornication (I mean idolatry) as to carnal fornication?'* The fact that this conflation of idolatrous indiscretion with carnal indulgence was taken up in popular Protestant propaganda against the 'spiritual fornication' of Romish image-worship should not mask the theoretical basis to the view of images underlying the analogy. It is only within the context of Reformation debates on the legitimacy of images as an aid to Christian worship that the concupiscence of the Bower of Bliss assumes its full impact as an idolatrous transgression and a perversion of metaphor within the allegorical text.

A central feature of Protestant aversion to the veneration of images concerned attempts to create a comprehensive classification of idols and icons in which the whole universe was turned into a gradual hierarchy of images. The primary distinction between *latria* (the honour due to God alone) and *dulia* (the service offered to the creature), first drawn up in ninth century Byzantium by the Nicene Council, became a particular focus of attention.[20] For Catholic apologists, the spiritual devotion rendered to the supreme God was quite distinct from the inferior reverence for holy images. To Protestant theologians like Bishop Jewel the distinction was spurious and dangerous:

> And by such a simple distinction it is thought the whole matter is well salved. But what if the simple people understand no Greek, and cannot so learnedly discern *latria* from *doulia*, but take the one adoration for the other? Verily, as it now fareth in the church of Rome, they use them both universally without difference.... Ye will not have your adoration of images called *latria*, but only *doulia*. But, sir, do you by this distinction any thing abate *idolatria*?[21]

Jewel is in no doubt; the distinction between *latria* and *dulia* is not sustainable. If it was devised as a concession to the nature of ordinary men to enable their souls to worship the one God invisible and immaterial, in practice it was liable to cause confusion by leading to the adoration of the Creator and the creature with one honour. For Augustine, it was precisely this inability to distinguish between the love of the things of the earth for the sake of God and for the sake of themselves that distinguished charity from cupidity:

> I call 'charity' the motion of the soul toward the enjoyment of God for His own sake, and the enjoyment of one's self and of one's neighbor for the sake of God; but 'cupidity' is a motion of the soul toward the enjoyment of one's self, one's neighbor, or any corporal thing for the sake of something other than God.
> (*On Christian Doctrine*, III. x. 16)

Once idolatry and cupidity are acknowledged as involving a similar withdrawal by the Christian from the quest towards God in favour of the pleasures of the here and now, it is possible to see how the two chief protagonists of intemperance Guyon meets in Book II both tempt him with forms of cupidity which are also inherently idolatrous. Mammon seeks to replace the love of God with the avaricious desire of wealth for its own sake, while Acrasia aims to supplant the love of God with an intemperate indulgence in lust for its own sake. The enemies of temperance are idolaters precisely because they exchange the proper enjoyment of the things of this world for the illicit pleasures of material reward and fleshly sensuality as ends in themselves. What both Mammon and Acrasia offer, as A. Bartlett Giamatti argues, are false forms of earthly bliss in place of the true bliss of heavenly beatitude.[22] Mammon's vaunts are unmistakably idolatrous:

> God of the world and worldlings I me call,
> Great *Mammon*, greatest god below the skye.
>
> (II. vii. 8)

Guyon in resisting the 'idle offers' of his 'golden fee' (II. vii. 9) avoids the idolatry of avaricious cupidity with which Mammon seeks to tempt him in words which could be used to paraphrase Augustine:

> Loe here the worldes blis, loe here the end,
> To which all men do ayme, rich to be made.
>
> (II. vii. 32)

When Guyon turns to the 'Money God' and announces: 'all thine idle offers I refuse' (II. vii. 39), not only does he evoke the 'idle/idol' pun for the second time, he also invokes what amounts to an Augustinian concept of 'charity' to oppose to Mammon's 'cupidity'. In place of worldly riches as both the source and goal of earthly enjoyment Guyon postulates 'Another blis ... Another happinesse, another end' (II. vii. 33) and exposes the cheapness of Mammon's opulence compared with the pleasures of divine bliss for which it can never be more than an idle substitute.

The links between the cupidity of Mammon's Cave and that on display in Acrasia's Bower are still more apparent once it is noticed that the language of desire is common to both avarice and lust. Guyon's short history of man's descent into covetousness tells a story of 'licentious lust' in which the rape of the earth's 'quiet wombe' to extract her 'hid treasures' from 'her sacred tombe' is depicted as an act of 'Sacriledge' climaxing in a description which deftly conflates sexual and material desire:

> Then auarice gan through his veines inspire
> His greedy flames, and kindled life-deuouring fire.
>
> (II. vii. 17)

There is no difference between this conception of the effects of avarice and the depiction of the lustful fires associated with uncontrolled sexual desire such as those which consume Malecasta in the Castle Ioyeous:

> Like sparkes of fire, which fall in sclender flex,
> That shortly brent into extreme desire,
> And ransackt all her veines with passion entire.
>
> (III. i. 47)

Mammon's material cupidity is only superficially different from Acrasia's sexual cupidity since both involve essentially the same turning away from the spiritual enjoyment of God for the immediate pleasures of this world. In this sense, their appeal is similarly idolatrous because it seeks to make physical objects of desire the ultimate goal of human endeavour. Mammon's offer of limitless wealth and Acrasia's promise of carnal fulfilment amount to very much the same thing. Indeed, Mammon's last bid to weaken Guyon's resolve actually bridges the gap between material and sexual reward when he presents his daughter Philotime with the pledge: 'Thy spouse I will her make, if that thou lust' (II. vii. 49). 'Lust' for Mammon has become a synonym for all physical 'desire'. He tempts Guyon with a form of cupidity which links the love of money with the pleasures of the flesh since both lead to the immersion of the individual in the rewards of this world.

Mammon's attempt to usurp the place of the divine Creator by filling the heart of man with the love of gold rather than the love of God finally declares its idolatrous kinship with Acrasia's Bower in the presence of its own imitation paradise. The Garden of Proserpina signals the ultimate ambition of the false god to create a paradise of earthly bliss to appeal to human desire. But like the rest of Mammon's Cave, its attraction is limited; there is little to delight in for its true nature, as a living hell imprisoning tormented souls, appears only too plainly. If there is some doubt concerning the symbolic presence of Tantalus and Pilate in Mammon's river of hell,[23] the allegorical message as a whole is unambiguous: cupidity is an offence against God and the 'mind intemperate' (II. vii. 60) that is attracted to it will be punished with eternal damnation.

Guyon's faint on returning from his three-day ordeal in Mammon's dark underworld is specifically explained as a consequence of his 'want of food, and sleepe' (II. vii. 65) rather than the struggle to resist temptation. From start to finish Mammon's riches, like Pilate's hands, are portrayed as 'filthy feculent' (II. vii. 61) and deserving of the contempt they receive from Guyon. There is nothing in the Cave of Mammon to attract Guyon or the reader, and in exposing avarice for what it is – a depraved moral vice – the allegory does its job. Or does it? For there is a sense in which the presentation of the morally repugnant nature of avarice is in danger of misrepresenting its actual material attraction. When allegory embodies an abstract moral evil like avarice and depicts it as wholly repulsive and abhorrent, it ignores the very qualities which in reality make the lust for riches so appealing to human desire. Here, allegory is brought face to face with the traditional dilemma concerning the representation of evil in art: how are the temptations of vices to be mimetically represented without either distorting their appearance to facilitate their condemnation, or making them so inherently appealing to the reader that the moral perspective might be lost altogether? There are no easy solutions to this problem, since the allegorist either faces representational compromise or the risk of contaminating the purity of the text's own metaphors. If allegory chooses to play safe, revealing hidden moral truths in allegorical figures which disguise the attractiveness of evil to humans, it preserves its devotion to moral truth at the expense of mimetic truth. But alternatively, if allegory once dares to step down from its moral high ground in an attempt to do justice to the reality of the evils with which it battles, it brings into question the morality of its own figurative intentions. This then is the ironic cost of the true poet's commitment to allegorical truth; in his quest to make allegory a vehicle for discerning truth from falsehood, he must accept the need to question allegory's capacity to maintain a distinction between its own proper and improper use of figurative language.

As moral allegory, the Cave of Mammon plays safe; it represents the abstract quality of material cupidity through an allegorical figure and an allegorical environment which both ensure Guyon and the reader reject all they have to offer. There is nothing here to disturb a dispassionate and truly temperate response to the textual encounter with cupidity because the allegory embodies the spiritual monstrosity of covetousness not the actual attraction of what is coveted. In this respect, the allegory gives a true but experientially partial understanding of avarice; the cupidity it inspires is morally rejected but it has not been emotionally experienced or resisted. If cupidity were, like Mammon, self-evidently unattractive it would not constitute a real threat to individual or social morality. Guyon's victory over Mammon is, in this sense, achieved too easily; the bliss he is offered in Mammon's idolatrous kingdom manifestly fails to challenge its heavenly counterpart. In exposing cupidity for what it is morally the allegory avoids confronting it as a real source of human temptation.

FROM ICONOMACH[24] TO ICONOCLAST

The Bower of Bliss takes allegory into a far more treacherous region where its representation of the appeal of sexual cupidity highlights the actual attractions of lust and idolatry. It completes the Book of Temperance in an act of allegorical honesty which, in seeking a more intimate knowledge of the allurements of concupiscence, risks opening up the poem's own metaphoric enterprise to accusations of idolatrous intemperance in its excessive devotion to the sensual image of cupidity. A passage from Augustine, in which he develops his own metaphor for the pleasures of cupidity, will help to clarify the threat Acrasia represents not just for the virtue of temperance championed by Guyon but also for the poem's faith in the rectitude of its metaphoric project:

> Suppose we were wanderers who could not live in blessedness except at home, miserable in our wandering and desiring to end it and to return to our native country. We would need vehicles for land and sea which could be used to help us to reach our homeland, which is to be enjoyed. But if the amenities of the journey and the motion of the vehicles itself delighted us, and we were led to enjoy those things which we should use, we should not wish to end our journey quickly, and,

entangled in a perverse sweetness, we should be alienated from our country, whose sweetness would make us blessed.
(*On Christian Doctrine*, I. 4. 4)

This metaphor of the wanderer in search of a homeland, which Augustine introduces to reveal cupidity as an abandonment of the ultimate goal of heavenly blessedness for the enjoyment of the immediate pleasures of the world, could almost have been designed to encapsulate the conflicting desires of allegory in *The Faerie Queene*. All the poem's eponymous figures of virtue, as errant knights, are wanderers whose return to the homeland of the court of Gloriana is promised only after the fulfilment of their quest. More than any other knight, Guyon, as the Knight of Temperance, confronts enemies who try to engineer his defeat simply by distracting him with the pleasures they put in his path along the way. Guyon must proceed resolutely, for to do otherwise is to start to enjoy the journey for its own sake, retarding his progress and tempting him to forget his ultimate destination altogether. This is why Guyon's archetype, recalled in the perils of his sea voyage to the Bower of Bliss, is the traveller Odysseus, whose epic tale tells of the journey back to his homeland in Ithaca, or more accurately, as Tzvetan Todorov suggests, of his deliberate attempts to postpone his homecoming:

> If Odysseus takes so long to return home, it is because home is not his deepest desire... Odysseus resists returning to Ithaca so that the story can continue. The theme of the *Odyssey* is not Odysseus' return to Ithaca; this return is, on the contrary, the death of the *Odyssey*, its end. The theme of the *Odyssey* is the narrative forming the *Odyssey*, it is the *Odyssey* itself.[25]

Spenser's Odyssean archetype needs to be carefully reworked if *The Faerie Queene* is to avoid the implied cupidity of poetic self-obsession. While Christian allegory must recognize that its quest towards the revelation of divine truth will inevitably be endlessly postponed, it should not allow a narcissistic delight in its own images to become a substitute for that ultimate destination that should remain its deepest desire. In allegory, metaphor is indeed a figure of transport, a vehicle providing a means of journeying on the quest of spiritual predication. The danger for the allegorist, if Augustine's metaphor for cupidity is applied to poetic composition, is that in enjoying the pleasures of his own metaphoric vehicle, he may lose sight of the purpose for which it was employed in the first place and commit what amounts to an act of poetic idolatry.

Spenser knew only too well the terms in which his work would be dismissed by its detractors:

> Of some th'aboundance of an idle braine
> Will iudged be, and painted forgery.
>
> (II. Proem. 1)

The Proem to Book II initiates the dual criticism of the idleness that invents allegory and the idolatry its counterfeit images enact,[26] but it is not until Guyon enters Acrasia's garden that the idolatrous potential of poetic self-indulgence reaches its culmination. After all, if 'aboundance' is a sign of literary idleness, then not only does the Bower of Bliss house the figure of Excesse, but its description generates the most prolix canto in the entire poem. And if this excessive prolongation of sensual and aesthetic pleasure is to be resisted, condemned, and ultimately destroyed, it is precisely because the experience of reading it threatens to expose the corruptibility of the metaphors of Christian allegory. Where the allegorical journey should lead towards spiritual revelation, progress through Acrasia's garden of delights is constantly arrested and the text's metaphoric surface increasingly becomes an end in itself. Every time a particular attraction is lingered over, the reader becomes more fully entangled in the textual equivalent of that 'perverse sweetness' which Augustine warns against as the source of alienation from the blessedness of divine truth.

Augustine's conception of cupidity as the 'perverse sweetness' enjoyed when carnal human desire willingly embraces earthly pleasures, even though those pleasures are known to be illicit, encapsulates the conflicting responses characteristic of the poetic experience evoked within the Bower of Bliss. As Stephen Greenblatt astutely remarks, the reader 'can master the iconography, read all the signs correctly, and still respond to the allure of the Bower.'[27] This is what makes Acrasia's particular brand of 'perverse sweetness' such a dangerously subversive challenge to the temperate discourse demanded of Christian allegory. Once poetic images are acknowledged to be capable of exhibiting their moral depravity while still appealing aesthetically to the reader, then the potentially confused responses they generate begin to undermine the oppositional conceptual systems readers of allegory normally rely on to interpret the text. It was evident from the history of Jason and Medea, depicted in the ivory of the entrance gate, that art is capable of producing ambivalent responses to the scenes it portrays:

> And other where the snowy substaunce sprent
> With vermell, like the boyes bloud therein shed,
> A piteous spectacle did represent,
> And otherwhiles with gold besprinkeled;
> Yt seemd th'enchaunted flame, which did *Creüsa* wed.
>
> (II. xii. 45)

The 'piteous spectacle' of Medea scattering the pieces of her brother's body on the surface of the sea and the equally brutal immolation of Creüsa are fashioned in such a way that the horror of the events is lost beneath the aesthetically pleasing surface of the work of art. But Acrasia's art desires more than emotional manipulation of readers; it aims to distort their perception of art itself.

In this respect, the relationship between art and nature in the Bower of Bliss epitomizes a blurring of boundaries that highlights the religious anxieties inherent in an aesthetic creed that puts its faith wholeheartedly in the figurative power of poetry to achieve moments of spiritual revelation. If art is capable of granting a vision of perfected nature, it is possible to envisage poetry replacing religion altogether as a way back to God. Derek Attridge locates a crisis point for Renaissance literary theory in this dilemma, which generates unease whenever it surfaces in Elizabethan texts, and which is most acute when 'art ceases to be distinguishable by its distance from nature and takes on the appearance of nature itself'.[28] Attridge reveals how easily the apparent stability of the opposition between art and nature can evaporate, even in a text like Puttenham's *The Arte of English Poesie*, which strives to maintain its belief in the supplementary relationship of art to nature. In the Bower, where Acrasia aims to obliterate all means of distinguishing art from nature, we witness a poetics of religious substitution turning itself into an act of idolatry.

Acrasia is actively engaged in constructing a version of creation capable of replacing God's original paradise with her own artificial replica. If she is successful in creating a prelapsarian world here and now, then there is no need to wait or strive for the distant promise of man's ultimate perfectibility in divine reconciliation. But, at the precise moment when the idolatrous potential of art to construct an earthly form of bliss to replace heavenly bliss is envisaged, the limits of metaphor are reasserted. In a stanza constructed as a climactic list comparing the Bower with legendary scenes of natural beauty it is described as:

> More sweet and holesome, then the pleasaunt hill
>   Of *Rhodope*, on which the Nimphe, that bore
>   A gyaunt babe, her selfe for griefe did kill;
>   Or the Thessalian *Tempe*, where of yore
>   Faire *Daphne Phoebus* hart with loue did gore;
>   Or *Ida*, where the Gods lou'd to repaire,
>   When euer they their heauenly bowres forlore;
>   Or sweet *Parnasse*, the haunt of Muses faire;
> Or *Eden* selfe, if ought with *Eden* mote compaire.

(II. xii. 52)

The comparative process that elevates the Bower of Bliss above the level of Parnasse, the home of the Muses and source of poetic inspiration, is collapsed at the point where its audacious transgression becomes truly idolatrous. The rhetorical flow of the stanza as a whole lulls the reader into an increasingly unquestioning acceptance of the sequence of comparisons. They are introduced as natural alternatives to each other, so that when the last line, following the same grammatical pattern as the preceding lines, begins 'Or *Eden* selfe', the act of profanation it represents, at first, goes unnoticed. Any such idolatrous misreading of the passage is simultaneously made explicit and challenged by the suppositional clause which follows: 'if ought with *Eden* mote compaire.' Yet, although the implication is clear that nothing can be compared to Eden, let alone surpass it, there is also tacit recognition that the comparison, while unacceptable, has been made and may have been momentarily accepted. The reader's susceptibility to the transgressive potential of metaphoric comparison to blur distinctions between the secular and the sacred and the human and the divine makes plain the idolatrous nature of the entire episode.

The importance of metaphor as a means of obliterating distinctions between art and nature in the Bower of Bliss becomes increasingly evident. If Acrasia is to succeed in supplanting heavenly bliss with her earthly substitute, she must ensure that it is impossible to distinguish her crafted version of a natural paradise from '*Eden* selfe'. She need not surpass nature; indeed it is important that she does not, since to do so would still ensure the perception of differences between the two. Her art must instead strive to achieve a form of perfect mimesis – to hold a mirror up to nature to produce an image that is designed to be indistinguishable from the original it reflects. An art, however, which suppresses all trace of difference between the original it copies and its own representation fundamentally misunderstands the basis of the relationship between art and nature that underlies the concept of mimesis. Mimesis accepts the secondariness of art's imitation of the nature it reflects and, furthermore, recognizes nature itself as fallen and consequently only an imperfect image of nature in its prelapsarian or ideal state. Acrasia's artistic rebellion, in questioning the relationship between art and nature at the first of these levels, threatens to dismantle the structured system of difference on which divine transcendence relies at the second level. The full impact of her revolutionary enterprise is consequently double-edged, and seeks to overturn artistic and religious creeds in a single stroke.

In her grand act of religious trespass Acrasia enlists the support of metaphor as a powerful figure of verbal transgression in its own right. Yet, metaphoric predication, in recognizing the similarity of dissimilars, accepts difference alongside its perception of likeness and always stops short of identity. Acrasia's idolatrous misuse of images which pretend to be synonymous with the prototype they imitate perverts metaphor every bit as much as it corrupts art. When Harry Berger Jr refers to Acrasia as 'a demonic allegorist', he rightly characterizes her opposition to God as an inversion of Christian allegory.[29] Figurative language consequently participates in her plan to make art seem as natural as nature by making nature seem more artificial than art. This double inversion of natural relationships is particularly obvious in the grapes adorning the vine of Excesse's porch:

> Some deepe empurpled as the *Hyacint*,
> Some as the Rubine, laughing sweetly red,

Metaphor as an Act of Idolatry

> Some like faire Emeraudes, not yet well ripened.
>
> And them amongst, some were of burnisht gold,
>   So made by art, to beautifie the rest,
>   Which did themselues emongst the leaues enfold.
>
> (II. xii. 54–5)

The grapes made of 'burnisht gold' mingle with the fruit on the vine and enfold themselves in the natural foliage, but what stops them from seeming out of place are the similes comparing the colours of the real grapes to gemstones. Art may be seen to be actively engaged in copying nature but it is nature itself which seems to increase in lustre from being associated with the artificial splendour of jewels. The figurative language of the description accomplishes the subtle blurring of distinctions between the real and the unreal, the natural and the artificial in a commingling of identities which, in merging art and nature so cunningly, begins to enact the etymology of Acrasia's own name.

While Acrasia represents incontinence generally, her name derives from a complex field of meaning associated with its Greek root including the word *krasis*: a mixing, compounding or blending.[30] Her paradise of incontinence is consequently most fully realized in its celebration of the collapse of difference as art and nature become indistinguishable:

> One would haue thought, (so cunningly, the rude,
>   And scorned parts were mingled with the fine,)
>   That nature had for wantonesse ensude
>   Art, and that Art at nature did repine;
>   so striuing each th'other to vndermine,
>   Each did the others worke more beautifie.
>
> (II. xii. 59)

Art and nature appear to function as one and the relationship between them is now so close that it is possible to see them as equal partners in a process of perfect creation; possible, that is, were it not for the corrective presence of the initial interjection: 'One would haue thought' and its bracketed extension. This prefatory remark counteracts Acrasia's perverse allegory of Edenic restoration by reminding us that the impression it gives of artistic innocence is merely a contrivance designed to disguise the idolatry of the false images it has created. Spenser thus seems able to protect his own poetry from similar accusations of idolatry so long as he can differentiate the moral effects of a mode of allegory based on verbal interaction with the reader from the sensual appeal of a primarily visual mode of allegory like Acrasia's.

Where Guyon has the Palmer to correct any momentary aberration, the reader can, in addition, turn for guidance from the poet's moral commentary planted in the verbal description of the enchantments of the garden. That Spenser should follow a Protestant poetics based on the power of the word to repress the deceptions of visual appearance seems only natural in an age when painted images in churches were whitewashed and replaced by the written text of Scripture.[31] Michael O'Connell refers to Spenser's use of such intervention in the narrative as representative of a poetics in which 'language is represented as the only reliable index of reality',[32] while for Harry Berger Jr, Spenser's morally charged language actually delivers us from evil in the Bower of Bliss where 'confronted by the images rather than words, we would no doubt succumb.'[33] The presence of a moral discourse opposed to the dissolute images is not in question; what is debatable, however, is the extent to which these images retain their capacity to seduce the reader despite the poem's condemnatory internal commentary. There is more uncertainty, perhaps even fear, regarding the verbal medium of poetry in The Faerie Queene than critics are sometimes willing to admit.

Where the accumulation of moral censure might be expected to produce increasing revulsion, the pleasure of the text is experienced with growing intensity as the reader makes progress through the Bower and its inner secrets are revealed. What is also noticeable is that as the nature of the reading experience becomes ever more sexual, the eroticism of the text appropriates a language associated with the description of allegorical writing, as in the case of the 'naked Damzelles' (II. xii. 63) wrestling in the waters of the fountain:

> The whiles their snowy limbes, as through a vele,
> So through the Christall waues appeared plaine:
> Then suddeinly both would themselues vnhele,
> And th'amorous sweet spoiles to greedy eyes reuele.

(II. xii. 64)

Metaphor as an Act of Idolatry 149

The sexual disclosure of the maidens as they expose their bodies from beneath the watery veil is reminiscent of images which have been associated with the allegorical quest toward poetic revelation. This disconcerting link between the veiled truths of allegory and the provocative antics of the bathing maidens invites comparison between the promise of interpretational penetration of textual mysteries and the discovery of the sexual secrets of the female body. For Camille Paglia, such 'scopophilia is one of the most characteristic moods of *The Faerie Queene*',[34] and once the pleasure of textual revelation is viewed as a form of voyeurism, as here in the Bower of Bliss, then the poem's allegory as a whole is endangered.

When the nymphs 'vnhele' their 'sweet spoiles' to Guyon, the association of their willingness to make themselves visible with the process of metaphoric discovery spoils any naive belief in the incorruptibility of Spenser's allegory. Suddenly, readers are forced to confront the allegorical representation of concupiscence as a full-blooded embodiment of venerean enticements capable of kindling prurient desires in them as well as Guyon. When Guyon starts to 'slacke his pace' in order to look and see more, his display of sexual self-indulgence gratifies the libidinous weakness of the reader for continued erotic titillation climaxing in the maidens' invitation to approach ever nearer for further revelation:

> Their wanton meriments they did encreace,
> And to him beckned, to approch more neare,
> And shewd him many sights, that courage cold could reare.
>
> (II. xii. 68)

The allegory exposes the loss of control Guyon experiences over the erected spirit of his temperate manhood as his sexual desires rise up. But, if Guyon's self-control is questioned by the episode, then a similar question is asked of the reader (particularly the male reader) concerning the extent to which his own willingness to indulge himself erotically draws him away from the path of temperate reading. Once sexual desire is established as a metaphor for textual interpretation, then the potentially carnal enjoyment of the attempt to penetrate the veil of allegory becomes apparent. It is an acknowledgement which, in alluding to the similarities between the pleasures of sexual and allegorical gratification, recognizes that concupiscence and the spiritual whoredom of idolatry are both potential metaphors for the poem's own figurative discourse.

An uneasiness concerning the response not just of Guyon but also of the reader to the erotic exhibitionism of the 'naked Damzelles' surfaces with unusual starkness in the uncomfortable commentary which follows:

> On which when gazing him the Palmer saw,
>   He much rebukt those wandring eyes of his,
>   And counseld well, him forward thence did draw.
>   Now are they come nigh to the *Bowre of blis*
>   Of her fond fauorites so nam'd amis.
>
> (II. xii. 69)

Surprisingly, there is no clear definition of the vice which has been displayed, nor is there any indication of how the Palmer 'rebukt' Guyon, or of what he said in his good counsel. The Palmer is anxious to draw Guyon past this particualr temptation as quickly as possible; but the poem itself seems to have lost faith in the reader's capacity to interpret the metaphoric environment. The narrative voice steps in to provide a curious reminder that the genitive metaphor that named Acrasia's garden 'the Bowre of *Blisse*' in the forty-second stanza derives falsely from the Bower's own deluded inhabitants. The reader must be clearly informed that the '*Bowre of blis*' is not to be mistaken for a site of true bliss (a point reinforced by the lack of capitalization of the word '*blis*' this time). The sudden need to reassert the Bower's metaphoric status and to impose its correct interpretation only serves to heighten the fear that idolatry may be intrinsic to the allegorist's figures. In the Bower of Bliss, where eroticism intensifies the sensual appeal of the poetry to such an extent that readers not only observe how lust affects Guyon but experience the effects of lust through their own response to the poem, the idolatrous appeal of poetry is witnessed first hand.

Linda Gregerson has proposed a useful functional distinction between what she terms 'exemplary' and 'catalytic' modes of allegorical representation.[35] In the first case, an allegorical figure is a direct embodiment of the condition it represents; in the second case, an allegorical figure causes the condition it represents to appear in other characters. The concupiscence displayed in the Bower of Bliss constitutes an extreme form of catalytic allegory, where the precipitation of the vice extends beyond the poem's internal characters and is actually activated in the reader. The proposed educative function of the moral allegory is brought to the verge of collapse by this idolatrous transgression in which figured concupiscence is experienced as actual concupiscence. Acrasia's perverse allegory generates metaphoric confusion, blurring distinctions between figurative representations and the literal responses they invite. Here then is the ultimate example of the sign being mistaken for the thing signified, the idolatrous abuse of the image that comes to replace its own prototype.

Where one might expect a clear distinction to be drawn between the idolatrous allegory generated by Acrasia and the poet's controlling figurative discourse, Spenser's similes comparing the bathing nymphs to the emergent Venus in fact reinforce the impression of beauty:

> As that faire Starre, the messenger of morne,
> His deawy face out of the sea doth reare:
> Or as the *Cyprian* goddesse, newly borne
> Of th'Oceans fruitfull froth, did first appeare:
> Such seemed they, and so their yellow heare
> Christalline humour dropped downe apace.
> Whom such when *Guyon* saw, he drew him neare.

(II. xii. 65)

Acrasia contrives to present herself in the guise of the earthly Venus, whether as *Venus Pandemos* embodying natural beauty in the material world or as *Venus Genetrix* representing the power of generation and natural plenitude. The Venerean image she cultivates throughout her garden, and which culminates with her leaning over Verdant on a bed of roses in a virtual tableau of Venus's disarming of Mars, seems to grow out of her own self-conscious artistry. Here, however, the comparisons with Venus derive from the poet's narrative commentary and there is no hint of irony behind the reference to the rising morning star or the birth of the goddess from the sea. The stanza gives the impression that the perception is Guyon's and that the similes describe what he 'saw'; but, since the basis of the comparison is not visual but conceptual this is merely a narrative illusion. The transformation of a display of unabashed sexual provocation into an image of Venereal beauty has been achieved by the poet's own figurative language which, far from counteracting Acrasia's false allegory, has shown how easily it can start to merge with it.

The danger of such momentary loss of distinct boundaries between the corrupt allegory perpetrated by Acrasia and the poet's corrective intervention is that it questions the poem's capacity to provide spiritual guidance. The transgressive powers of figurative discourse must be seen to be kept in check by the poet's master allegory if the reader's faith in the revelatory powers of the poetry is to be maintained. In the Bower of Bliss metaphoric transgression threatens to run riot as distinctions between earthly pleasure and divine bliss are dissolved in an allegorical paradise where metaphor knows no bounds. The garden's music epitomizes the idolatrous potential of metaphor to replace divine perfection with an earthly simulacrum. John Hollander has shown how Spenser mingles various categories of sound and brings together the literal forms of vocal and instrumental human music with a figurative 'music' of natural sounds in a single harmonious concert.[36] Not surprisingly, this subtle act of metaphoric transgression takes place at the entrance to Acrasia's inner sanctum:

> The ioyous birdes shrouded in chearefull shade,
>   Their notes vnto the voyce attempred sweet;
>   Th'Angelicall soft trembling voyces made
>   To th'instruments diuine respondence meet:
>   The siluer sounding instruments did meet
>   With the base murmure of the waters fall.
>
> (II. xii. 71)

What is most significant about this blending of literal and metaphoric forms of music is that it denies the ascending hierarchy of musical production from the level of 'natural music' to the *musica instrumentalis* of the human level up to the *musica mundana* of heavenly concord. Literal music is in fact produced only at the level of *musica instrumentalis*, the sounds of nature and the transcendent *harmonia mundi* of divine origin are only conceived figuratively as music. Here, however, literal music merges into figurative music at both ends of the hierarchy with the result that *musica instrumentalis* can be confused with *musica mundana*.

The simulation of heavenly harmony in Acrasia's earthly ensemble simply continues the metaphoric process that turns the noise of birds into 'notes' and the sound of water into a 'base murmure' giving to the 'waters fall' a sense of musical cadence. The only difference is that instead of natural sounds imperceptibly merging with human music, human voices and instruments assume the heavenly qualities of the 'Angelicall' and 'diuine'. This unearthly music extends the metaphoric illusion from the sights to the sounds of the Bower. The idolatrous attempt to replace divine perfection with her simulated pleasures is shown to involve more than visual appearances, for Acrasia's idolatry is not primarily a matter of false images but of false figures.[37] It is an act of metaphoric deception, a verbal contrivance that often gives the impression that it is visual for the simple reason, recognized by Aristotle, that many of the most effective metaphors can be said to set the scene before our eyes.

The scene in which Acrasia projects a Venerean image of herself associates cupidity ever more closely with the metaphoric veil of allegory:

> Vpon a bed of Roses she was layd,
>   As faint through heat, or dight to pleasant sin,
> And was arayd, or rather disarayd,
>   All in a vele of silke and siluer thin,
>   That hid no whit her alablaster skin,
> But rather shewd more white, if more might bee.
>
> (II. xii. 77)

Moral mediation is subdued in this passage where the reader experiences concupiscence as 'pleasant sin', a call to lustful self-indulgence, wrapped in a poetry that confuses ethical and aesthetic responses. Acrasia's idolatrous allegory is a thinly veiled appeal to replace the soul's quest towards God with the cupidity of earthly pleasures whether in the form of sexual or poetic gratification. The rose song which accompanies the final baring of the vice amounts, in this respect, to the Bower's hymn in celebration of poetic idolatry. As a *carpe florem*, with its call to 'Gather the Rose of loue, whilest yet is time' (II. xii. 75), the lyric puts its faith in the enjoyment of present pleasure as a means of alleviating the consequences of mortal decay. It follows a tradition devoted to the here and now and extols the ephemeral joys of temporal existence in place of the eternal bliss of spiritual regeneration. Most significantly of all, Spenser's 'louely lay' (II. xii. 74), as a lay of love, emphasizes the link between cupidity and concupiscence through the sexual personification of the rose:

> Ah see the Virgin Rose, how sweetly shee
> Doth first peepe forth with bashfull modestee,
> That fairer seemes, the lesse ye see her may;
> Lo see soone after, how more bold and free
> Her bared bosome she doth broad display;
> Loe see soone after, how she fades, and falles away.
>
> (II. xii. 74)

The natural beauty of the 'Virgin Rose' is prostituted by the unnatural appeal of the sexual metaphor. The flower's modest charm and development towards full bloom is provocatively enhanced by comparison with the seductive self-exposure of the female body that recalls the immodesty of the earlier bathing maidens. This amorous personification displays once more how figurative tropes are enlisted to increase the appeal of cupidity in the Bower. Yet, the metaphor of the 'Rose of loue' is not primarily designed to eroticize nature, its real purpose is to play down the sin of carnality. After all, if intemperate sexual intercourse is equivalent to plucking the budding rose, then far from being condemned, it should be encouraged as a preferable deflowering to the ravages of time. Immorality can be hidden just as easily as it can be exposed by metaphoric discourse, and the final irony of the rose song rests in its willingness to finish on a note of disapproval:

> Gather the Rose of loue, whilest yet is time,
> Whilest louing thou mayst loued be with equall crime.
>
> (II. xii. 75)

'Equall crime' is not a phrase applied to the intemperate love of the Bower of Bliss from a moral perspective outside, it is the conclusion to the lay dedicated to the celebration and encouragement of the Bower's promiscuity. Robert Durling has suggested that there may be an echo of 'Aquinas' discussion of intemperance, where we read, "The intemperate man rejoices in having sinned, because the sinful act has become connatural to him."'³⁸ A more sinister view than this is possible, however, for the confessional reference to intemperate love as a 'crime' might stem from confidence rather than indifference. In other words, the song acknowledges the sinfulness of the concupiscence it promotes precisely because the pleasures of its lyric charm are strong enough to outweigh the reminder of its sinfulness.

The aesthetic appeal of poetry is clearly capable of enhancing the sensual appeal of concupiscence in a dangerous liaison that implicates literary figures and sexual pleasures equally in the carnal enjoyment of corporal things for their own sake. Where the allegorical text ought to be enjoyed for the truth it leads towards but which it can only hope to glimpse in moments of metaphoric vision, Acrasia provides an allegorical paradise in which pleasure is metaphorically generated as an alternative to the distant promise of divine revelation. Her idolatrous allegory, that would substitute the figurative sign for the transcendental signified, is a perverse inversion of the proper heuristic function of metaphoric predication.

The enchanting delights of the succubus threaten to disarm the poet of his figurative defence of poetry as completely as they have divested Verdant of his 'warlike armes' (II. xii. 80). If Spenser's poetry is to be more than the 'idle instruments' (II. xii. 80) of idolatrous lyric pleasure[39] then it is not enough to meet the Circean idolatress[40] with the disapproval of an iconomach; Acrasia's carnal images must be destroyed with the full vigour of an iconoclast:

> But all those pleasant bowres and Pallace braue,
> *Guyon* broke downe, with rigour pittilesse;
> Ne ought their goodly workmanship might saue
> Them from the tempest of his wrathfulnesse,
> But that their blisse he turn'd to balefulnesse:
> Their groues he feld, their gardins did deface,
> Their arbers spoyle, their Cabinets suppresse,
> Their banket houses burne, their buildings race,
> And of the fairest late, now made the fowlest place.
>
> (II. xii. 83)

What are we to make of the ruthless demolition of the Bower of Bliss? The catalogue of devastation lists the acts of Guyon's iconoclasm with relentless force. Yet, does his 'rigour pittilesse' itself verge on an over-zealous response that is not only difficult to reconcile with temperate action but which perhaps stems from the iconoclast's anxieties concerning his own response to the idol? Luther argued on this point that images were merely *adiaphora*, that is, not important in themselves but significant because others made them so.[41] He believed that the physical removal of imagery was secondary to the suppression of the idolatry of the heart. Guyon's violent uprooting of the external image can be seen as a displacement of a deeper fear concerning his own attraction to the carnal pleasures of idolatry. The need to preserve the sanctity of the self from the inner corruption it has experienced risks tainting the act of iconoclasm with the suspicion of its own fetishism in the act of destroying the idol. And, if Guyon's merciless ravaging of Acrasia's seductive images reflects the force of his own carnal desires, it also reveals an unease about the nature of allegory and the potentially idolatrous enjoyment of metaphor for its own sake.

There is something truly grotesque therefore about the introduction of Grill that has nothing to do with his 'hoggish forme' (II. xii. 86). It is the need to use him in an act of poetic iconoclasm that surpasses even the puritanical zeal of Guyon's savagery. Grill is introduced to assert the poem's voice of moral authority with a devastating bluntness that replaces the dynamic metaphoric process of moral exploration with a fixed moral emblem. Yet, as a solution to the problems raised by the Bower's idolatrous appeal to 'the mind of beastly man' (II. xii. 87), it is inadequate. At the moment of crisis, the imposition of the voice of moral correction, in attempting to assert ethical control, draws attention to the realization that its authority may already have been lost. Just as Guyon and the Palmer can transform Grill physically back to his former state but are powerless to alter his 'hoggish mind' (II. xii. 87), so all acts of iconoclasm are destined to destroy the object of idolatry without necessarily influencing the mind of the idolater. The dilemma confronting the Christian allegorist is not just that moments of moral intervention in the poem take on the intrusive violence of the iconoclastic act but that their corrective influence may prove to be ineffective. The struggle between the sensual power of idolatrous poetic figuration and the iconoclastic reassertion of moral authority becomes increasingly problematic once idolatry is seen to involve both the creation and the reception of the image. Iconoclasm, despite its display of ruthless power, provides no solution; ultimately it is impotent against an idolatry that originates in the eye of the idolater.

IDYLLS OF ALLEGORY

The sexual metaphors of the Bower of Bliss expose the thin line separating poetry from idolatry and mark a recurrent anxiety concerning the poem's capacity to guide readers towards moral or spiritual revelation. Moments of intense visionary experience are often problematized in *The Faerie Queene* by their association with acts of sexual violation. As Susanne Wofford has argued 'threatened rapes become disruptive analogies that undermine the poet's efforts to represent or embody vision.'[42] These analogies draw attention to the transgressive similarities between the experiences and discourses of poetry, sexuality and religion that threaten to infect the poem's allegorical quest for visionary fulfilment. Nowhere are the dangers attendant on the poetic desire for divine revelation more apparent than in the sequence of motifs of rings and centres which climax in Calidore's visionary encounter on Mount Acidale in Book VI. The scenes of Calidore's amorous rapture on first beholding Pastorella amidst the shepherds and his later visionary ravishment on witnessing the Graces dancing before Colin Clout both recall implicit parallels with the description of Serena stripped naked before the encircling 'savage nation' (VI. viii. 35). The savages' perverse blend of rapture, rape and idolatry offers a disturbing preface to the theme of contemplative cynosure in the pastoral idyll which follows.

The sacrifice of Serena envisaged at the end of the eighth canto is rooted in primitive religious impulses and the carnal instincts of idolatry. Aspects of the priest's ceremonial preparations, such as the composition of his 'garland ... Of finest flowres' (VI. viii. 39) and the washing of his 'bloudy vessels' (VI. viii. 39), suggest an element of satire directed against Catholic ritual generally, while the prospect of eating Serena perhaps parodies the Roman belief in the Real Presence of the body and blood of Christ in the sacraments of the Eucharist.[43] Regardless of the specificity of the episode as an example of Protestant contempt for the practices of Catholic worship, it enacts an archetypal descent of religious devotion into idolatry:

> Then when she wakt, they all gaue one consent,
> That since by grace of God she there was sent,
> Vnto their God they would her sacrifize,
> Whose share, her guiltlesse bloud they would present,
> But of her dainty flesh they did deuize
> To make a common feast, and feed with gurmandize.

(VI. viii. 38)

The cannibals' initial desire to worship their God through the sacrifice of Serena degenerates into a beastly ceremony because they are unable to distinguish spiritual celebration from the gratification of their own fleshly tastes. Serena, while seen as a gift of grace, is perceived both as a means of displaying adoration for the God who sent her, but also as an object of sensual pleasure in her own right. To their God the cannibals offer merely a share of the trophy: Serena's 'guiltlesse bloud', while for themselves they reserve the feast of 'her dainty flesh'. This division of Serena into the innocent blood of her inner being and the outward appearance of her fleshly body demarcates an essential distinction similar to that which leaves the status of images in the service of religion permanently open to abuse. Where the spirit of man can be drawn up to the lofty adoration of God through a visible form of an invisible grace, it can also be dragged down into the low and material idolization of the creature. The confusion between the spiritual reverence due to God and the respect owed to God's creatures reduces both aspects of the ceremony to a grotesque perversion of all religious veneration. The cannibals embody the 'fleshly-minded' and 'beastly' nature of 'natural man' whose conception of God is divorced from the things of the 'Spirit'.[44]

What is more disturbing, from the perspective of the defence of poetic discourse, is the incriminating association of the cannibals' appetite for carnal idolatry with what Cheney terms 'the language of a love-religion.'[45] Where the love poet feasts his eyes on the physical attractions of woman, the cannibals intend to turn this feast for the eyes into a feast for their stomachs:

> So round about her they them selues did place
> Vpon the grasse, and diuersely dispose,

As each thought best to spend the lingring space.
Some with their eyes the daintest morsels chose;
Some praise her paps, some praise her lips and nose;
Some whet their kniues, and strip their elboes bare.

(VI. viii. 39)

The feeding imagery of the love poet is here obscenely literalized into the barbarous reality of sharpened knives and bared forearms. The association between carnal appetite and poetic praise is then taken a stage further as Serena, having been violently stripped of her clothing, is exposed to the lascivious eyes of her captors:

Now being naked, to their sordid eyes
The goodly threasures of nature appeare:
Which as they view with lustfull fantasyes,
Each wisheth to him selfe, and to the rest enuyes.

Her yuorie necke, her alablaster brest,
  Her paps, which like white silken pillowes were,
  For loue in soft delight thereon to rest;
  Her tender sides, her bellie white and clere,
  Which like an Altar did it selfe vprere,
  To offer sacrifice diuine thereon;
  Her goodly thighes, whose glorie did appeare
  Like a triumphall Arch, and thereupon
The spoiles of Princes hang'd, which were in battel won.

Those daintie parts, the dearlings of delight,
  Which mote not be prophan'd of common eyes,
  Those villeins vew'd with loose lasciuious sight,
  And closely tempted with their craftie spyes;
  And some of them gan mongst themselues deuize,
  Thereof by force to take their beastly pleasure.

(VI. viii. 41–3)

The description takes the form of a blazon (a commonplace of Elizabethan love poetry) in which the parts of the woman are anatomized from the head down. Traditionally, the power of such catalogues derived, as Anne Ferry has shown, both from its use of repetition linking it to the verbal devices of prayer and specifically from the archetypal biblical source of such lists in the Song of Solomon, otherwise known to Elizabethans as the Song of Songs.[46] The blazon was consequently seen as a form of verse directly associated with the inspiration of poetic language, capable of disseminating sacred mysteries through the almost miraculous power of similitude. Ironically, the eroticism of the form, sanctioned by its biblical prototype, could all too easily slide from the sublime ecstasy of spiritual contemplation into the lewd excitement of sexual voyeurism.

In the most extensive blazon to be found in The Faerie Queene, introducing Belphoebe as a representation of Elizabeth into the poem, a crisis is reached when the description threatens to profane the royal image as respectful encomium momentarily borders on discourteous sexual intrusion in the presentation of her 'silken Camus':

> Which all aboue besprinckled was throughout
> With golden aygulets, that glistred bright,
> Like twinckling starres, and all the skirt about
> Was hemd with golden fringe
>
> (II. iii. 26)

The unfinished alexandrine at the end of the stanza shies away from completing a provocative line of thought that jeopardizes the act of poetic tribute through the infringement of sexual disclosure. If, as Louis Montrose wittily suggests, 'the narrator's gaze skirts the fringes of Belphoebe's secret parts',[47] the suggestive textual lacuna left by such a narrative evasion cannot cover up the embarrassing poetic silence. The equation of the revelatory powers of the blazon with the exposure of female sexuality thus surfaces even at a moment when courtly decorum might be expected to keep it firmly out of sight. Where, in the portrait of Belphoebe, the violative impulse of the blazon must be repressed even at the cost of aesthetic impairment, the defilement of Serena, by exposing her 'daintie parts' so barbarously to common view, openly displays the transgressive potential of all blazons. Once more, poetry capable of inspiring reverence for virtuous contemplation appears to be perilously close to poetry that appeals to the impure desires of carnal appetites.

The problem is by no means exclusive to The Faerie Queene among

Elizabethan poems. The same dilemma structures Sidney's *Astrophil and Stella*, where the elevation of spiritual love and the degradation of bodily desire struggle for mastery over the sonneteer's poetic motivation. No matter how strongly the argument for the superiority of the love of the virtuous soul is presented, as in sonnet fifty-two, physical love refuses to be denied 'Her eyes, her lips, her all' and in the last line of the sonnet still urges: 'that body graunt to us.' Astrophil's sensual love translates effortlessly into the language and actions of idolatry. In the first song, the list of Stella's parts turns the blazon's anatomy of the female body into an idolatrous hymn celebrating her life-giving powers which appropriates the terminology of Christian devotion for its own earthy purposes:

> Who hath the breast whose milke doth passions nourish,
> Whose grace is such, that when it chides doth cherish?
> To you, to you, all song of praise is due,
> Onelie through you the tree of life doth flourish.[48]

Astrophil's hymn to Stella masks the carnal appeal of the blazon in its superficial vocabulary of sublimation; but no such deceit is attempted in the anatomy of Serena. Here, the sexual focus of the catalogue is highlighted. While conforming to the traditional pattern of movement down the woman's body, this blazon chooses to ignore Serena's head altogether, narrowing the range of its gaze to those parts lying between her neck and thighs. Serena appears topless, her identity reduced to the sum of her sexual parts, in a blazon that seems to be the product of the lewd imaginings of primitive male 'fantasyes'.

The disclosure of Serena's helpless nakedness is shocking not just because it manifests the savage nature of men's sexual aggression towards women but because it threatens to lay bare the same vile cupidity exhibited by the cannibals beneath the civilized veneer of the courtly poet's blazon. Where poetry should evolve from virtuous thoughts and seek to inspire noble actions through its quest for the revelation of spiritual perfection, this blazon emerges from 'lustfull fantasyes' (VI. viii. 41) and participates in a ceremony of ritual violation inciting rape. There is no getting away from the disturbing potential of even an archetypal mode of sublime poetic comparison, such as the blazon, to succumb to the temptations of concupiscence and idolatry. This adulteration of the mystical similitudes of the catalogue through association with the sexual fetishism of a pagan rite contrives the perverse simile of a sacrificial altar for Serena's belly and actually borrows the likeness of thighs to pillars adorned with trophies directly from the Song of Solomon.[49] As a result, the attempted violation of Serena's maidenhead is strangely entangled with the profanation of a poetic tradition originating in the figurative revelation of sacred verse. Calepine, in rescuing Serena from the lascivious clutches of a savage people, is also charged with the task of wresting the poem's figurative discourse from the perils of carnal idolatry and restoring the serenity of poetic contemplation.

Calepine arrives on the scene as if to perform the necessary act of providential intervention. Yet, from the moment he first witnesses the detestable abuses of the sacrifice, his understanding of the situation and response to it remain darkly ambiguous:

> There by th'vncertaine glims of starry night,
> And by the twinkling of their sacred fire,
> He mote perceiue a litle dawning sight
> Of all, which there was doing in that quire:
> Mongst whom a woman spoyld of all attire
> He spyde, lamenting her vnluckie strife.
>
> (VI. viii. 48)

Serena's identity is hidden from Calepine whose 'litle dawning sight' perceives only 'a woman spoyld of all attire'. At this moment, he is an outsider looking in, and his secretive observation is not without the suggestion of an element of voyeurism in the use of the word 'spyde'. There is the hint of a sexual subtext in the description of Serena's rescue which raises a suspicion of doubt about the purity of Calepine's actions. On viewing the priest's 'naked knife' (VI. viii. 48) about to enter Serena, Calepine 'thrusts into the thickest throng' (VI. viii. 49) where his violent wrath displays something of the destructive vigour of repressed passion associated with Guyon's demolition of the Bower of Bliss. But, if Calepine's reaction to the sacrificial ritual is slightly open to question, his attitude towards the naked damsel he has saved becomes far more problematic in the closing stanzas of the canto:

> From them returning to that Ladie backe,
>   Whom by the Altar he doth sitting find,
>   Yet fearing death, and next to death the lacke
>   Of clothes to couer, what they ought by kind,
>   He first her hands beginneth to vnbind;
>   And then to question of her present woe;
>   And afterwards to cheare with speaches kind.
>   But she for nought that he could say or doe,
> One word durst speake, or answere him a whit thereto.
>
> So inward shame of her vncomely case
>   She did conceiue, through care of womanhood,
>   That though the night did couer her disgrace,
>   Yet she in so vnwomanly a mood,
>   Would not bewray the state in which she stood.
>   So all that night to him vnknowen she past.
>   But day, that doth discouer bad and good,
>   Ensewing, made her knowen to him at last:
> The end whereof Ile keepe vntill another cast.
>
>   (VI. viii. 50–1)

The failure of the lovers to recognize each other and the deferral of their moment of rapturous reunion has been viewed as a consequence of Serena's ingratitude and 'shame at her own sin'.[50] While it is true that we cannot know whether Serena recognizes Calepine or not, the reason for her continued silence seems straightforward enough: her embarrassment at the immodesty of her nakedness. Calepine, on the other hand, knows one thing for certain about the woman sitting before him: she has been stripped of all her clothing. Before judging Serena's silence, it is worthwhile considering her reticence in the context of Calepine's bolder response to the indelicacy of her predicament.

On the surface, Calepine behaves with decent courtesy and, having untied Serena's hands, attempts to cover her state of undress with his cheerful 'speaches kind'. However chivalrous his discourse, one cannot help but feel that a real cloak would serve Serena better than Calepine's cloak of words. Nothing Calepine says or does covers the disgrace of Serena's condition; her nudity continues under cover of darkness, allowing her, temporarily at least, to remain 'to him unknowen'. At this especially charged moment, the sexual connotation of the phrase reminds us that it is not just her identity that Serena is trying to protect. If Spenser chooses to leave Calepine and Serena literally and metaphorically in the dark, it is only after the promised reunion has been tinged with the sinister possibility that, for Calepine, awaiting the revelatory light of day holds out the promise of sexual satisfaction. The 'litle dawning sight' that first gave him a glimpse of 'a woman spoyld of all attire' anticipates the brighter light of dawn that will make 'her knowen to him at last'. Whether day will discover bad or good in Calepine is left open to speculation by the canto's inconclusive ending. Calepine redeems Serena from the cannibals' boorish carnality, but by withholding the reunion of the lovers Spenser chooses not to endorse the spiritual purity of their relationship. Once more, the poem seems to have lost faith in its ability to figure forth a moment of genuine unity and closure, free from doubts as to whether its own metaphoric quest to attain revelatory disclosure can in fact be distinguished from the yearnings of concupiscent idolatry.

In Book VI, where narrative disjunction features so significantly,[51] the postponement of Calepine's reunion with Serena positions a crisis for the poem's faith in the metaphoric language of allegory as a medium for divine contemplation just before the resumption of Calidore's narrative history. The allegory has reached an impasse from which the allegorical idyll of Calidore's pastoral sojourn must seek to find an escape if the poem is to restore confidence in the predicative validity of its figurative discourse. The stark alternatives mapped out through Calepine, between using allegory as an idolatrous surrogate for true spiritual contemplation, and avoiding the dangers of idolatrous transgression only by choosing to maintain the mystical obscurity of allegory's veil of darkness, leave the poem's faith in the veracity of metaphoric language seriously in doubt.

The Legend of Sir Calidore or of Courtesy is the last 'complete' Book of *The Faerie Queene* and is noticeably more embedded in the world of romance than any of the earlier books. Romance motifs abound and the poem increasingly gives the impression that it has chosen to retire from the ardours of worldly questing in order to reflect on the issue of its own origin in an ultimate romance of romance.[52] The Book of Courtesy turns out to be *The Faerie Queene*'s Book of Genesis, returning to focus on questions of poetic conception and contemplation that have been present from the beginning. The poem's self-referential concern with its own implications is intensified and, as Jacqueline Miller demonstrates, Calidore is the courtly figure through whom Spenser conducts 'an anatomy of his own allegory in *The Faerie Queene*'.[53]

Miller points out that the conflation of courtly behaviour and courtly rhetoric in Elizabethan courtesy theory allowed Puttenham in *The Arte of English Poesie* to recognize the same ability to dissemble cunningly in both allegory and the courtier: 'for so as I remember it was concluded by us setting foorth the figure *Allegoria*, which therefore not impertinently we call the Courtier.'[54] In the light of Puttenham's analogy, it is easy to see how Calidore becomes the means of conducting a joint investigation into the nature of both courtesy and allegory. Calidore is, in this sense, the most dubious of Spenser's knights, for not only is he a personification of courtesy, but as the Knight of Courtesy he is also a personification of allegory. Puttenham's equation of the cloaked speech of allegory with the duplicity of court manners points to the anxieties underlying Spenser's allegorical figure of the ideal courtier. Sir Calidore is in danger of either infecting his own courteous manner with the guileful deceits of allegory or alternatively, corrupting allegory's metaphoric quest to reveal sacred truth with the dissimulation of courtly self-interest.

Calidore's stay among the shepherds thus brings the analysis of allegory and the poem's questioning of its own metaphoric faith to a simultaneous climax. Entry into the world of pastoral simplicity, while marking a generic return to an originary mode for Spenser, neither presents a simpler nor a purer form of allegorical poetry. On the contrary, as Louis Montrose points out, 'Puttenham's courtier dissembles most cunningly when he is masked as a gentle shepherd.'[55] The literary and political complexities of pastoral poetry are part of an ironic mode that is quite alien to the innocent pastoral associated with the activities of real shepherds. When Calidore abandons his quest to 'follow the foule *Blatant Beast*' (VI. x. 1) for the more pleasing pursuit of Pastorella, the poem, far from withdrawing from its exploratory metaphoric quest, intensifies its investigation into the nature of poetic revelation. Indeed, Calidore enacts a favourite rhetorical metaphor for metaphor when he doffs his suit of armour and dresses himself in the borrowed robes of a rustic.[56] The courtly figure requires a reflective pasture in which the noble nature of allegory can be identified in courteous relationship to the truth it seeks to serve. This is why the initial criticism of Calidore's apparent truancy at the start of the tenth canto soon turns into the muted tones of 'Ne certes mote he greatly blamed be' (VI. x. 3), and the declaration of the visionary idyll's superiority over the 'false blisse' of more earthly delights:

> For what hath all that goodly glorious gaze
>   Like to one sight, which *Calidore* did vew?
>   The glaunce whereof their dimmed eies would daze,
>   That neuer more they should endure the shew
>   Of that sunne-shine, that makes them looke askew.
>   Ne ought in all that world of beauties rare,
>   (Saue onely *Glorianaes* heauenly hew
>   To which what can compare?) can it compare;
>   The which as commeth now, by course I will declare.
>
> (VI. x. 4)

Calidore's 'one sight' on Mount Acidale is the visionary core of Book VI in which the figure of allegory is brought face to face with its own function in the text of poetic revelation. Yet significantly, this first indication of the importance of the encounter pointedly draws attention to the inadequacies of the comparative process of metaphor as a means of embodying the transcendent object of faith. Spenser, like all Christian writers, knows that the language of men is part of the same imperfect material world with which he must work as a shadowy manifestation of the divine source. The poet's declaration that further disclosure will follow cannot disguise the underlying recognition that all earthly comparisons with sacred truth are ultimately inadequate. The bracketed reference to '*Glorianaes* heauenly hew' seems to soften the sense of exclusion from supernal bliss, but the adjective 'heauenly' is merely figurative, and Gloriana herself, as a figurehead of earthly glory, while celebrated, is never realized in the body of the poem. And what is worse, the elevation of Gloriana into an image of a vision of divine perfection is itself open to the same accusations of idolatry that can be levelled against the construction of the Marian Cult of the Virgin Queen at a time when the veneration of Romish saints was being suppressed.[57]

In the Proem to Book VI, Spenser establishes the grounds of the debate concerning the correct use of poetry in the service of divine truth that he revisits on Mount Acidale. From the beginning, the ravishing sights and sounds of his own verse are recognized as both a source of support and a potential distraction on the journey toward spiritual enlightenment:

> The waies, through which my weary steps I guyde,
>   In this delightfull land of Faery,
>   Are so exceeding spacious and wyde,
>   And sprinckled with such sweet variety,
>   Of all that pleasant is to eare or eye,
>   That I nigh rauisht with rare thoughts delight,
>   My tedious trauell doe forget thereby;
>   And when I gin to feele decay of might,
> It strength to me supplies, and chears my dulled spright.
>
>   (VI. Proem. 1)

Whether the pleasures of Spenser's poetic composition provide him with necessary succour along the way or, to revive Augustine's metaphor, entangle him in the idolatrous enjoyment of the 'sweet perverseness' of the activities of the journey for its own sake, remains open to question. But, while the unwary traveller can be misled by the allurements of the 'delightfull land of Faery', access to 'the sacred noursery / Of vertue' is only available to one trained in the arts of poetry and visited with poetic inspiration:

> Such secret comfort, and such heauenly pleasures,
>   Ye sacred imps, that on *Parnasso* dwell,
>   And there the keeping haue of learnings threasures,
>   Which doe all worldly riches farre excell,
>   Into the mindes of mortall men doe well,
>   And goodly fury into them infuse;
>   Guyde ye my footing, and conduct me well
>   In these strange waies, where neuer foote did vse,
> Ne none can find, but who was taught them by the Muse.
>
> Reuele to me the sacred noursery
>   Of vertue, which with you doth there remaine,
>   Where it in siluer bowre does hidden ly
>   From view of men, and wicked worlds disdaine.
>
>   (VI. Proem. 2–3)

The poet's invocation of the Muses recognizes that the poetry of revelation is in danger of profaning the divine source of truth by exposing sacred secrets to mortal view. The need to protect 'heauenly pleasures' from worldly disdain is openly acknowledged, but Spenser's supplication admits an element of unease concerning his and his poetry's fitness to act as a spiritual conduit. The plea for guidance places emphasis on the steps required to attain revelation rather than the moment of visionary fulfilment itself. It is assistance in keeping his 'footing' and direction through 'strange waies' that is desired. The Muses alone can show the way, but what is to ensure, as Spenser asks, that they will 'conduct me well'? The phrase seems to marry the older meaning of 'conduct' in the sense of guide, lead, or teach with the more modern sense of conducting oneself in moral behaviour.[58] There is a tension here between the poet's professed wish to attain the hallowed site of spiritual initiation through verse and his consciousness that poetry capable of revealing 'heauenly pleasures' has the potential to appeal instead to the earth-bound senses. Establishing a clear distinction between the elevated poetry of holy beatitude and the debased poetry of carnal idolatry remains as difficult as ever.

Mount Acidale, as 'a place, whose pleasaunce did appere / To passe all others, on the earth which were' (VI. x. 5), is evidently another *locus amoenus* providing the ground for further discussion of poetic pleasure in the service of divine truth. Inevitably, many of the sights and sounds imitated by Acrasia's false pleasaunce in the Bower of Bliss are present in Venus's genuine earthly retreat. The trees in continual bud are filled with bird song while the 'gentle flud' (VI. x. 7) produces soft cadences to accompany the 'Nymphes and Faeries' (VI. x. 7) by its banks. But this is a paradise where order rather than mere profusion prevails: where 'all trees of honour stately stood' (VI. x. 6) and where the birds conform to their natural place in the hierarchy of creation. Just as in the Mutabilitie Cantos the cynosural scene on Arlo Hill is kept from 'confusion and disorder' by 'Natures Sergeant (that is *Order*)' (VII. vii. 4), so on Mount Acidale it is order that allows true pleasure to flourish:

> Ne ought there wanted, which for pleasure might
> Desired be, or thence to banish bale:
> So pleasauntly the hill with equall hight,

Did seeme to ouerlooke the lowly vale;
Therefore it rightly cleeped was mount *Acidale*.

(VI. x. 8)

Proportion, like correctness, is not just a matter of geography here, it is a question of the appropriateness of language. Mount Acidale, as a rising hill, physically embodies its own etymology and appears to signify, as Isabel MacCaffrey notes, 'that it is a place where language is in control.'[59] Unlike the falsely named Bower of Bliss, the Mount of Venus is the natural seminary of Spenser's art in which the pleasures of poetry lead towards the contemplation of divine perfection and spiritual completion. It is essential that this sublime pleasure is clearly distinguished from the sensual enjoyment of more earthly delights. And yet, the conflicting desires that give rise to both the poet's highest aspirations for the revelatory status of his work and his deepest misgivings concerning his poetry's proximity to idolatrous transgression are both discernible in the etymology of Mount Acidale. The name suggests a possible derivation from the Greek *a-kedes* meaning that 'which displaces care'. The displacement of worldly cares is, of course, a necessary concomitant to ascetic contemplation, but a carefree life is also lived by those who simply abandon responsibility. This latter interpretation is also brought to mind by the possible reference of Acidale to the sin of *accidia* or sloth, of which Calidore can be accused for abandoning his quest for the Blatant Beast. All too easily, the certainties of nomination in this controlled linguistic environment dissolve into the uncertainties of etymological corruption. There seems to be nothing to prevent a site of transcendental vision from being mistaken for a place of idleness in which the pleasure of the poetry becomes idolatrously enjoyed for its own sake.

The contradictory etymologies of Mount Acidale epitomize the difficulties Spenser confronts in seeking to present an allegorical representation of visionary fulfilment untainted by idolatry. Ultimately, how is the poet to prevent readers of the poem from treating his exalted vision as an immediate source of sensual gratification? Indeed, if idolatry occurs as a result of the way in which images are perceived, and not just as a result of the manner in which they are created, then what matters most is not the intention of the poet but the interpretation of the reader. The defence of allegory, based on the distinction between good and bad exponents of the art, now finds itself confronting a new source of criticism against which there is no obvious counter. Whereas the poet can take responsibility for the authorship of his writing, he cannot authorize the way in which it is read and interpreted. Once the abuse of poetic figuration is seen to originate at the point of its reception, regardless of the intentions of the poet at the time of its conception, then all but perhaps the most rigidly didactic allegory is in peril of inciting idolatry.

There is no avoiding this critical dilemma which, rather like the indiscriminate slander of the Blatant Beast, threatens all poetry with universal condemnation. The time has come for the poem to reflect on the function of allegory in relation to the interpretation of its readers. Calidore's encounter with the Graces is, in this respect, an unparalleled passage of poetic contemplation on the nature of visionary poetry, precisely because of the importance it attaches to the response of the audience. The Dance of the Graces is as much a meditation on the interpretation of allegory as it is a presentation of allegorical sublimation.

Debra Belt suggests that Calidore is used throughout Book VI to explore the virtues of the courteous reader in much the manner of preface writers of the sixteenth century.[60] But, on Mount Acidale, it is Calidore himself who seems to lack the necessary skills to respond appropriately to the visionary performance of poetry:

> There he a troupe of Ladies dauncing found
> Full merrily, and making gladfull glee,
> And in the midst a Shepheard piping he did see.
>
> He durst not enter into th'open greene,
> For dread of them vnwares to be descryde,
> For breaking of their daunce, if he were seene;
> But in the couert of the wood did byde,
> Beholding all, yet of them vnespyde.
> There he did see, that pleased much his sight,
> That euen he him selfe his eyes enuyde,
> An hundred naked maidens lilly white,
> All raunged in a ring, and dauncing in delight.
>
> (VI. x. 10–11)

Although Calidore comes across this scene by accident and not by stealth, there is no other obvious difference between the way he secretly observes the 'naked maidens' from the 'couert of the wood' and the overt prurience of a figure like Faunus in the Mutabilitie Cantos who hides in a bush and leers at Diana while she bathes. The pleasure they both take is purely visual, and fails to achieve spiritual insight because it leaves their eyes fixed firmly on the rewards of the physical senses. What Faunus sees 'pleased much his eye' (VII. vi. 46), while the event which Calidore witnesses 'pleased much his sight'. The verbal echo between these phrases emphasizes the voyeuristic aspect of Calidore's behaviour which is every bit as transgressive as Faunus's 'foolish thought' (VII. vi. 46). Calidore looks on with the same 'hungry eye' (VI. ix. 26) with which he earlier devoured the sight of Pastorella. His lustful appetite for visual satisfaction, in a manner disturbingly akin to the carnal idolatry of the cannibals, prevents him elevating his eyes from the immediate pleasures of the here and now towards the higher rewards of transcendental contemplation.

Calidore fails to recognize the mystical nature of the vision because he treats it as an experience of ordinary sight rather than as a moment of spiritual revelation. This is not a dance to be appreciated by the eye, it is a performance to be contemplated in the eye of the mind. The poem moves to correct Calidore's visual perspective by introducing a comparative and conceptual mode that requires a radically different response from the reader:

> All they without were raunged in a ring,
>   And daunced round; but in the midst of them
>   Three other Ladies did both daunce and sing,
>   The whilest the rest them round about did hemme,
>   And like a girlond did in compasse stemme:
>   And in the middest of those same three, was placed
>   Another Damzell, as a precious gemme,
>   Amidst a ring most richly well enchaced,
> That with her goodly presence all the rest much graced.
>
> Looke how the Crowne, which *Ariadne* wore
>   Vpon her yuory forehead that same day,
>   That *Theseus* her vnto his bridale bore,
>   When the bold *Centaures* made that bloudy fray,

> With the fierce Lapithes, which did them dismay;
> Being now placed in the firmament,
> Through the bright heauen doth her beams display,
> And is vnto the starres an ornament,
> Which round about her moue in order excellent.
>
> (VI. x. 12–13)

These stanzas enact a moment of metaphoric transformation that initiates an attempt to redefine the contemplative function of poetic allegory. What begins as a description of the concentric circles of dancing maidens, as if sustaining the penetrative gaze of Calidore, gradually shifts the reader's perception through the similes of 'a girlond' and 'a precious gemme' at the centre of an ornamental ring. At first, this movement from visual perception to conceptual reflection is masked by the similes themselves which can still be treated as ornamental figures appealing predominantly to the eye. It is not until the introduction of the extended comparison of Ariadne's crown that visionary insight is shown to depend on the verbal rather than the visual aspects of metaphor. Physical sight is insufficient, even though the mythological simile is announced with the exclamation 'Looke'; its interpretation does not rely on what we see in any literal sense but on how we conceptualize metaphorically. The passage conflates the marriage of Theseus and Ariadne with the battle between the Centaurs and the Lapiths which took place at the marriage of Pirithous and Hippodamia when Theseus fought against the Centaurs. A scene of turbulent discord is imported into the midst of an image of cosmic concord so that the presentation of Ariadne's wedding crown, 'placed in the firmament' as a symbol of celestial 'order excellent', is also a record of the 'bloudy fray' of human affairs. The construction of an idealized visualization of astral harmony is brought down to earth by the complications of Spenser's version of a myth that demands a balance between the visual and conceptual modes of metaphor.

The need to counteract the potentially erotic and idolatrous appeal of visionary poetry to the eye is paramount if the quest for conceptual comprehension is to replace the desire for perceptual possession. The allegorical vision can only be approached as allegory; that is to say it must be understood in its own terms as a predicative exploration and not simply a visual incarnation of abstract concepts. Calidore, however, manifestly lacks the capacity to respond appropriately to the mysterious representations of allegory which consequently dissolve before his eyes:

> Much wondred *Calidore* at this straunge sight,
>   Whose like before his eye had neuer seene,
>   And standing long astonished in spright,
>   And rapt with pleasaunce, wist not what to weene;
>   Whether it were the traine of beauties Queene,
>   Or Nymphes, or Faeries, or enchaunted show,
>   With which his eyes mote haue deluded beene.
>   Therefore resoluing, what it was, to know,
> Out of the wood he rose, and toward them did go.
>
> But soone as he appeared to their vew,
>   They vanisht all away out of his sight,
>   And cleane were gone, which way he neuer knew.
>
> (VI. x. 17–18)

It is Calidore's continued reliance on physical sight that ironically excludes him from seeing further into the nature of the graceful dance. Rapt with the pleasure of what he sees, Calidore has allowed sensual gratification to obscure spiritual fulfilment. His resolution to know 'what it was' in a material sense, blinds him from a philosophical consideration of what it is to know in an ontological sense. The knowledge Calidore desires is limited by his corporeal response to transcendental experience and as such remains linked to the more obviously carnal tastes of the cannibals. The similarity lies in the transgressive attempt to experience divine presence through the physical senses. Where the cannibals swopped spiritual devotion for fleshly consumption, Calidore, in stepping towards the figuration of dancers, displays an equally physical desire for literal rather than symbolic communion with the divine essence. And once this step has been taken there is no going back; the vision is violated by Calidore's material approach and vanishes from his idolatrous sight.

At a narrative level, Calidore is responsible for the destruction of Colin Clout's poetic vision, but the withdrawal of the vision from the reader's view actually occurs prior to Calidore's physical intrusion into the scene. The presentation of Mount

Acidale is characterized, from the outset, by anxieties concerning the revelatory status of allegory and the necessity of protecting the poet's figurative representation of divine mysteries from the abuses of misinterpretation. Calidore's response to the configuration of dancers is symptomatic of an idolatry he shares with readers of allegory who mistake the figurative signs of poetry for the subject of signification. The temptations of the sensual pleasures of literal reading cannot be denied but they must be controlled. The determination to distance the reader from the secret voyeurism of Calidore's predominantly visual observations requires a different sort of engagement with the poet's visionary creation. As readers, we consequently see very little of what we are told Calidore saw. This is a vision that is not visually rendered but mediated (even before the introduction of Colin Clout's extended explication) by the authoritative intervention of poetic commentary:

> Those were the Graces, daughters of delight,
> Handmaides of *Venus*, which are wont to haunt
> Vppon this hill, and daunce there day and night:
> Those three to men all gifts of grace do graunt,
> And all, that *Venus* in her selfe doth vaunt,
> Is borrowed of them.
>
> (VI. x. 15)

No attempt is made to describe the appearance of 'this goodly band, / Whose sundry parts were here too long to tell' (VI. x. 14). The traditional rhetorical disclaimer allows descriptive detail to be replaced by detailed exposition. The visionary moment is kept at a safe distance to ensure that it is received as a symbolic incarnation of divine perfection, untainted by the idolatry of materially minded readers. But, like all such moments of vision, it still teeters on the brink of idolatry; the human yearning for revelation to carnalize the spiritual can never be wholly eradicated. The dangers are ever present as the terms A. Bartlett Giamatti uses to celebrate Spenser's miraculous visions indicate:

> When in chivalric romance the moment of vision or revelation occurs, we are summoned from shimmering vistas of magic to stable peaks of miracle.... The poet constantly returns to these

moments because Spenser's whole impulse is to flesh out the ideal, to grapple, or moor, the visionary to the real world; he is forever seeking a language, a grammar, that will be sufficiently suggestive and rare, even incantatory, and yet supple and generously mundane enough to capture and hold these moments of revelation intact.[61]

The vocabulary Giamatti employs to distinguish between 'magic' and 'miracle' ends up sounding all too familiar to anyone versed in theological discourses against idolatry, where to speak of an 'impulse' to 'flesh out the ideal, to grapple, or moor, the visionary to the real world' is to suggest a carnality deserving severe censure. Verbs like 'grapple', 'capture' and 'hold' appear to consider spiritual revelation in terms of a desire for physical incarnation underlying the visionary language of Spenserian allegory. Giamatti's belief that Spenser 'wants to reform our sight from that of *voyeurs* to that of *voyants*, from the gaze of spies to the vision of seers'[62] draws attention to the idolatrous impulse that threatens to keep the poet's metaphoric figures weighed down by the cloying materialism of the senses.

The visionary episode on Mount Acidale seems designed to protect inspired poetry from the profanation of unspiritual reading; but the shift from sensually gratifying forms of visual allegory to a more conceptual metaphoric mode no longer provides an adequate defence against the abuses of misinterpretation. Even if the poet believes in the purity of his metaphors as a means of mediating sacred mysteries, a fear that their figurative integrity can be compromised by the corruptions of misreading demands that the medium of allegorical revelation is rigorously controlled. The ecstasy of divine contemplation is to be differentiated from the visual or verbal dissection of an eroticized female body. The Dance of the Graces displaces the visual and sexual gratification of the blazon by transforming its fixed observation of a static object of devotion into a movement around a deferred centre. The key to the nature of the metaphoric dance of allegory is its circularity, its willingness to explore a subject, while avoiding the idolatrous desire to penetrate towards a visually or mentally determined core. The 'metaphoric miracle' of Spenserian allegory lies in, and relies upon, the poet's ability to sustain figurative exploration in its predicative relation to the subject. Spenser's vision of visionary allegory reveals the investigative restlessness of the heuristic metaphoric enterprise at the same time as it exposes its susceptibility to violation by erroneous interpretation.

Paradoxically, allegory in its purest visionary form, unmediated by the voice of poetic commentary, is most vulnerable to misinterpretation. When Calidore resolves to approach the vision of allegory, it is with a conviction that the mysteries of metaphoric revelation contain a kernel of knowledge, a truth, that can be extracted and possessed. Even after the dancers have 'vanisht all away' he draws near to Colin Clout in the expectation 'that he the truth of all by him mote learne' (VI. x. 18). Calidore assumes that the meaning of the dance can be retrieved through the language of explication and persists in his demand for definitive explanation, unaware that interpretative commentary is secondary to, and divorced from, the actual moment of poetic epiphany. Colin's ensuing exposition, far from explaining the mysteries of the vision, seems designed to rectify Calidore's misconceptions about visionary experience and its translation into the figures of allegorical poetry. Colin Clout reasserts the secondariness of inspired poetic contemplation in its relationship to sacred truth. As he moves towards consideration of the figure at the centre of the dance, Colin acknowledges the inevitable loss experienced in the contemplation of the divine subject through the chain of transmission from vision into poem. John Guillory has argued that this loss amounts to an admission of the poet's inability to recover divine origin, which leaves the poem to contemplate the loss of divine presence rather than divine presence itself. For Guillory, what Spenser stages on Mount Acidale is 'a scene of pure inspiration, excluding entirely from this scene its consequence: the poem.'[63] In other words, the poem does not contemplate visionary oneness; it remains shut off from the moment of union with a sacred origin, locked in a state of limbo where it is condemned to meditate on its own longing for a state of completeness it can never attain. Guillory concludes his discussion of the image of source in *The Faerie Queene* by spelling out the apparent consequences of such an acceptance of loss for the sacred poet:

> The last movement of *The Faerie Queene* completes its critique of origins by giving up the truth claims of allegory as a veil behind which lies a putative sacred origin. The text that emerges from this critique is the secular text, and the question that

immediately presents itself concerns the authority of these human words. What authority can such a text have if it is created in the continual absence of a speaking God?[64]

Guillory presents Mount Acidale as the moment when *The Faerie Queene* abandons its sacred quest 'by giving up the truth claims of allegory'. But to say that 'truth claims' have been given up is to assert that they were once made in the first place. There is no reason to view Mount Acidale as a sudden renunciation of the poem's belief in the sacred authority of allegory, rather than as a culmination of the same radical scepticism concerning the relation of allegory and divine truth that has been present throughout *The Faerie Queene*. Guillory's absolute distinction between the sacred and the secular text is in danger of oversimplifying the complexities of the Spenserian text. That Spenser reveals the impossibility of manifesting truths beneath the veiled voice of allegory does not necessarily constitute the abandonment of a belief in the existence of that truth or in the validity of the metaphoric text as a medium for the contemplation of sacred origin. Once the experience of loss is accepted as the inevitable condition of the sacred text, then the quest to comprehend divine truth through the metaphors of allegorical poetry relies on a sacred belief in metaphor itself as a means of meditating on the nature of divine essence in the absence of divine presence.

The justification of religious allegory on the grounds that it is a means of manifesting divine truth, far from preserving the sacred text from becoming secular, exposes metaphor in the service of Christian revelation to the charge of idolatry. The sacred allegorist must retain faith in the figures of poetry as a means of contemplating divinity without ever mistaking the figurative other of allegory for the actual presence of spiritual truth. On Mount Acidale, the vision of union with the object of desire is withdrawn and replaced by Colin's discourse on the visionary figure of perfection in the form of his own 'countrey lasse' (VI. x. 25):

> But that fourth Mayd, which there amidst them traced,
> Who can aread, what creature mote she bee,
> Whether a creature, or a goddesse graced
> With heauenly gifts from heuen first enraced?

(VI. x. 25)

The poet's explanation raises more questions than it answers. Colin's dilation finally comes to rest on the primary problem of interpretation – 'who can aread'? And who can read 'aread'? Is this a general statement of interpretational uncertainty? Or is 'aread' being used in the sense of advise, as a reminder that exegesis is the responsibility of each individual reader? The 'fourth Mayd, which there amidst them traced' epitomizes the tracings of the dance of allegory.[65] The metaphoric presence of the image of divinity implanted within her is only realized through the acceptance of its literal absence. This is the metaphoric act of faith demanded of the reader by *The Faerie Queene*: a belief in metaphor as metaphor, free from the idolatry that seeks to transform symbolic presence into real presence.

In the final stanzas devoted to the elucidation of the figure of the unnamed 'Damzell', Colin places the allegorist's vision back in its rightful place as a divine gift of metaphoric contemplation:

> Another Grace she well deserues to be,
>   In whom so many Graces gathered are,
>   Excelling much the meane of her degree;
>   Diuine resemblaunce, beauty soueraine rare,
>   Firme Chastity, that spight ne blemish dare;
>   All which she with such courtesie doth grace,
>   That all her peres cannot with her compare,
>   But quite are dimmed, when she is in place.
> She made me often pipe and now to pipe apace.
>
> Sunne of the world, great glory of the sky,
>   That all the earth doest lighten with thy rayes,
>   Great *Gloriana*, greatest Maiesty,
>   Pardon thy shepheard, mongst so many layes,
>   As he hath sung of thee in all his dayes,
>   To make one minime of thy poore handmayd,
>   And vnderneath thy feete to place her prayse,
>   That when thy glory shall be farre displayd
> To future age of her this mention may be made.
>
>   (VI. x. 27–8)

Appropriately, the episode concludes by tracing patterns of earthly and 'Diuine resemblaunce'. The 'Mayd' who excells 'the meane of her degree' emphasizes the doubleness of metaphor that enables figurative communion with the originary Being to be contemplated. To function at all, metaphor recognizes degrees of comparison which establish resemblance and difference simultaneously through the perception of the similarity of dissimilars. This 'Mayd' whose 'peres cannot with her compare', shines all the more brightly by comparison with her peers who 'are dimmed' when set by her side. Similarly, 'Great *Gloriana*', the 'Sunne of the world', is compared with a lesser light in order that her incomparable glory can be displayed in its full brightness. The comparative process which structures chains of resemblance relies on such degrees of excellence to establish the ascending hierarchy of contemplative allegory towards the figure of the Godhead. Just as Gloriana is shown to be without compare through comparison with her 'poore handmayd', so sacred truth is revealed to be without compare, though contemplatable through the allegorist's figures of 'Diuine resemblaunce'.

The duality of metaphoric signification protects Colin's poetic theology from the transgressive impulses of idolatry. For Colin, the Graces are his Muses, uniting theological grace and poetic grace in the circular tracings of the contemplative dance of allegory. The holy gift of metaphor allows the mystery of the divine subject to be approached, though never wholly divined, by the figures which circle it. What Colin teaches is an acceptance of humanity's relationship to God and the proper role of sacred poetry within that relationship. Poetry for the allegorist is, in this sense, a true vocation, a spiritual calling, to strive to deliver communion with God through the grace of metaphor.[66] Spenser's Christian faith is tantamount to a faith in metaphor and the 'darke conceit' of 'continued Allegory' as an instrument of revelation. Acknowledgement that divine presence cannot be fully retrieved or manifested in the text of allegory should not be mistaken for a crisis of poetic faith. As allegory, *The Faerie Queene* has always known that it inhabits a world of otherness, a world of signs, where its wanderings are destined to be continued endlessly, since full presence is not possible though easily confused with the false bliss of idolatry.

The 'endlesse worke' of comparative predication is based on a belief in metaphor as an act of faith which 'enables us to believe things which we know to be untrue.'[67] The leap of faith that puts the 'to be' and 'not to be' of metaphor beyond question trusts in allegory as a quest of exploration rather than discovery, to figure forth illuminations of sacred truth. The allegorical text that is *The Faerie Queene* exists between the monstrous forms of faithless misreading which frame Books I to VI. The dragon Errour and the Blatant Beast, as forms of erroneous interpretation and critical calumny, threaten to disfigure the poem by confusing metaphoric disclosure with false forms of absolute closure. But the figures of allegory must be accepted for what they are in full knowledge of the *allos* of allegorical alterity. To forget that Redcrosse is and is not Holiness or that Calidore is and is not Courtesie is to lose faith in metaphor and to turn allegory into an act of idolatry.

4
Meta-Metaphors

MUTABILITIE'S MUTATION

In 1609, a decade after Spenser's death, a folio edition of *The Faerie Queene* was published by a bookseller Matthew Lownes. After the six books which had been published before, were '*Two Cantos of Mutabilitie: Which, both for Forme and Matter, appeare to be parcell of some following Booke of the Faerie Queene, Vnder The Legend of Constancie. Neuer before imprinted.*' Many questions surround the publication of this volume and the relationship of the Mutabilitie Cantos to the rest of the text of *The Faerie Queene*. How they came into Lownes's possession, on what basis he placed and numbered them along with two last stanzas in a third 'unperfite' canto and why he linked them to 'The Legend of Constancie' must remain unknown, though it is worth noting Lownes's own apparent uncertainty, implied in his use of the word 'appeare'. When they were written, and how they should be interpreted, however, are matters for textual and critical analysis. Here the debate concerning their date, though hampered by a desire to romanticize the biography of the poet's last years,[1] has tended towards a view of their late composition.

On the key question of the relation of the Mutabilite Cantos to the rest of *The Faerie Queene*, four main positions are possible: firstly, they could be viewed as a separate and self-contained poem; secondly, as an abandoned or reworked part of an earlier Book of the poem; thirdly, as a part of a later Book of the poem; and fourthly, as a deliberate conclusion to the whole *Faerie Queene*.[2] How one chooses to view the Mutabilitie Cantos inevitably depends on one's interpretation of the whole text of the poem, since the relation between the two cannot be definitively established. The ambiguity surrounding their entire production raises problems concerning the status of the text and of its interpretation, which threaten to undermine any attempt at exegesis before it even begins.

The Mutabilitie Cantos, whether by accident or design, force the hermeneutic act to proceed ever more self-consciously and self-referentially, bearing in mind its own fallibility and the possibility of alternative interpretations all the time it strives to establish its own authority. Ironically, this would transform the Mutabilitie Cantos into a fitting climax to a poem which, beginning *in medias res*, set out with Redcrosse on a hermeneutic quest, that led immediately into Errour/error and a constant re-examination of the problematics of the metaphoric text. If the Mutabilitie Cantos are to be read as a metaphoric coda to the rest of *The Faerie Queene*, a sort of meta-metaphor for the metaphoric text, then some of their most striking features seem appropriate. In order to comment on the rest of the text, it is important that they should be clearly distinguishable from it, and to some extent self-contained. This, of course, means that they need not be bound to the rest of the text by characters or plot. Indeed, the very fact that they move outside the poem's normal compass and operate within a cosmic and philosophical framework is in keeping with such an enterprise. Yet, all these features may equally well be explained by other means. In attempting to perform a reading of the Mutabilitie Cantos that explores them as an allegory of metaphoric investigation it is as well to remember the hermeneutic problems testified to by their own existence.

Throughout *The Faerie Queene*, the attempt to establish a correct procedure for the use and interpretation of the metaphoric text has been threatened by false metaphorizers within the text itself. Their attempt to undermine the heuristic metaphoric quest has been characterized by an inversion of the metaphoric act. Instead of the metaphoric description of its subject required of true metaphor, there is the attempt to create a replica to stand literally in place of the subject. When metaphor forgets the distinction between itself and its subject and turns itself from description into copy, it literalizes itself and brings about its own destruction. The figure of False Florimell bore witness to the futility of metaphor forgetting its predicative function. The moment she stood alongside the true Florimell, her attempt at false nomination melted into the emptiness of the act which had generated her. All attempts to invert metaphor in this way are destined to fail, since metaphoric meaning is born out of 'the blockage of any literal interpretation of the statement'.[3]

The attempt to literalize metaphor, to reduce its figurative exploration of the world to a pointless parody of truth is not the only danger metaphor must guard against, though the one most prevalent in the text of *The Faerie Queene*. Once metaphor has triumphed over its own literalization, an attempt to unite or be as one with its subject, metaphor must still confront the equally destructive attempt to shut it off from its subject altogether. Here, the figurative and predicative nature of metaphor is no longer questioned; instead its own endless search to describe its subject becomes an end in itself. This form of metaphoric abuse, instead of attempting to replace its subject directly, subverts the metaphoric act by denying its primary purpose and transforming its own ceaseless activity into the principle of its existence. It is this second form of the abuse of metaphor that the Mutabilitie Cantos confront.

In order to understand the relationship between the two forms of metaphoric abuse, and why the defeat of the second is left until the Mutabilitie Cantos, it is necessary to recognize the underlying link between the Mutabilitie Cantos and Book I of *The Faerie Queene*. The Mutabilitie Cantos place the metaphoric debate back into an overtly theological context. Redcrosse's quest involved learning to accept the multiplicity of true metaphoric interpretation rather than the tempting univocity of his adversaries, in order to rediscover the true nature of his relationship to God and the divine order.[4] In this way, the text of the poem united metaphoric faith with Christian faith, and a hermeneutics of the metaphoric text with a Christian interpretation of the physical world. The Book of the World and poetic discourse both became metaphoric texts to be approached metaphorically but not literally translated into a metaphoric equivalent. The spiritual and metaphoric acts of faith destroyed the temptation to replace the predicative quest with a nominative idol. This Christian metaphoric thus accepted the impossibility of exhausting the routes of the predicative quest, without forsaking its belief in its ultimate goal.

In placing metaphor in this paradoxical relationship to truth, however, it brought into existence an inverse threat. Defeating the attempts to construct a metaphoric copy to replace truth, by relying on an act of faith to validate the metaphoric act, distanced that act from the professed source of its own activity. Resisting the temptation of one form of metaphoric abuse opens the door to another. If metaphor is in one sense divorced from its source and uncertain of its ability to become reunited with it, the temptation now is to abandon its heuristic enterprise and transform its own predicative convolutions into a universal and self-generating activity. The Mutabilitie Cantos confront this second hermeneutic and theological threat, which is all the more dangerous because, instead of limiting the power of metaphor, it seeks to extend it. The defence of metaphor which has for so long fought to establish its figurative powers of predication, must now define those powers as part of a process of predicative interpretation, subordinate to the thing it ultimately strives to understand descriptively.

The following interpretation of the Mutabilitie Cantos accepts them as a product of what Josephine Waters Bennett terms 'the revived and Christianized Neo-Platonism of the Renaissance'.[5] Her article 'Spenser's Venus and the Goddess Nature of the Cantos of Mutabilitie' provides a detailed explanation of their philosophical content which coincides with my own investigation of the Mutabilitie Cantos as an allegory of metaphoric exegesis. The most important distinction between a Neoplatonic and a Lucretian interpretation centres on the extent of Mutabilitie's challenge.[6] Since this issue is central to the metaphoric, as well as the theological debate, I shall quote Josephine Waters Bennett's conclusion:

> It is essential to observe that the rule of Mutability can extend no further than the celestial world. There is no suggestion that she has any place in the eternal, super-celestial realm which is inhabited only by such immutable beings as God, the angels, and the Platonic Ideas.[7]

Mutabilitie does not threaten the *primum mobile*; the debate does not take place at this level. What is at stake in her argument is the interpretation of the structure of the two lower or visible worlds, and whether they are governed by a movement of degeneration or perfection. In challenging Jove, Mutabilitie is attempting to claim dominion over the whole of the created universe. The Supreme Deity is outside of the created universe; it is not his existence which is brought into question, but the divorce of his creation from His own perfection. It is clear from Mutabilitie's willingness to accept Nature's judgement in the matter of her claim, that she accepts there are powers greater than herself. What she seeks to have confirmed is that the celestial and sublunar worlds are governed by laws of change which they exhibit in every aspect of their existence and which run contrary to the laws of the supercelestial world of permanence.

The force of Mutabilitie's claim lies in her ability to draw upon the 'ancient idea of the decay of the world', (which as George Williamson has argued underlies the whole of late sixteenth and seventeenth century melancholy)[8] and to align it with the arguments of the new astronomy. In claiming sway over the celestial world, Mutabilitie carries the doctrine of decay into a sphere previously considered permanent. Her triumph here would appear to confirm her thesis on the general decay of nature, set on a path of degeneration taking it ever further from the state in which it was originally created. The amplification of Mutabilitie's plea begins in earnest in the fourteenth stanza of the seventh canto. Mutabilitie begins by examining 'the Earth':

> That only seems vnmov'd and permanent,
> And vnto *Mutability* not thrall;
> Yet is she chang'd in part, and eeke in generall.

(VII. vii. 17)

This same argument, that the nature of the parts governs the nature of the whole, even when the whole is not or cannot be perceived in itself, is repeated by Mutabilitie when she comes to examine the heavens later on:

> To whom, thus *Mutability*: The things
>   Which we see not how they are mov'd and swayd,
>   Ye may attribute to your selues as Kings,
>   And say they by your secret powre are made:
>   But what we see not, who shall vs perswade?
>   But were they so, as ye them faine to be,
>   Mov'd by your might, and ordred by your ayde;
>   Yet what if I can proue, that euen yee
> Your selues are likewise chang'd, and subiect vnto mee?

(VII. vii. 49)

Mutabilitie argues from the specific to the general, and that a theory based on the perception of the known is superior to a mystical belief. The strength of Mutabilitie's position lies in her ability to provide detailed descriptions and apparently incontrovertible evidence of the changeableness of the created universe, knowing that 'what we see not, who shall vs perswade?'

She presents before Nature's court a catalogue of change and decay. It begins with the earth and 'all that from her springs, and is ybredde' (VII. vii. 18), and having dealt with plants, beasts and man moves on to the elements. Each one in turn is shown to be 'tost, and turned, with continuall change' (VII. vii. 21) and to be further proof of the role of alteration. Then, it is the 'times and seasons of the yeare that fall' (VII. vii. 27) which are paraded before the court, followed by 'the *Day*, and *Night* (VII. vii. 44), 'the *Howres*' and 'after all came *Life*, and lastly *Death*' (VII. vii. 46). The facts are clear enough:

> Wherefore, this lower world who can deny
> But to be subiect still to *Mutabilitie*?

(VII. vii. 47)

When Jove accepts Mutabilitie's evidence of her rule over the lower world it is in expectation of distinguishing the celestial world as a distinct domain governed by a separate principle of existence:

> Then thus gan *Iove*; Right true it is, that these
> And all things else that vnder heauen dwell
> Are chaung'd of *Time*, who doth them all disseise
> Of being: But, who is it (to me tell)
> That *Time* himselfe doth moue and still compell
> To keepe his course?

(VII. vii. 48)

But the same type of evidence which Mutabilitie presented to claim sway over the sublunar world, having been accepted by Jove then, can now be turned against the celestial sphere. If the visible parts of it, including Jove and the sky, can themselves be shown to change, then Mutabilitie's case rests. She therefore turns her attention to the celestial gods, establishing in several cases their mortal nature and showing the conflicts that exist between them, causing their 'owne natures change ... By others opposition or obliquid view' (VII. vii. 54). Mutabilitie's speech reaches its culmination as she moves from the spheres to undermine the entire firmament:

> Onely the starrie skie doth still remaine:
> Yet do the Starres and Signes therein still moue,
> And euen it self is mov'd, as wizards saine.
> But all that moueth, doth mutation loue:
> Therefore both you and them to me I subiect proue.

(VII. vii. 55)

Mutabilitie, having couched her arguments all along in the emotive rhetoric associated with descriptions of the decay of nature, is finally able to switch from knowledge of the physical world to the findings of astronomy. The evidence of astronomers, pointing to change taking place in the eighth sphere of the Ptolemeic system, is used by Mutabilitie to establish the presence of decay even in the fixed stars and constellations. Jove, having accepted the decay of the parts as evidence of the principle of decay underlying the whole for the lower world, is confronted with precisely the same evidence when it comes to the celestial world. The principle of universal decay has been established, Mutabilitie's mutation is complete, she can claim her victory over Jove:

> Then since within this wide great *Vniuerse*
> Nothing doth firme and permanent appeare,
> But all things tost and turned by transuerse:
> What then should let, but I aloft should reare
> My Trophee, and from all, the triumph beare?

(VII. vii. 56)

What then are the implications of Mutabilitie's mutation for metaphor? Mutabilitie has sought to establish herself as a principle of degeneration governing the whole of creation. The universe, far from reflecting the divine order of its Creator, mirrors the chaos from which it sprang. Degeneration has set in and creation moves ever further from its original condition. The Supreme Deity, the Platonic Ideal, is not denied; what is questioned is the relationship between divine perfection and the imperfect creation. For, if the creation is degenerating, how can it hope to recapture its perfection out of the ruins of its disorderly state? Man, as part of decaying creation, is prevented from reading in his own nature, or the nature of his universe, the original plan of his Creator. Shut off from God, locked into a world of endless change, mutability takes over as a process with its own defining principle, completely independent from any external force.

When mutability, as the principle of change, is translated into metaphor, the figure of change, metaphoricity is seen to be governed by a principle of figurative degeneration. Instead of moving towards a fuller understanding of its subject, metaphor weaves a confused and confusing pattern of meanings that drifts ever further from its professed goal of predication. Metaphor, in so far as it must function through difference, can only stray further away from the object of its perception. The inherent illogicality of the metaphoric statement becomes proof of the impossibility of its achieving its desired end. Metaphor cannot hope to achieve a static union with its subject; the nominative and predicative domains are permanently separated. All metaphor can do is accept its changing nature and fall in love with mutation, the principle of its own being. Metaphor must forget its heuristic dream and come to terms with its endless proliferation of meaning. The metaphoric text consequently becomes an impenetrable confusion of potential interpretations and the author's original intention becomes lost in the reader's endless exegetic wanderings. The text can no longer be trusted; the link between author and reader is destroyed. The defence of metaphor collapses; if the author cannot control the metaphoric work he has brought into being, he can no longer vouch for the moral efficacy of its effect. The reader's hermeneutic quest is condemned as an act of futility, seeking an answer to a riddle that has no ultimate solution. Mutabilitie's mutation traps the reader inside the world of the text, unable to progress beyond the confines of its own self-governing metaphoric principle of chaos.

THE NATURE OF THE POEM

The poem has allowed Mutabilitie to present an argument logically and coherently which threatens to undermine the poet's professed aim of transmitting morality through verse.[9] It is no wonder, therefore, having brought the poem to a philosophical and literary crisis so near its end, that Mutabilitie's appeal to the final judgement of the 'greatest goddesse trew' (VII. vii. 56) should be followed by a pregnant pause:

> So hauing ended, silence long ensewed,
>   Ne *Nature* to or fro spake for a space,
>   But with firme eyes affixt, the ground still viewed.
>   Meane while, all creatures, looking in her face,
>   Expecting th'end of this so doubtfull case,
>   Did hang in long suspence what would ensew,
>   To whether side should fall the soueraigne place:
>   At length, she looking vp with chearefull view,
> The silence brake, and gaue her doome in speeches few.
>
> (VII. vii. 57)

The consequences of the situation are dramatically presented for the reader who, like the creatures on Arlo Hill, must wait in suspense viewing Nature, whose ensuing silence and downcast eyes seem to leave the verdict uncertain. Suddenly, however, the atmosphere of the stanza is transformed completely, prior to Nature's verbal response, by the sudden revelation of her 'chearefull view'. Nature's visage speaks louder than words, for before her speech breaks the silence, her face, by breaking the tension, prepares the way for the final judgement.[10] Nature's 'doome' follows and, in direct contrast to the lengthy protestations of Mutabilitie, is uttered 'in speeches few.' But the actual text of Nature's reply must wait, so that it is understood in the context of the "vast dramatic irony" of which Mutabilitie is the victim, and which perhaps explains Nature's mixed feelings at the end.

The Mutabilitie Cantos are structured to undermine Mutabilitie's ultimate claim from start to finish, though the frames of reference offered for viewing her change considerably.[11] The process begins with the poet's unfolding of Mutabilitie's 'linage ancient':

> As I haue found it registred of old,
> In *Faery* Land mongst records permanent.
>
> (VII. vi. 2)

The very records in which the history of Mutabilitie's 'antique race' are stored, and which give stature to her personage, by their permanence, stand against her claim. The details of her descent themselves reveal significant features concerning the status Mutabilitie aims to establish for herself. Mutabilitie is not born of Chaos, but of the union of Chaos's daughter, Earth, with Saturn's eldest son, Titan. While her claim to challenge Jove as the offspring of usurped authority has some credibility (as Jove is forced to admit when he is deemed unfit to judge a case in which he in his 'owne behalfe maist partiall seeme' [VII. vi. 35]), her aspirations are also confounded by her origin as Josephine Waters Bennett has argued:

> She did not originate solely from Chaos, but was a part of creation. She does not exist in spite of the spiritual ordering force of creation at work upon chaos, but as a part of it. Mutability is not simply the degeneration of stubborn matter, but has a definite place in the scheme of things.[12]

Mutabilitie's lineage simultaneously magnifies her stature while reducing her ultimate threat to the structure of the universe. In this respect, it is typical of a strategy at work throughout the Mutabilitie Cantos and aiming to attest to the power of mutability without granting it the status of a self-governing principle. The ambiguous nature of Mutabilitie's status is consequently an essential part of the outcome of the debate within the poem on which the status of poetry itself ultimately rests. Mutabilitie cannot be dismissed completely or allowed to hold complete sway; her power must be integrated within a universal plan. To achieve this end, the poem strives structurally and linguistically to create a meaningful tension.

Mutabilitie is a Titaness engaged in an epic struggle, and yet, the narrative of her ascent is perpetually on the verge of degenerating into a mock heroic parody. The extended simile used to describe the effect of her appearance on the other gods, epic in construction, is comic in intention:

> Whil'st she thus spake, the Gods that gaue good eare
>   To her bold words, and marked well her grace,
>   Beeing of stature tall as any there
>   Of all the Gods, and beautifull of face,

> As any of the Goddesses in place,
> Stood all astonied, like a sort of Steeres;
> Mongst whom, some beast of strange and forraine race,
> Vnwares is chaunc't, far straying from his peeres:
> So did their ghastly gaze bewray their hidden feares.
>
> (VII. vi. 28)

Yet, despite the deflating effect of the bovine comparison on the tone of the passage, the object of the humour is not Mutabilitie, but the gods. Furthermore, the stanza attributes to Mutabilitie physical stature and beauty at least on a par with the gods she is challenging and testifies to the impact her presence has created. There is an even more subtle irony, however, contained in the simile which, on closer inspection, proves to be inappropriate not on the grounds of tone but of logic. If, as the rest of the stanza asserts, the gods are astonished as a result of Mutabilitie's likeness to themselves, then the simile's comparison to creatures disturbed by the arrival of a 'strange and forraine' beast is an inversion of the situation of the subject it purports to describe. If the simile is just there to deflate the tone or to focus attention on the reaction of the gods regardless of its cause, then the illogicality of the comparison need not matter. The primary importance would appear to be to display the gods 'hidden feares.' These fears presumably involve their recognition that Mutabilitie really does constitute a threat to their order. The strange simile, that in describing their hidden fear makes it known, perhaps also describes the real threat of Mutabilitie to metaphoric discourse, while at the same time mysteriously controlling it.

Simile, unlike metaphor, does not create an immediate semantic problem: all similes are logically true just as all metaphors are literally false. But this simile, in creating a comparison that so directly inverts its subject, brings into question the validity of its own statement. The simile, in straying too far from the source that generated it, has undermined the basis of its initial comparison. If simile, which is not initially distanced from its subject, can so easily degenerate in this way, then what chance does metaphor have, which is? The divorce of the figurative comparison from its source, threatened by Mutabilitie's rebellion, surfaces again.

The defence of the figurative rests precisely on its ability to triumph over its own illogicality and in a peculiar way this simile draws attention to how that process is achieved. The significance of this simile is not in terms of its veracity to the whole of what it describes but merely to a part of it. In other words, the simile highlights one aspect of the gods (their shock) at the expense of another (its cause). The inherent contradiction does not deny the force of the ultimate insight, which is all the more significant because it reveals what the gods wish to keep hidden. In structuring itself on contradiction, this simile moves closer towards the nature of metaphor, and in triumphing over its own illogicality points towards the ability of metaphor to reveal truths about its subject out of the semantic clash of its structure. The literal contradiction is the necessary sacrifice for the figurative insight. At the very moment when the poem admits to the impressiveness of Mutabilitie it has built in a miniature defence of the figurative language her enterprise potentially threatens. In this manner it indicates the way an act of apparent confusion can paradoxically be part of a purposeful and controlled structure, and prepares the way for Nature's eventual judgement against Mutabilitie.

The simile discussed above is a typical strategy adopted to maintain and contain Mutabilitie's power. Ultimately, her enterprise is founded on a misunderstanding of her own nature, which she herself unwittingly reveals before Nature finally steps in to state it more directly. After all, as Jove and several commentators note, if she truly did control the heavens, why is she having to claim dominion over that which she already says she rules?

The main paradox confronting Mutabilitie surfaces most strongly in the seventh canto where she presents her case so convincingly. For, while the poem demands the dramatic pause preceding Nature's verdict, the final outcome has never been in doubt. Suspense is only ever partial in *The Faerie Queene*, momentarily evoked within a larger providential structure. The opening stanza of the seventh canto has told us of the 'fortunate successe, / And victory' obtained by Jove 'against that *Titanesse*', and as the spectators are marshalled in for the great debate, the thronging multitude is prevented from falling into 'much confusion and disorder' by '*Natures* Sergeant (that is *Order*)' (VII. vii. 4). If the setting and the issue to be considered recall the scene of the marriage 'Twixt *Peleus*, and dame *Thetis*' (VII. vii. 12), when the apple of discord was thrown down, then it is not going to subdue the 'great ioyance' of the occasion or Nature's 'chearefull view' at the end. When Mutabilitie later seeks permission from Nature to present the pageant of the year the request, while granted, does not suggest it is likely to produce the sense of confusion it is supposed to:

> *Nature* did yeeld thereto; and by-and-by,
> Bade *Order* call them all, before her Maiesty.
>
> (VII. vii. 27)

Order brings them in and it is order not chaos that underlies the procession of subjects who are supposedly in thrall to Mutabilitie. And what is true of the cycle of the months is true of Mutabilitie's entire case. The more she strives to present her arguments and witnesses in a coherent form before the court, the more her evidence paradoxically weighs against her.

Mutabilitie, in presenting such a highly structured display in her own defence of the forces of discord, is inevitably hoist by her own petard. This underlying irony that has been present from the moment Mutabilitie set forth on her challenge provides the grounds for Nature's confident response when she looks up from the ground to give it:

> I well consider all that ye haue sayd,
>   And find that all things stedfastnes doe hate
>   And changed be: yet being rightly wayd
>   They are not changed from their first estate;
>   But by their change their being doe dilate:
>   And turning to themselues at length againe,
>   Doe worke their owne perfection so by fate:
>   Then ouer them Change doth not rule and raigne;
> But they raigne ouer change, and doe their states maintaine.
>
> Cease therefore daughter further to aspire,
>   And thee content thus to be rul'd by me:
>   For thy decay thou seekst by thy desire;
>   But time shall come that all shall changed bee,
>   And from thenceforth, none no more change shall see.
>
> (VII. vii. 58–9)

Nature's reply is brief and to the point: Mutabilitie for all her changes, can change nothing. Nature's argument is rooted in a Neoplatonic conception of the relation between the 'first estate' and the changing forms of the 'states' in which it appears in the mundane world. The apparently endless changes of the form do not alter the nature of the 'first estate' (the original 'Being' of Platonic Ideas). Instead the changes of form are the means by which the form 'dilates' its 'Being' in a process of 'Becoming' that allows it to return to its original condition. Change is not a pointless and chaotic process but a fulfilment of a preordained pattern of existence, in which the finite world through self-dilation imitates the infinite. Mutabilitie's inconstancy is paradoxically transformed into an expression of the universal permanence in which she unknowingly participates.

Nature's solution draws on the Plotinian concept of 'dilation', which in *The Enneads* is developed to encompass layerings of resemblance between forms and things. Through this principle, as Rosalie L. Colie has argued, Spenser creates a union between pure form and matter, that allows the imperfect creation to enact in its variable nature the principle of its perfect Creator.[13] This self-dilation, as Plotinus argues, not only allows things to imitate but also to approach gradually closer to the source of their existence:

> To the lowest of things the good is its immediate higher; each step represents the good to what stands lower so long as the movement does not tend awry but advances continuously towards the superior: thus there is a halt at the Ultimate, beyond which no ascent is possible: that is the First Good, the authentic, the supremely sovran, the source of good to the rest of things.[14]
>
> (VI. vii. 25)

For Plotinus, matter can dilate itself through the convoluted sequence of resemblances but cannot ultimately desire to become its own form, since that would amount to denying its own essence:

> Universally what approaches as a good is a Form; Matter itself contains this good which is Form: are we to conclude that if Matter had will it would desire to be Form unalloyed?
> No: that would be desiring its own destruction whereas every-

thing seeks what will do it good. But perhaps Matter would not wish to remain at its own level but would prefer to attain Being and, this acquired, to lay aside its evil.

(VI. vii. 28)[15]

This is akin to the message contained in the second part of Nature's address. Having explained how mutation enacts the eternal principle of 'stedfastnes', she warns Mutabilitie against seeking her own destruction which raising herself to the position of a universal truth would entail. There is only one Truth and were she to achieve her own complete dilation, Mutabilitie would have exhausted change and become constant. Matter and Form, Being and Becoming are at one and the same time united in a common expression of good, though distinguished as different levels of existence.

Mutabilitie cannot escape her own nature, which paradoxically expresses permanence, not change, in the wondrous variety of its own dilation. Mutabilitie's ceaseless alteration, far from distancing her from her original state, is the one thing which allows her, in realizing her nature, to be permanently reminded of it. This is why her beauty has never been denied, for, as part of the creation which reflects the nature of its Creator, she, along with the changing world she has presented, displays the greater glory of their God. Mutabilitie is put down but not humiliated, belittled or destroyed. She is not evil like Duessa and vile beneath the surface or false and empty like the imitation Florimell. Her sin is a failure to understand herself, a loss of faith in an order that gives purpose to the created world, while existing beyond it.

Mutabilitie cannot be excluded, though her self-destructive desire must be opposed. The whole tone of Nature's speech is not condemnatory but explanatory, her attitude towards Mutabilitie, whom she calls 'daughter', is motherly and corrective, without being severe. There is a place for Mutabilitie in the scheme of things, for it is only with the apocalyptic change, when the whole creation is to be finally consumed, that Mutabilitie too will rest and 'none no more change shall see.' This promised end, which Nature intimates to her assembled audience, is the Christian addendum added to the otherwise Neoplatonic solution to the problem of mutability. It is a promise of the ultimate perfection of the imperfect creation, which must accept its fallen existence as a state in which it must strive to become itself more fully through perpetual dilation.

Mutabilitie's claim is denied, though her rule in the lower world is confirmed where her power has never been questioned, if we recall the opening stanza of the Mutabilitie Cantos:

> What man that sees the euer-whirling wheele
>   Of *Change*, the which all mortall things doth sway,
>   But that therby doth find, and plainly feele,
>   How *MVTABILITY* in them doth play
>   Her cruell sports, to many mens decay?

(VII. vi. 1)

Though the Mutabilitie Cantos do not deny the sway of Mutabilitie in mortal matters, they deny her universal supremacy. She is not a degenerative influence but the means by which creation expresses its perfectibility in the midst of the flux in which it must exist. The perpetual alteration of matter, in its perpetual self-dilation, is its only way to move towards a fuller knowledge of itself and its own ideal form.

Mutabilitie has learnt what it is to be herself. But she has also shown that far from being condemned to a world of figurative confusion, metaphor is the created world's means of dilating through numerous transformations towards a fuller description of its subject. Metaphor itself has thus been rescued from a life of aimless predicative wandering, and is now blessed with the knowledge of its semantic power. Mutabilitie, as the figurative embodiment of a view of metaphor as a self-defining principle, has proved inadequate in so far as she only half understands her own nature. An alternative figure encompassing the totality of metaphoric duality must replace Mutabilitie as the poem's meta-metaphor. Nature, as the representative of 'the highest him, that is behight / Father of Gods and men' (VII. vi. 35), is an authority to whom both Mutabilitie and Jove acquiesce. The 'God of Nature' remains above Nature, but she alone can be called on directly to pass judgement in this cosmic dispute. As an intermediary between the perfect Creator and His fallen creation, can Nature herself be viewed as the poem's final metaphoric figure, the ultimate metaphor for metaphor?

Nature is certainly a very mysterious figure. She enters the poem at the request of Mutabilitie, and when she eventually makes her appearance the description which follows emphasizes and re-emphasizes the difficulty of describing 'her'. Although the poem ascribes the epithets 'great goddesse' and 'great dame' to Nature, and while her physical stature is more impressive than 'any of the gods or Powers on hie':

> Yet certes by her face and physnomy,
> Whether she man or woman inly were,
> That could not any creature well descry:
> For, with a veile that wimpled euery where,
> Her head and face was hid, that mote to none appeare.
>
> (VII. vii. 5)

We recall how Una too wore a veil that hid her face from view, and how the image of Venus and of the union of the lovers in the first ending to Book III were both described as hermaphroditic figures. It is as if Nature embodies these ultimate images of truth and love which the poem has struggled to approach and which can, at best, only be seen or half seen through the mysterious metaphoric veil of allegory. Nature, as the image of metaphor, must at one and the same time embody the revelatory and incomprehensible aspects of metaphor, whose very existence creates a figurative possibility that defies literal translation. Nature and metaphor simultaneously promise access through revelation to a truth that can never be fully revealed. The choice of the word 'descry' is in this sense quite precise for it carries the meaning of an attempt to disclose what should be kept secret.

The presentation of Nature thus begins by limiting her accessibility through description, and then proceeds to distance that description by turning from the poet's own direct attempt, through a process of deferral and professed poetic limitation, towards other literary authorities. This process begins with a typical Spenserian evocation of unknown personages' opinions concerning the purpose of Nature's veil and the nature of her visage:

> That some doe say was so by skill deuized,
>   To hide the terror of her vncouth hew,
>   From mortall eyes that should be sore agrized;
>   For that her face did like a Lion shew,
>   That eye of wight could not indure to view:
>   But others tell that it so beautious was,

And round about such beames of splendor threw,
That it the Sunne a thousand times did pass,
Ne could be seene, but like an image in a glass.

(VII. vii. 6)

Right from the start of this stanza, we are in the world of theory and assumption: 'some doe say ... But others tell that'. The two main views given at first seem contradictory: Nature's face must be covered, either because it is too terrifying for 'mortall eyes', or because it is too beautiful and bright to be viewed directly and can at best 'be seene, but like an image in a glass.' On closer inspection these two opinions converge in important ways and paradoxically imply a common belief underlying their differing interpretations. In the first description, the terror Nature's appearance would inspire is not caused by hideousness but strangeness. Her 'hew' is described as 'vncouth', a word with the primary meanings of things unknown or persons to whom one is unaccustomed. Nature in this interpretation cannot be observed clearly because she is too different for her sight to be tolerated and understood. In the second description she must remain hidden because the 'beames of splendour' issuing from her are so bright that they will dazzle if seen directly. In either case, the observer cannot endure the vision, and must be guarded against it. There is agreement, therefore, about the purpose of the veil which is to protect the observer rather than to conceal the truth of what lies behind. This is a crucial distinction, since it implies that the need for partial comprehension grows out of the nature of what mortal beings cope with and not a desire for supreme truth to remain hidden.

There is a further aspect of the two descriptions which links them and their subject together in an even more startling manner. They both agree that a full view of Nature is beyond human endurance, but when it comes to displaying their own partial view of her true being, they both realize the need to adopt the same method and turn to the figurative language of simile: firstly, describing her face as 'like a Lion' and secondly, as only to be seen indirectly 'like an image in a glass.' The visual veil is the linguistic figure that hides the truth, paradoxically, to allow it to be seen at all. And now the reason for the images themselves, the capitalized 'Lion' and 'Sunne', becomes clearer. The lion and the sun are both symbols of Christ and, as such, link Nature to Christian grace and the means by which fallen creation can re-attain its perfect state. Christian hope is again united with Spenser's metaphoric hope and turns once more towards the emerging heliotropic metaphor, which as Derrida has argued, is the most potent metaphor for metaphor:

> Now the sun, from this point of view, is a sensible object par excellence. It is the paradigm of what is sensible *and* of what is metaphorical: it regularly turns (itself) and hides (itself). The trope of metaphor always implies a sensible kernel, or rather something which, like what is sensible, may always fail to be present actually and in person. And the sun, in this respect, is above all the sensible signifier of what is sensible, the sensible model of the sensible (the Form, paradigm, or parable of the sensible). For these reasons, the orbit of the sun is the trajectory of metaphor. Indeed, of bad metaphor which gives only improper knowledge. But since the best metaphor is never absolutely good, since otherwise it would not be a metaphor, does not bad metaphor always provide the best example? Metaphor therefore means heliotrope, both movement turned to the sun, and the turning movement of the sun.[16]

Derrida later shies away from making metaphor a form of truth, Spenser does not. The difference centres on the notion of bad metaphor. What for Derrida is an admission of the limitations of metaphoric truth is for Spenser the crucial link with truth. Metaphor is neither entirely good nor entirely bad, it is the thing that is both turned towards the sinful condition of fallen creation and the perfection of its Creator. It is by nature paradoxical, only able to speak and to be spoken of paradoxically. Metaphor can never describe fully, but only metaphor can describe at all. The sun, as the sensible paradox, thus begins to describe metaphor in attempting to describe the nature of Nature. Metaphor as partaking of the divine in its own mystical communion with the divine must accept paradox as both its medium and its ultimate message. For, as Rosalie L. Colie says: 'What is relevant to that realm goes so far beyond human categories and classifications that it can be expressed only in physical, emotional, logical, or rhetorical paradoxes.'[17] The sun, like metaphor, reveals and conceals itself, for like Nature's face which is a thousand times brighter than the sun, it cannot be viewed directly since it would only blind the observer. Blindness and insight are the necessary concomitants of metaphor. It is better to see a little than to seek to see too much and end in blindness. The metaphoric veil, like Nature's own miraculous cover, hides that we may begin to see, 'like an image in a glass.' In this final simile, the possibility of encapsulating the paradoxes of metaphoric truth are figuratively displayed: what we read is a simile of reflection to describe a metaphor for a metaphor for metaphor, and this we must remember is only offered as hearsay.

Nature's nature like the nature of metaphor itself can never be fully known. It effortlessly incorporates contradictions in the expression of its own being as in the final description given of Nature before Mutabilitie's case is heard:

> This great Grandmother of all creatures bred
> Great *Nature*, euer young yet full of eld,
> Still moouing, yet vnmoued from her sted;
> Vnseene of any, yet of all beheld.
>
> (VII. vii. 13)

The description here is as paradoxical as Nature's judgement that follows, and is a summation of the essential duality that is the essence of the metaphoric utterance. The perception of Nature is both possible and impossible, reflecting, as only she can, the double nature of metaphor which constructs figurative sense out of literal nonsense. We see and we do not see, for to see both is to see nothing.[18]

Spenser knows the impossibility of describing such absolutes only too well. But the figure of Nature is perhaps as much a source of literary authority for his own poetic limitation as she is a means of defining metaphor itself. He therefore takes time out from his own descriptive efforts to discuss the representations of others in the literary tradition:

> So hard it is for any liuing wight,
>   All her array and vestiments to tell,
>   That old *Dan Geffrey* (in whose gentle spright
>   The pure well head of Poesie did dwell)
>   In his *Foules parley* durst not with it mel,

> But it transferd to *Alane*, who he thought
> Had in his *Plaint of kindes* describ'd it well:
> Which who will read set forth so as it ought,
> Go seek he out that *Alane* where he may be sought.
>
> (VII. vii. 9)

Ironically, Spenser does not refer directly to a source to which the reader may turn. What he does is to turn to Chaucer in order to show how even the 'pure well head of Poesie' declined to meddle with the subject of Nature's clothes and himself referred to an earlier literary model, which Spenser refers the reader to in the vaguest of terms: 'Go seek he out that *Alane* where he may be sought.' The point of this deferred reference would seem to be to point out the tacit agreement within the literary tradition not to attempt more than it 'durst'.

When confronted with an ideal or divine vision there would seem to be no language in which the poet can describe it:

> Her garment was so bright and wondrous sheene,
> That my fraile wit cannot deuise to what
> It to compare, nor finde like stuffe to that,
> As those three sacred *Saints*, though else most wise,
> Yet on mount *Thabor* quite their wits forgat,
> When they their glorious Lord in strange disguise
> Transfigur'd sawe; his garments so did daze their eyes.
>
> (VII. vii. 7)

Even metaphor has its limitations; there are those ultimate truths that defy comparison, and the poet must in all humility acknowledge the limitations of his art. And yet, in describing the nature of the limitation, a negative comparison emerges which paradoxically includes the indescribable within the terms of the overall analogy. Spenser, in being unable to describe Nature's garment, compares himself to the saints who found themselves unable to describe the transfiguration of Christ because of the brightness of His garments. Analogy, of course, does not just construct a single system of comparison. Spenser is like the saints because he cannot describe something and, consequently, the thing he cannot describe is like the thing the saints could not describe;

Nature's garments are like Christ's and Nature is like the transfigured Christ. The figurative comparison, phoenix like, rises out of the ashes of the expression of its own limitation. Through the description of Nature, the description of metaphoric truth and the description of religious truth once more converge, since for Spenser there can be no final differentiation between them. It is no accident that this ultimate comparison should focus on the transfiguration of Christ to identify Him more completely with metaphor as the figure of change. Following His transfiguration, Christ then delivered to Peter, James and John knowledge of His resurrection, and with it the promise of the restoration of fallen man. The same promise of future restoration is contained in Nature's own final words, a promise that unites spiritual and metaphoric deliverance as a mutually inclusive vision.

No sooner is her promise made than Nature vanishes, 'whither no man wist' (VII. vii. 59). No more can be said, the ultimate union with truth must remain as nothing more than a future promise, a hope that is either believed in or not. The metaphoric act of faith demands belief in the veracity of metaphor itself. Belief is either held or it is not. Mutabilitie has enacted the plot of disbelief and, in doing so, sought to condemn herself and metaphor to an existence without purpose. Nature has taught Mutabilitie to see in her own state of alteration the means of attaining singularity through diversity. In this sense, Mutabilitie moves in the Mutabilitie Cantos towards a fuller understanding of her own nature which expresses itself fully through dilation. Mutabilitie is like *The Faerie Queene*, which is only able to move towards a fuller understanding of the truth it embodies if it believes in the veracity of the metaphoric transformations which generate its being. The Mutabilitie Cantos bring the poem full circle to recognize its wholeness in holiness: metaphor is an act of faith.

There can be no further revelation beyond this: metaphor is truth, truth metaphor – and dare one say: 'that is all / Ye know on earth, and all ye need to know.' Nothing remains to be told, the narrative must cease as the lady vanishes. And yet, the poet has one last metaphor to play; for if metaphor is an act of faith, its faith can only hope to be maintained through prayer, and it is in two final supplicatory stanzas that Spenser expresses his own poetic faith:

When I bethinke me on that speech whyleare,
  Of *Mutability*, and well it way:
  Me seemes, that though she all vnworthy were
  Of the Heav'ns Rule; yet very sooth to say,
  In all things else she beares the greatest sway.
  Which makes me loath this state of life so tickle,
  And loue of things so vaine to cast away;
  Whose flowring pride, so fading and so fickle,
Short *Time* shall soon cut down with his consuming sickle.

Then gin I thinke on that which Nature sayd,
  Of that same time when no more *Change* shall be,
  But stedfast rest of all things firmely stayd
  Vpon the pillours of Eternity,
  That is contrayr to *Mutabilitie*:
  For, all that moueth, doth in *Change* delight:
  But thence-forth all shall rest eternally
  With Him that is the God of Sabbaoth hight:
O that great Sabbaoth God, graunt me that Sabaoths sight.

(VII. viii. 1–2)

The stanzas look back at the Mutabilitie Cantos in order to look forward beyond the limits of the poem. The doctrine put forward by Nature to explain the temporal immutability of change struggles to convince when weighed against the evidence of Mutabilitie whose sway still seems so vast in all things below the heavens. Ironically, therefore, more confidence can be put in Nature's promise of eternal rest from change than in her proof of constancy through change: in the unseen rather than the seen. For, as Mutabilitie, Nature and now the poet all agree: 'all that moueth, doth in *Change* delight', and steadfastness, if expressed through the dilation of creation, is not and cannot be the experience of creation from within that change. The vision of the permanence of the universe is a sight that is granted only to a perspective from outside. Thus, the final 'Sabaoths sight' is the vision of the eternal rest from which eternal rest can alone be seen. Perspectives merge in a final paradox which is complicated by the textual inconsistency of the spellings of 'Sabaoth' ('armies' or 'host') and 'Sabbaoth' ('rest').[19]

The final prayer enacts once more the nature of metaphor which alone triumphs over its own apparent inconsistency. The tension between the literal and figurative built into the structure of metaphor, like this last linguistic wobble, relies upon the presence of two apparently different intentions to arrive at a conclusion which subsumes the two. In the end, the sight of eternal rest is identical to the saintly sight of the heavenly host, from which perspective alone, truth can be viewed singularly; the one implies the other. The 'imperfections' of the poem, the textual doubts, remain to haunt the reader to the end. There can be no final hermeneutic release, no ultimate statement, merely a prayer, an act of faith uniting structurally and semantically for the last time the poet's trust in God and metaphor.

Notes

INTRODUCTION

1. Cited by Paul Ricoeur in *The Rule of Metaphor: Multi-disciplinary Studies of the Creation of Meaning in Language*, trans. Robert Czerny (Toronto: Toronto University Press, 1977), pp. 33–4.
2. Sir Philip Sidney, *An Apology for Poetry*, ed. Geoffrey Shepherd (Manchester: Manchester University Press, 1989), p. 101. All quotations from *An Apology for Poetry* are from this edition and are cited parenthetically in the text.
3. Rosemond Tuve discusses the influence of the 'Horatian half-quotation' on Renaissance theories of imagery. See Rosemond Tuve, *Elizabethan and Metaphysical Imagery: Renaissance Poetic and Twentieth-Century Critics* (Chicago: Chicago University Press, 1968), pp. 50–60.
4. Aristotle, *Poetics*, in *The Basic Works Of Aristotle*, ed. Richard McKeon, trans. Ingram Bywater (New York: Random House, 1941), p. 1479.
5. William Shakespeare, *Antony and Cleopatra*, ed. M.R. Ridley (London: Methuen, 1978), pp. 85–7.
6. For a fascinating examination of the history of the rhinoceros in art see T.H. Clarke, *The Rhinoceros from Dürer to Stubbs: 1515–1799* (London: Sotheby's Publications, 1986).
7. E.H. Gombrich, *Art and Illusion: A Study in the Psychology of Pictorial Representation* (London: Pantheon, 1960), p. 81.
8. Gombrich, *Art and Illusion*, p. 73.
9. George Lakoff and Mark Johnson, *Metaphors We Live By* (Chicago: Chicago University Press, 1980), p. 157.
10. This sonnet, and all further quotations from Elizabethan sonnets, can be found in Maurice Evans (ed.), *Elizabethan Sonnets* (London: Dent, 1977).
11. Lawrence Babb, *The Elizabethan Malady: A Study of Melancholia in English Literature from 1580–1642* (East Lansing, Mich.: Michigan State College Press, 1951), p. 138.
12. The use of the term 'sequence' has been discussed by W.T. Going and Lawrence A. Sasek. Between them they have found three examples of the use of the term 'sequence' to describe a group of linked sonnets in the poetry of George Gascoigne. In these examples, however, the sonnets have a clear narrative progression and in some cases use grammatical connectives to link one sonnet to the next. Gascoigne's sequences, in this sense, are unlike the larger collections of other Elizabethans, who do not appear to have applied the term sequence to their work. The term sequence would appear to have been applied retrospectively after it gained currency when applied by Victorian poets to their own very different form of 'sonnet sequence'. The relevant articles are: W.T. Going, 'The Term Sonnet

Sequence', *Modern Language Notes*, 62 (1947) 400–2; W.T. Going, 'Gascoigne and the Term "Sonnet Sequence"', *Notes and Queries*, 199 (1954) 189–91; Lawrence A. Sasek, 'Gascoigne and the Elizabethan Sonnet Sequences', *Notes and Queries*, 201 (1956) 143–4.
13. Evans (ed.), *Elizabethan Sonnets*, Introduction, p. xi.
14. Germaine Warkentin, '"Love's sweetest part, variety": Petrarch and the Curious Frame of the Renaissance Sonnet Sequence', *Renaissance and Reformation*, 11 (1975) 14–23 (p. 16).
15. Tuve, *Elizabethan and Metaphysical Imagery*, p. 121.
16. Tuve, *Elizabethan and Metaphysical Imagery*, p. 122.
17. A. Leigh DeNeef, *Spenser and the Motives of Metaphor* (Durham, NC: Duke University Press, 1982), p. 69.
18. DeNeef, *Motives of Metaphor*, p. 70.
19. G. Wilson Knight, 'The Spenserian Fluidity', in Paul J. Alpers (ed.), *Edmund Spenser* (Harmondsworth: Penguin, 1969), pp. 222–32 (p. 228).
20. Knight, 'Spenserian Fluidity', p. 227.
21. Harry Berger Jr, 'The Discarding of Malbecco: Conspicuous Allusion and Cultural Exhaustion in the *Faerie Queene* III. ix–x', *Studies in Philology*, 66 (1969) 135–54 (pp. 146–7).
22. The relevant passage can be found in Plato, *Phaedrus*, trans, C.J. Rowe (Warminster: Aris and Phillips, 1986), pp. 125–7. The inference is that a Garden of Adonis is an environment where one is at liberty to develop ideas freely, as a means of entertainment, without worrying about the restrictions more formal settings impose on the uses of language and writing.
23. The classical topos of the pleasance or *locus amoenus* is discussed in detail by E.R. Curtius, *European Literature and the Latin Middle Ages*, trans. Willard R. Trask (New York: Pantheon, 1953), pp. 195–200.

CHAPTER 1

1. The proverb was well established by the Elizabethan age. Tilley records its usage from 1546 onwards (W733). The other proverb alluded to: 'He has lost himself in a Wood', meaning he is puzzled or bewildered, is first located by Tilley in 1608 (W732), though the proverb must have been in use before this date. See Morris Palmer Tilley, *A Dictionary of the Proverbs in England in the Sixteenth and Seventeenth Centuries* (Ann Arbor: Michigan University Press, 1950), pp. 749–50.
2. Douglas Brooks-Davies cites probable sources for the catalogue of trees as Ovid's *Metamorphosis* X. 90ff. and Chaucer's *Parlement of Foules* 176ff. See Douglas Brooks-Davies, *Spenser's 'Faerie Queene': A Critical Commentary on Books I and II* (Manchester: Manchester University Press, 1977), p. 17.
3. All quotations from *The Faerie Queene* are from *Spenser's 'Faerie Queene'*, ed. J.C. Smith, 2 Vols (Oxford: Clarendon Press, 1909, rpt. 1978).
4. This sort of aporetic question is similar to the Megarian paradoxes

of the ancient world, of which Rosalie L. Colie gives the following examples: 'The Bald Man: "Is a man with one hair bald?" Answer: "Yes." "With two hairs?" "Yes." "With three?" – and so on. Another, much like it, is the Heap: "Is one grain of barley a heap?" "No." "Two grains, then?" "No." – and so on.' See Rosalie L. Colie, *Paradoxia Epidemica: The Renaissance Tradition of Paradox* (Princeton, NJ: Princeton University Press, 1966), p. 12.

5. 'One of the six often deliberately seductive charms of landscape recognised by rhetoricians since late Antiquity: Curtius, 197; the implication is that the wood is in the tradition of the *locus amoenus* or pleasant place.' See Brooks-Davies, *Critical Commentary*, p. 16. J. Nohrnberg cites Petrarch writing about the opening of Virgil's *Aeneid* as an interpretation of the symbolic environment Spenser is drawing on. See J. Nohrnberg, *The Analogy of 'The Faerie Queene'* (Princeton, NJ: Princeton University Press, 1976), pp. 138–9.

6. Here and throughout the chapter emphasis is given to what I.A. Richards called 'a wide and open metaphoric sense' of words like see and perceive rather than the literal sense. See I.A. Richards, *The Philosophy of Rhetoric* (New York: Oxford University Press, 1950), pp. 131–2.

7. Maureen Quilligan, *The Language of Allegory: Defining the Genre* (Ithaca, NY: Cornell University Press, 1979), p. 36.

8. Quilligan, *Language of Allegory*, p. 33.

9. Quilligan, *Language of Allegory*, p. 33.

10. An interesting discussion of the interplay of these two tendencies is provided by B. Rajan, *The Form of the Unfinished: English Poetics from Spenser to Pound* (Princeton, NJ: Princeton University Press, 1985), pp. 5–10 and 44–95. Rajan argues that the whole poem grows out of 'the evolving engagement between pattern and procession' which 'both in its own dispositions and in the invitations it issues to the reader situates the poem around an internal dialogue about its nature which it can initiate and explore but not conclude' (p. 83).

11. J. Nohrnberg reads the opening episode as what he terms 'the symbol of the threshold, a threshold peculiar to the theme of knight errantry' and 'the whole theme of the emergence of a dragon slayer'. See Nohrnberg, *Analogy*, p. 136. But as he states in conclusion, the symbolism of the episode works on various levels which he interprets as corresponding to 'Aristotle's six parts of poetry', where 'the *lexis*, or basis for the figurative rhetoric of the episode, may be found in the etymology of the word *error* itself', but which only constitutes one of the six parts. See Nohrnberg, *Analogy*, pp. 149–51.

12. Paul J. Alpers uses the lines to discuss the surface ambiguity of Spenser's language, where it is not certain whether the pain is felt by Redcrosse or Errour. This ambiguity functions at both the literal and figurative levels, drawing attention to the strength of will necessary to comprehend the nature of Errour. See Paul J. Alpers, *The Poetry of 'The Faerie Queene'* (Princeton, NJ: Princeton University Press, 1967), pp. 85–6.

13. George A. Miller points to a connection between metaphor and

nonsense, in which he says the reader's 'truth assumption' desires to make sense of an apparent lack of logic. See George. A. Miller, 'Images and Models, Similes and Metaphors', in Andrew Ortony (ed.), *Metaphor and Thought* (Cambridge: Cambridge University Press, 1979), pp. 202–50 (esp. pp. 210–14).
14. Lewis Carroll, *The Complete Works of Lewis Carroll*, ed. Alexander Woollcott (London: Nonesuch, 1939), p. 142.
15. Carroll, *Complete Works*, p. 196.
16. Nohrnberg, *Analogy*, p. 150.
17. Ariosto, *Orlando Furioso*, VI. 23–56. All quotations are from Ariosto, *Orlando Furioso*, eds Santorre Debenedetti and Cesare Segre (Bologna: Commissione per i Testi di Lingua, 1960). The translation used is by Guido Waldman (London: Oxford University Press, 1974). Further references to *Orlando Furioso* are cited parenthetically in the text. Other relevant passages from Spenser's sources are listed in *The Works of Edmund Spenser: A Variorum Edition*, ed. Edwin Greenlaw et al., 11 vols (Baltimore: Johns Hopkins University Press, 1932–57), Vol. I, pp. 202–4.
18. Hallet Smith, *Elizabethan Poetry: A Study in Conventions, Meaning, and Expression* (Cambridge, Mass.: Harvard University Press, 1952), p. 293.
19. Douglas Brooks-Davies comments that: 'In addition the roses – by attraction to Fraelissa's name (= Italian *fralezza*, frailty) – symbolise frailty and mutability.' See Brooks-Davies, *Critical Commentary*, p. 34.
20. William Langland, *The Vision of Piers Plowman*, ed. A.V.C. Schmidt (London: Dent, 1982), p. 231.
21. J. Nohrnberg, *Analogy*, pp. 161–2. Nohrnberg provides a detailed account of the scriptural influences and references of Spenser's symbolism in this episode. See Nohrnberg, *Analogy*, pp. 158–73.
22. *Spenser's 'Faerie Queene'*, ed. Smith, Vol. II, p. 485.
23. Ernest Sirluck, 'A Note on the Rhetoric of Spenser's "Despair"', *Modern Philology*, 47 (1950) 8–11 (p. 8).
24. Sirluck, 'Note on Rhetoric', p. 8.
25. William Nelson provides a detailed study of the effects of accusations of untruthfulness on sixteenth and seventeenth century literature in *Fact or Fiction: The Dilemma of the Renaissance Storyteller* (Cambridge, Mass.: Harvard University Press, 1973).
26. A rigorous application of this type of reading is provided by Maurice Evans, *Spenser's Anatomy of Heroism: A Commentary on the 'Faerie Queene'* (Cambridge: Cambridge University Press, 1970). Evans argues that the key to understanding the poetry of *The Faerie Queene* is to see it as a 'psychological allegory'. In Book I, where it is in its purest form, he argues that Redcrosse is the only 'real' character, who sets out on his quest with characters who personify those aspects of his own nature which are relevant to his quest. The characters around him are consequently read as projections of himself, acting out the allegory of his mind.
27. F.E. Sparshott, '"As," or the Limits of Metaphor', *New Literary History*, 6 (1974) 75–94 (p. 80).
28. Ernest Sirluck explains the relationship between the two Covenants

which Despair suppresses during the dialogue with Redcrosse. See Sirluck, 'Note on Rhetoric'.
29. Spoken by Bosola in *The Duchess of Malfi*, I. ii. 215, in *John Webster: Three Plays*, ed. D.C. Gunby (Harmondsworth: Penguin, 1979). The particular device Despair uses is also expressed in the proverbs 'The Devil can cite Scripture for his purpose' and 'The Devil sometimes speaks the truth'. See Tilley, *Dictionary of Proverbs* (D230 and D266), pp. 150–1 and 153.
30. Brooks-Davies, *Critical Commentary*, p. 90.
31. Brooks-Davies, *Critical Commentary*, pp. 90–1.
32. Roland Barthes, *Mythologies*, trans. Annette Lavers (Aylesbury: Paladin, 1985), p. 12.
33. Roland Barthes, 'The Death of the Author', in David Lodge (ed.), *Modern Criticism and Theory: A Reader* (Harlow: Longman, 1988), pp. 167–72 (pp. 171–2).
34. Spoken by Brachiano in Webster's *The White Devil*, V. iii. 108.
35. Barthes, 'Death of the Author', p. 171.
36. Alpers, *Poetry of 'The Faerie Queene'*, p. 335.
37. DeNeef, *Motives of Metaphor*, p. 98.
38. Douglas Brooks-Davies lists the celebrated instances of faith: 'Joshua 10:12ff. (Joshua commanding the sun to stand still); 2 Kings 20:10ff. (Hezekiah and the dial of Ahaz: see iv.4n.; significantly, a symbol of deliverance); Judges 7 (Gideon's victory over the Midianites with only three hundred men); Exodus 14:21–31 (the passage of the Israelites over the Red Sea, typologically Christ's baptism and His delivery of fallen man from sin) ... and Matthew 21:21 (the faith that will move mountains)'. See Brooks-Davies, *Critical Commentary*, p. 96.
39. Raymond Klibansky, Erwin Panofsky and Fritz Saxl, *Saturn and Melancholy: Studies in the History of Natural Philosophy, Religion, and Art* (London: Nelson, 1964), p. 244.
40. Klibansky, Panofsky and Saxl, *Saturn and Melancholy*, p. 247.
41. Paul de Man, *Blindness and Insight: Essays in the Rhetoric of Contemporary Criticism* (London: Methuen, 1983), p. 18.
42. The idea of absence constituting the source and ultimate goal of both literature and criticism is examined by Tzvetan Todorov with reference to short stories by Henry James. Todorov looks closely at the story 'The Figure in the Carpet', in which a critic attempts to unravel a writer's works. Todorov shows that what is to be found is 'the existence of a secret', which turns out to be 'nothing other than the quest itself.' See Tzvetan Todorov, *The Poetics of Prose*, trans. Richard Howard (Oxford: Blackwell, 1977), pp. 143–77.
43. Max Black's work in *Models and Metaphors: Studies in Language and Philosophy* (Ithaca, NY: Cornell University Press, 1962) explores the importance of metaphor in scientific and philosophical investigation.
44. Lakoff and Johnson, *Metaphors We Live By*, pp. 10 and 12–13.
45. de Man, *Blindness and Insight*, p. 8.
46. Frank Kermode, *The Sense of an Ending: Studies in the Theory of Fiction* (New York: Oxford University Press, 1966), p. 7.
47. In a chapter entitled 'Narrative Men', Tzvetan Todorov examines

The Thousand and One Nights as an example of story-telling where 'narrative equals life; absence of narrative, death.' Todorov, *Poetics of Prose*, p. 74.
48. Kermode, *Sense of an Ending* , pp. 57–8.
49. Michel Tournier, *The Erl-King*, trans. Barbara Bray (London: Methuen, 1983), p. 11.
50. Sir Walter Raleigh, *The History of the World*, ed. C.A. Patrides (London: Macmillan, 1971), pp. 86–7.

CHAPTER 2

1. Patricia Parker, 'The Metaphorical Plot', in David S. Miall (ed.), *Metaphor: Problems and Perspectives* (Brighton: Harvester, 1982), pp. 133–57.
2. Referring to the stanzas describing the dead body of the dragon (I. xii. 9–11) A. Leigh DeNeef talks of Spenser's ability to strip his own metaphors of allegorical equivalences: 'The dragon, as a result, both is and is not Satan or the serpent; Redcross is and is not Christ bruising the serpent's head; and the garden he regains both is and is not Eden.' See DeNeef, *Motives of Metaphor*, p. 102.
3. Sparshott, 'Limits of Metaphor', p. 86n.
4. Wallace Stevens, 'The Man with the Blue Guitar', *Collected Poems of Wallace Stevens* (London: Faber, 1984), p. 165.
5. Paul Ricoeur, 'The Metaphorical Process as Cognition, Imagination, and Feeling', in Mark Johnson (ed.), *Philosophical Perspectives on Metaphor* (Minneapolis: Minnesota University Press, 1981), pp. 228–47 (p. 232).
6. Thomas Elyot, *Dictionary 1538*, ed. R.C. Alston (Menston: Scolar Press, 1970).
7. The phrase was first used by Monroe C. Beardsley in 'The Metaphoric Twist', *Philosophy and Phenomenological Research*, 22 (1962) 293–307.
8. Arthur Golding, *Shakespeare's Ovid: The Metamorphosis*, ed. W.H. Rouse (London: Centaur Press, 1961), p. 17.
9. The source of the character is discussed by Jortin: 'This is taken from a Dialogue in Plutarch ... where Gryllus, one of the companions of Ulysses, transform'd into a hog by Circe, holds a discourse with Ulysses, and refuses to be restored to his human shape.' Cited in *Spenser Variorum*, ed. Greenlaw, Vol. II, p. 394.
10. *Spenser Variorum*, ed. Greenlaw, Vol. III, p. 286.
11. *Spenser Variorum*, ed. Greenlaw, Vol. III, p. 287.
12. The word *becco* is used specifically to mean a cuckold in John Marston's *The Malcontent*:

    Malevole: Duke, thou art a *becco*, a *cornuto*.
    Pietro: How?
    Malevole: Thou art a cuckold.

    (I. iii. 88–90)

    John Marston, *The Malcontent*, in *The Selected Plays of John Marston*,

eds MacDonald P. Jackson and Michael Neill (Cambridge: Cambridge University Press, 1986), p. 205.
13. Ricoeur, 'Metaphorical Process', p. 240.
14. William Blake, *The Marriage of Heaven and Hell*, *The Complete Poems of William Blake*, ed. W.H. Stevenson (New York: Norton, 1971), p. 118.
15. Alpers, *Poetry of 'The Faerie Queene'*, p. 224.
16. Angus Fletcher, *Allegory: The Theory of a Symbolic Mode* (Ithaca, NY: Cornell University Press, 1964), p. 289.
17. Jay L. Halio, 'The Metaphor of Conception and Elizabethan Theories of the Imagination', *Neophilogus*, 50 (1966) 454–61 (p. 455).
18. Mark Antony's speech is discussed above in the Introduction.
19. Philip Sidney makes the same equation between the poet and God while recognizing that he is treading on dangerous ground:

> Neither let it be deemed too saucy a comparison to balance the highest point of man's wit with the efficacy of Nature; but rather give right honour to the heavenly Maker of that maker, who having made man to His own likeness, set him beyond and over all the works of that second nature: which in nothing he showeth so much as in Poetry, when with the force of a divine breath he bringeth things forth far surpassing her doings, with no small argument to the incredulous of that first accursed fall of Adam: since our erected wit maketh us know what perfection is, and yet our infected will keepeth us from reaching unto it. But these arguments will by few be understood, and by fewer granted.

See Sidney, *An Apology for Poetry*, p. 101.
20. Judith C. Ramsay discusses the critical problems surrounding the merger of narrative and metaphysical elements in this section. See Judith C. Ramsay, 'The Garden of Adonis and the Garden of Forms', *University of Texas Quarterly*, 35 (1966) 188–206 (pp. 193–4).
21. Harry Berger Jr, 'Spenser's Gardens of Adonis: Force and Form in the Renaissance Imagination', *University of Texas Quarterly*, 30 (1961) 128–49 (p. 134).
22. Patricia Parker cites the metaphor of clothing as one of the most common metaphors for metaphor in rhetorical discussions of the trope. See Parker, 'Metaphorical Plot', p. 131.
23. Berger, 'Gardens of Adonis', p. 137.
24. Berger, 'Gardens of Adonis', p. 137.
25. Berger, 'Gardens of Adonis', p. 138.
26. Ramsay, 'Garden of Adonis', p. 193.
27. This intense debate particularly characterized assessment of the Garden of Adonis completed during the 1920s and 1930s. The ebb and flow of the argument can be followed through a sequence of articles. See Edwin Greenlaw, 'Spenser and Lucretius', *Studies in Philology*, 17 (1920) 439–64; Josephine Waters Bennett, 'Spenser's Garden of Adonis', *PMLA*, 47 (1932) 46–80; Brents Stirling, 'The Philosophy of Spenser's "Garden of Adonis"', *PMLA*, 49 (1934) 501–38; Josephine Waters Bennett,

'Spenser's Garden of Adonis Revisited', *Journal of English and German Philology*, 41 (1942) 53–78.

28. Maureen Quilligan explores this allegorical technique with reference to *Piers Plowman* and explains sudden narrative shifts as the natural outcome of 'metaphor compared to the literal truth inherent in the words of the text'. See Quilligan, *Language of Allegory*, p. 68.
29. Milton Miller also sees the Garden of Adonis as a fusion of two conflicting principles in which the forces of permanence and alteration are brought into each other's presence: 'The fixed principle itself would give us perfection; mutability itself would give us dissolution; both together give us the Garden of Adonis.' See Milton Miller, 'Nature in *The Faerie Queene*', *English Literary History*, 18 (1951) 191–200 (p. 197).
30. A.C. Hamilton goes so far as to say '"melt": suggests orgasm, but goes beyond it.' See *Edmund Spenser: 'The Faerie Queene'*, ed. A.C. Hamilton (London: Longman, 1977), p. 421.
31. Patricia Parker examines the link between the words copula and copulation with reference to *Wuthering Heights*. See Parker, 'Metaphorical Plot', p. 136.
32. The *OED*, I. 1. d. cites H. Smith, *Sinful Mans Search* (1592) B6: 'That ye be not seduced to offer your petitions to strange gods as Saints, stocks or stones.'
33. Thomas P. Roche Jr, *The Kindly Flame: A Study of the Third and Fourth Books of Spenser's 'Faerie Queene'* (Princeton, NJ: Princeton University Press, 1964), p. 134.
34. Donald Cheney points out that all attempts to locate a specific statue have so far failed. See Donald Cheney, 'Spenser's Hermaphrodite and the 1590 *Faerie Queene*', *PMLA*, 87 (1972) 192–200.
35. Philip Sidney provides a typical example in *Astrophil and Stella*, sonnet 8: 'Whose faire skin, beamy eyes, like morning sun on snow'. Sidney's own emphasis in this sonnet, as frequently in the collection, falls on the 'coldness' of the lady towards her lover. Spenser uses the image of 'her snowy browes' himself in *Amoretti*, sonnet 64.
36. Comparisons of hair to gold or golden wire, and eyes to lamps shining in the firmament abound in Elizabethan sonnets. A typical example of the first is: B. Griffin, *Fidessa, more chaste then kinde*, sonnet 39: 'My Ladies haire is threads of beaten gold'. Spenser in *Amoretti*, sonnet 37, writes of the confusion caused when the lady wears a hair-net of gold: 'that which is gold or heare may scarse be told?' Other examples include Daniel in *To Delia*, sonnets 19, 33 and 36; and the anonymous *Zepheria*, sonnet 17. Examples of the second type are *Zepheria*, sonnet 8: 'Illuminating Lamps, ye Orbs christallite'; Sidney, *Astrophil and Stella*, sonnet 26 and Daniel, *To Delia*, sonnet 28. All these sonnets can be found in Evans (ed.), *Elizabethan Sonnets*.

CHAPTER 3

1. Augustine of Hippo (Saint Augustine), *On Christian Doctrine*, trans. D.W. Robertson Jr (Indianapolis: Bobbs-Merrill, 1958), III. 29. 40. Further references are cited parenthetically in the text.
2. On Renaissance views of 'poetic theology' as a means of protecting divine secrets from profanation, see Edgar Wind, *Pagan Mysteries in the Renaissance* (Harmondsworth: Penguin, 1967), pp. 17–25.
3. These quotations are cited in Keith Thomas, *Religion and the Decline of Magic: Studies in Popular Beliefs in Sixteenth and Seventeenth Century England* (London: Weidenfeld & Nicolson, 1973), pp. 53–4. Thomas gives a full account of the practical effects of the Reformation on what were increasingly seen as the magical beliefs of church ritual, pp. 51–77.
4. D. Douglas Waters, *Duessa as Theological Satire* (Columbia: Missouri University Press, 1970) discusses the poet's doctrine of the Eucharist in Book I stressing Duessa's unifying role as a symbol of the Roman Mass in the Mistress Missa tradition of popular culture.
5. C.S. Lewis, *The Allegory of Love: A Study in Medieval Tradition* (Oxford: Clarendon Press, 1936), pp. 322–3.
6. Cited by Margaret Aston, *England's Iconoclasts: Laws Against Images* (Oxford: Clarendon Press, 1988), pp. 436–7.
7. John Jewel, *The Works of John Jewel Bishop of Salisbury*, ed. Rev. John Ayre, 4 Vols (Cambridge: Parker Society, 1847), Vol. II, p. 594.
8. Most of the episodes from *The Faerie Queene* which I have focused on in previous chapters have themselves featured in readings concerned with idolatry. Nohrnberg argues that the devotions Duessa secures are idolatrous in the sense that 'all false faith is idolatry.' See Nohrnberg, *Analogy*, pp. 222–60. Linda Gregerson equates idolatry with a literalizing of figurative texts and focuses on Malbecco as the 'chief figure in Spenser's parable of dyslexia'. Her interest in Spenser's association of spiritual and lexical matters in terms of libidinous metaphors provides useful parallels with my reading of the Bower of Bliss. See Linda Gregerson, 'Protestant Erotics: Idolatry and Interpretation in Spenser's *Faerie Queene*', *English Literary History*, 85 (1991) 1–34. For a reading of the Garden of Adonis in terms of its resistance to both idolatry and iconoclasm, see Kenneth Gross, *Spenserian Poetics: Idolatry, Iconoclasm, and Magic* (Ithaca, NY: Cornell University Press, 1985), pp. 181–209.
9. W.B. Yeats epitomized the tendency to celebrate the sensuous appeal of the Bower of Bliss when he wrote: He [Spenser] is a poet of the delighted senses, and his song becomes most beautiful when he writes of those islands of Phaedria and Acrasia, which angered "that rugged forehead".' See W.B. Yeats, 'Edmund Spenser', Introduction to his edition of *Poems of Spenser* (1902), in Paul Alpers (ed.), *Edmund Spenser* (Harmondsworth: Penguin, 1969), pp. 172–8 (p. 174).
10. Stephen Greenblatt, *Renaissance Self-Fashioning: From More to Shakespeare* (Chicago: Chicago University Press, 1984), p. 179. Although Greenblatt's main discussion of the Bower of Bliss in relation to

the Reformation attack on images only accounts for four pages of the entire chapter, it exposes the inadequacy of colonial and iconoclastic violence as a means of resolving the inherent contradictions of the Elizabethan response to the appeal of other cultures or aesthetic images.
11. For a detailed examination of the sorts of activity considered appropriate in gardens in the Renaissance see Terry Comito, *The Idea of the Garden in the Renaissance* (Hassocks: Harvester Press, 1979), esp. Chapter III, 'Gardens of Poetry and Philosophy', pp. 51–88.
12. Gross, *Spenserian Poetics*, p. 182.
13. George Puttenham, *The Arte of English Poesie*, in G. Gregory Smith (ed.), *Elizabethan Critical Essays*, 2 Vols (London: Oxford University Press, 1950), Vol. II, p. 169.
14. C.S. Lewis in an appendix to *The Allegory of Love* entitled 'Genius and Genius' concludes his survey of the figure of Genius in ancient, medieval and Renaissance literature with a frank admission about Spenser's Genius in the Bower of Bliss: 'I have suggested a textual operation which would remove the confusion: but it remains very likely that Spenser was, in fact, confused.' Lewis, *Allegory of Love*, p. 363. A more productive view of the Bower's Genius is provided by Isabel MacCaffrey who begins from the premiss that these 'stanzas are self-referring in a complicated way' and that 'Bad Genius ... composes bad allegory, deceptive rather than revelatory'. See Isabel MacCaffrey, *Spenser's Allegory: The Anatomy of Imagination* (Princeton, NJ: Princeton University Press, 1976), p. 214.
15. Puttenham, *Arte of English Poesie*, in Smith (ed.), *Elizabethan Critical Essays*, Vol. II, p. 169.
16. Anne Ferry comments with reference to Peacham's *The Garden of Eloquence*: 'Here it is the art of making metaphors, which he demonstrates by using the traditional comparison – a variant of his book's title – of the "places" where metaphors may be found to "fields," the figures taken from them to "flowers."' Anne Ferry, *The Art of Naming* (Chicago: Chicago University Press, 1988), p. 90. She goes on to point out that this floral metaphor was also applied to 'verse or poesy itself (for which a common pun was posie)', p. 93. Puttenham provides a typical example of the use of 'flowers' as a metaphor for rhetorical tropes when he speaks of 'figures and figuratiue speaches, which be the flowers, as it were, and coulours that a Poet setteth vpon his language of arte'. See Puttenham, *Arte of English Poesie*, in Smith (ed.), *Elizabethan Critical Essays*, Vol. II, p. 143.
17. Spenser's awareness of the connection between the words 'Idle' and 'Idol' is specifically shown when the witch's son accompanies False Florimell into the forest:

> To walke the woods with that his Idole faire,
> Her to disport, and idle time to pas.
>
> (III. viii. 11)

Ernest B. Gilman comments with reference to Phaedria's island in the 'Idle lake' that 'the connection between "Idle" and Idol is no mere coincidence.' See Ernest B. Gilman, *Iconoclasm and Poetry in the English Reformation: 'Down Went Dagon'*, (Chicago: Chicago University Press, 1986), pp. 77–8.

18. For references to specific examples of the conjunction of lust and idolatry in the Bible, see Gregerson, 'Protestant Erotics', p. 8; Nohrnberg, *Analogy*, p. 223n.
19. These quotations from *The Second Book of Homilies* and the quotation which follows are cited by Waters, *Duessa as Theological Satire*, p. 43.
20. For a full account of the iconoclastic controversy in Eastern Christendom in which the major arguments of the Reformation debate had been rehearsed, see Jaroslav Pelikan, *The Christian Tradition: A History of the Development of Doctrine*, 5 Vols (Chicago: Chicago University Press, 1974), Vol. II, pp. 91–145.
21. Jewel, *Works*, Vol. II, p. 666.
22. A. Bartlett Giamatti, *The Earthly Paradise and the Renaissance Epic* (Princeton, NJ: Princeton University Press, 1966), pp. 232–90.
23. Hamilton comments that 'It is not known why Spenser links Tantalus and Pilate' (see *The Faerie Queene*, ed. A.C. Hamilton, p. 235), though there is some agreement amongst critics that they represent the profanation of the divine in so far as Tantalus questioned the divinity of the gods and Pilate denied God Himself. The combination of their blasphemies would create a religious vacuum which the self-professed god, Mammon, is ready to fill.
24. The term 'iconomach', which was commonly used in Reformation debates of the sixteenth century concerning the status of images, is revived by Margaret Aston to distinguish someone who was hostile to religious images from an 'iconoclast' or someone wishing to destroy religious images. See Aston, *England's Iconoclasts*, p. 18.
25. Todorov, *Poetics of Prose*, pp. 62–3.
26. Ernest B. Gilman takes the title for his chapter 'Spenser's "Painted Forgery"' from the Proem to Book II. His discussion of the debate between pictorialism and iconoclasm in *The Faerie Queene* focuses primarily on anxieties about visual imagery and views of painting and poetry as 'sister arts'. See Gilman, *Iconoclasm and Poetry*, esp. pp. 61–83.
27. Greenblatt, *Renaissance Self-Fashioning*, p. 172.
28. Derek Attridge, *Peculiar Language: Literature as Difference from the Renaissance to James Joyce* (London: Methuen, 1988), p. 39. It is interesting to note that while Attridge recognizes that the meditations on the relationship of nature and art in the Bower of Bliss dramatically present 'the division between Spenser's aesthetic and politico-religious beliefs', and bring the art/nature contradiction to a moment of acute danger, his discussion of the supplement in Renaissance literary theory relegates the only quotation from Spenser's poem to the supplementary status of a footnote, p. 38n. He states from the outset that Puttenham's treatise is 'especially useful' for his purposes precisely because, unlike Spenser's poem, 'it does not

exercise to the full the rhetorical and persuasive powers that are, in part, its subject', p. 19.
29. Harry Berger Jr, *The Allegorical Temper: Vision and Reality in Book II of Spenser's 'Faerie Queene'* (New Haven, Conn.: Yale University Press, 1957), p. 224.
30. For a discussion of the complex field of meaning associated with *krasis*, see Berger, *Allegorical Temper*, pp. 66–7.
31. On the practical effects of the Elizabethan royal injunctions on the interiors of churches and the return to the Edwardian policy of painting Scripture on the walls, see John Phillips, *The Reformation of Images: Destruction of Art in England, 1535–1660* (London: California University Press, 1973), pp. 128–39. On the idea of the gradual change from a culture of orality and image to one of print, see Walter J. Ong, *Orality and Literacy: The Technologizing of the Word* (London: Methuen, 1982) and for a view stressing the importance of Protestant ideology rather than the technological development of print, see Patrick Collinson, *The Birthpangs of Protestant England: Religious and Cultural Change in the Sixteenth and Seventeenth Centuries* (London: Macmillan, 1988). For an account stressing the continued role of visual communication in Protestant culture and the 'fruitful confrontation' of image and word, see Tessa Watt, *Cheap Print and Popular Piety 1550–1640* (Cambridge: Cambridge University Press, 1991), pp. 131–40.
32. Michael O'Connell, 'The Idolatrous Eye: Iconoclasm, Antitheatricalism, and the Image of the Elizabethan Theater', *English Literary History*, 52 (1985) 279–310 (p. 299).
33. Berger, *Allegorical Temper*, p. 239.
34. Camille Paglia, *Sexual Personae: Art and Decadence from Nefertiti to Emily Dickinson* (London: Yale University Press, 1990), p. 189.
35. Gregerson, 'Protestant Erotics', p. 5.
36. John Hollander, 'Spenser and the Mingled Measure', *English Literary Renaissance*, 1 (1971) 226–38. My reading of II. xii. 71 is informed by Hollander's insights.
37. Ray Frazer points out that the term 'image' must be carefully distinguished from the term 'figure' when discussing Renaissance poetry. He explains that for writers of the period:

> There was a special term (Icon) which meant a picture of something, and a general concept (Enargia) which meant the process of making the reader seem to see something.... The Renaissance poet, whose work was characteristically so full of imagery, didn't think of himself as using any. What he did think in terms of was 'figures' – the techniques of expression.

See Ray Frazer, 'The Origin of the Term "Image"', *English Literary History*, 27 (1960) 149–61 (pp. 149–50).
38. Cited by Robert M. Durling, 'The Bower of Bliss and Armida's Palace', *Comparative Literature*, 6 (1954) 335–47 (p. 342).
39. On the significance of Verdant's 'idle instruments' and their associ-

ation with the lyric impotence of poetry compared to more active sexual, martial and political pursuits, see Patricia Parker, 'Suspended Instruments: Lyric and Power in the Bower of Bliss', in *Literary Fat Ladies: Rhetoric, Gender, Property* (London: Methuen, 1987), pp. 54–66.
40. For citations showing that 'Spenser's analogy between the witchcraft of Circe and the works of the whore of Babylon is well established in Protestant polemic', see Nohrnberg, *Analogy*, pp. 244–5.
41. On the development of Luther's ideas on theology and religious art, see C.C. Christensen, *Art and Reformation in Germany* (Detroit, Mich.: Ohio and Wayne University Press, 1979), pp. 42–65.
42. Susanne Lindgren Wofford, *The Choice of Achilles: The Ideology of Figure in the Epic* (Stanford, Calif.: Stanford University Press, 1992), p. 359.
43. The comparison between cannibalism and the Real Presence in Protestant polemic is noted by Nohrnberg who cites Ridley's view that the doctrine 'confirmeth and maintaineth that beastly kind of cruelty of the "Anthropophagi," that is devourers of man's flesh.' As Nohrnberg goes on to say, this was also 'the technical position of Zwingli, in his *Commentary on True and False Religion*'. See Nohrnberg, *Analogy*, p. 712.
44. The words in inverted commas are used by Tyndale in his reply to More's *Dialogue Concerning Tyndale*. For a discussion of More's controversy with Tyndale in which these terms are cited and reference to the history of the introduction of false practices into the sacrificial ceremonies of the Jews, see Phillips, *Reformation of Images*, pp. 42–8.
45. Donald Cheney, *Spenser's Image of Nature: Wild Man and Shepherd in 'The Faerie Queene'* (New Haven, Conn.: Yale University Press, 1966), p. 106.
46. Anne Ferry provides an extensive discussion of the associations of the anatomical blazon with its biblical sources but also its potentially demonic links with charms and ritual. She specifically notes an echo from the Song of Songs in the Geneva Bible with the catalogue of Serena's 'daintie parts'. See Ferry, *Art of Naming*, pp. 154–68.
47. Louis Adrian Montrose, 'The Elizabethan Subject and the Spenserian Text', in Patricia Parker and David Quint (eds), *Literary Theory/Renaissance Texts* (London: Johns Hopkins University Press, 1986), pp. 303–40 (p. 327).
48. Sir Philip Sidney, *Astrophil and Stella*, in Evans (ed.), *Elizabethan Sonnets*, p. 28.
49. For reference to Spenser's use of the Geneva Bible version of the Song of Solomon in the blazon of Serena, see Naseeb Shaheen, *Biblical References in 'The Faerie Queene'* (Memphis, Tenn.: Memphis State University Press, 1976), p. 34.
50. Humphrey Tonkin, *Spenser's Courteous Pastoral: Book Six of the 'Faerie Queene'* (Oxford: Clarendon Press, 1972), p. 105.
51. Stanley Stewart says of Book VI: 'The primary feature of organization, it seems to me, is disjunction.' See Stanley Stewart, 'Sir Calidore

and "Closure"', *Studies in English Literature*, 24 (1984) 69–86 (p. 85).
52. This phrase is used by J. Nohrnberg in relation to Book VI where he writes: 'we find ourselves experiencing not the romance of faith or chastity, but the romance of romance itself.' See Nohrnberg, *Analogy*, p. 656. Patricia Parker uses the same phrase 'The Romance of Romance' as a subheading to a chapter on Spenser which provides an absorbing reading of Book VI as the poem's retrospective on its own implications. See Patricia Parker, *Inescapable Romance: Studies in the Poetics of a Mode*, (Princeton, NJ: Princeton University Press, 1979), pp. 101–13.
53. Jacqueline T. Miller, 'The Courtly Figure: Spenser's Anatomy of Allegory', *Studies in English Literature*, 31 (1991) 51–68 (p. 53).
54. This excerpt from Puttenham is cited by Miller, 'Courtly Figure', p. 53.
55. Louis Adrian Montrose, 'Of Gentlemen and Shepherds: The Politics of Elizabethan Pastoral Form', *English Literary History*, 50 (1983) 415–59 (p. 438).
56. For a discussion of rhetorical definitions of metaphor (including the imposture of disguise or false clothing) which become figures for metaphor, see Parker, 'Metaphorical Plot', pp. 36–9.
57. Robin Headlam Wells points out the apparent irony as well as the logic behind the rise of the 'sacred' image of Elizabeth the Queen developed in Marian iconography. See Robin Headlam Wells, *Spenser's 'Faerie Queene' and the Cult of Elizabeth* (London: Croom Helm, 1983), pp. 14–21.
58. Once the verb 'to conduct' becomes associated with moral guidance rather than just geographical guidance it only takes a small shift to emphasize the resultant behaviour instead of the initial act of instruction.
59. See MacCaffrey, *Spenser's Allegory*, p. 357n.
60. Debra Belt, 'Hostile Audiences and the Courteous Reader in *The Faerie Queene*, Book VI', *Spenser Studies*, 9 (1988) 107–35.
61. A. Bartlett Giamatti, 'Spenser: From Magic to Miracle', in Herschel Baker (ed.), *Four Essays on Romance* (Cambridge, Mass.: Harvard University Press, 1971), pp. 17–33 (pp. 18 and 25).
62. Giamatti, 'Magic to Miracle', p. 25.
63. John Guillory, *Poetic Authority: Spenser, Milton, and Literary History* (New York: Columbia University Press, 1983), p. 43.
64. Guillory, *Poetic Authority*, p. 45.
65. The primary meaning of the verb 'to trace' in the context of Spenser's description refers to the action of pacing or treading in a dance. Other meanings of trace relating to tracking footprints or signs suggest interesting readings in the context of the attempt to use metaphor as a means of figuratively 'tracing' divine presence in the knowledge of its literal absence.
66. For a fascinating discussion of the vocational complexities of Spenser's epic undertaking in *The Faerie Queene* which pays close attention to the episode on Mount Acidale and issues of poetry and nomination, see Elizabeth J. Bellamy, 'The Vocative and the Vocational:

The Unreadability of Elizabeth in *The Faerie Queene'*, *English Literary History*, 54 (1987) 1–30. I find Bellamy's arguments compelling, though her reading tends towards a secular rather than a sacred view of vocation. In a sacred context, Spenser must sustain metaphoric predication in order to avoid nomination precisely because it constitutes an act of idolatry when translated from the world of the secular epic into the realms of sacred allegory. The emphasis of my reading leads me to view *The Faerie Queene* as a celebration of predication rather than a failure of nomination.

67. This quotation, which applies so well to the necessity of repressing literal interpretation in order to allow metaphoric meaning to emerge, is taken from Bram Stoker's *Dracula* and is the definition of faith given by Dr. Van Helsing to Dr Seward. See Bram Stoker, *Dracula* (New York: Nelson Doubleday, 1987), p. 193.

CHAPTER 4

1. Judah L. Stampfer's article 'The Cantos of Mutabilitie: Spenser's Last Testament of Faith', *University of Texas Quarterly*, 21 (1951) 140–56, typifies the emotional aspect of such biographical criticism.
2. An informative discussion of the main critical views can be found in the introduction to S.P. Zitner's edition of the Mutabilitie Cantos. See *The Mutabilitie Cantos*, ed. S.P. Zitner (London: Nelson, 1968), pp. 5–10. A survey including more recent work can be found in *The Faerie Queene*, ed. Hamilton, pp. 711–13.
3. Ricoeur, *Rule of Metaphor*, p. 230.
4. Northrop Frye draws attention to the link between the Mutabilitie Cantos and Book I in terms of the Pisgah-vision experienced in them both. See Northrop Frye, *Anatomy of Criticism: Four Essays* (Princeton, NJ: Princeton University Press, 1957), p. 204.
5. Josephine Waters Bennett, 'Spenser's Venus and the Goddess Nature of the Cantos of Mutabilitie', *Studies in Philology*, 30 (1933) 160–92 (p. 160).
6. A Lucretian interpretation of the Mutabilitie Cantos can be found in Edwin Greenlaw, 'Spenser's "Mutabilitie"', *PMLA*, 45 (1930) 684–703.
7. Bennett, 'Spenser's Venus', pp. 162–3.
8. George Williamson, 'Mutability, Decay, and Seventeenth Century Melancholy', *English Literary History*, 2 (1935) 121–50 (p. 121). Williamson explains how the appearance of a bright star in the constellation of Cassiopeia, followed by its disappearance 16 months later, undermined Aristotle's doctrine of the incorruptibility of the heavens generally and of the fixed stars in particular.
9. Spenser expressed his moral purpose in the prefatory letter to Raleigh: 'The generall end therefore of all the booke is to fashion a gentleman or noble person in vertuous and gentle discipline.' See *Spenser's 'Faerie Queene'*, ed. Smith, Vol. II, p. 485.
10. William Blissett discusses this relaxation of tension prior to the final pronouncement. See William Blissett, 'Spenser's Mutabilitie', in Millar

MacLure and F.W. Watt (eds), *Essays in English Literature from the Renaissance to the Victorian Age: Presented to A.S.P. Woodhouse* (Toronto: Toronto University Press, 1964), pp. 26–42 (esp. pp. 38–40).
11. Several critics discuss ways in which the Mutabilitie Cantos are structured to undercut Mutabilitie. The pageant of the cycle of the months is dealt with in detail by Sherman Hawkins in 'Mutabilitie and the Cycle of the Months', in William Nelson (ed.), *Form and Convention in the Poetry of Edmund Spenser* (New York: Columbia University Press, 1961), pp. 76–102. A broader examination of the narrative pattern and the 'ironic balance of tone' is undertaken by Donald Cheney. See Cheney, *Spenser's Image of Nature*, pp. 239–47.
12. Bennett, 'Spenser's Venus', p. 189.
13. Colie, *Paradoxia Epidemica*, pp. 329–52.
14. Plotinus, *The Enneads*, trans. Stephen MacKenna, 4th edn revised by B.S. Page (London: Faber, 1969), p. 581.
15. Plotinus, *The Enneads*, p. 583.
16. Jacques Derrida, 'White Mythology: Metaphor in the text of Philosophy', *New Literary History*, 6 (1974) 5–74 (p. 52).
17. Colie, *Paradoxia Epidemica*, p. 345.
18. There is an interesting discussion of a visual paradox in art where a single shape represents two different images which are mutually exclusive in terms of the viewer's perception at any one time. The effect of such 'illusions' may have something in common with metaphor. See Gombrich, *Art and Illusion*, pp. 4–6. The artist whose paintings spring to mind in this context is Giuseppe Arcimboldo. In Giancarlo Maiorino's study of Arcimboldo he finds links between figures of eccentricity in rhetoric and Mannerism. I quote a passage in which Maiorino specifically draws attention to the 'metaphorical effects' which structure his portraits:

> Arcimboldo also made it possible for animals and vegetables to form a nose as long as their shapes were anatomically acceptable. To quote Roland Barthes, he never tired of using 'different forms to represent the same thing. Does he want to paint a nose? His multitude of synonyms proposes a branch, a pear, a pumpkin, corn, flowers, fish.' Interest is centered neither in the fish nor in the nose alone, but in teasing the very concept of reciprocity; every form is *like* and *unlike* other forms. Similitude became a Janus-like concept, and precedence was given to metaphorical effects.

Giancarlo Maiorino, *The Portrait of Eccentricity: Arcimboldo and the Mannerist Grotesque* (London: Pennsylvania State University Press, 1991), p. 34.
19. Patricia Parker comments on the associations created by the wording of the concluding lines with a final veiled reference to the name of the poem's dedicatee, Queen Elizabeth: 'The "Eli-sabbath," God of the Sabbath, is also, in the English Renaissance compliment, the etymology of "Elizabeth," so that Spenser manages once again both

to conceal and to reveal his sovereign within the "covert vele" of his poem.' See Parker, *Inescapable Romance*, p. 78. For a discussion emphasizing the problematic nature of Spenser's figurative fragmentation of Elizabeth's name in the final stanza, see Bellamy, 'The Vocative and the Vocational', pp. 22–4.

List of Works Cited

Alpers, Paul J. *The Poetry of 'The Faerie Queene'*. Princeton, NJ: Princeton University Press, 1967.
Ariosto. *Orlando Furioso*. Eds Santorre Debenedetti and Cesare Segre. Bologna: Commissione per i Testi di Lingua, 1960.
—— *Orlando Furioso*. Trans. Guido Waldman. London: Oxford University Press, 1974.
Aristotle. *The Basic Works of Aristotle*. Ed. Richard McKeon. Trans. Ingram Bywater. New York: Random House, 1941.
Aston, Margaret. *England's Iconoclasts: Laws Against Images*. Oxford: Clarendon Press, 1988.
Attridge, Derek. *Peculiar Language: Literature as Difference from the Renaissance to James Joyce*. London: Methuen, 1988.
Augustine of Hippo (Saint Augustine). *On Christian Doctrine*. Trans. D.W. Robertson Jr. Indianapolis: Bobbs-Merrill, 1958.
Babb, Lawrence. *The Elizabethan Malady: A Study of Melancholia in English Literature from 1580–1642*. East Lansing, Mich.: Michigan State College Press, 1951.
Barthes, Roland. *Mythologies*. Trans. Annette Lavers. Aylesbury: Paladin, 1985.
—— 'The Death of the Author'. In David Lodge (ed.) *Modern Criticism and Theory: A Reader*. Harlow: Longman, 1988, pp. 167–72.
Beardsley, Monroe 'The Metaphoric Twist'. *Philosophy and Phenomenological Research* 22 (1962) 293–307.
Bellamy, Elizabeth J. 'The Vocative and the Vocational: The Unreadability of Elizabeth in *The Faerie Queene*'. *English Literary History* 54 (1987) 1–30.
Belt, Debra. 'Hostile Audiences and the Courteous Reader in *The Faerie Queene*, Book VI'. *Spenser Studies* 9 (1988) 107–35.
Bennett, Josephine Waters. 'Spenser's Garden of Adonis' *PMLA* 47 (1932) 46–80.
—— 'Spenser's Venus and the Goddess Nature of the Cantos of Mutabilitie'. *Studies in Philology* 30 (1933) 160–92.
—— 'Spenser's Garden of Adonis Revisited'. *Journal of English and German Philology* 41 (1942) 53–78.
Berger, Harry Jr. *The Allegorical Temper: Vision and Reality in Book II of Spenser's 'Faerie Queene'*. New Haven, Conn.: Yale University Press, 1957.
—— 'Spenser's Gardens of Adonis: Force and Form in the Renaissance Imagination'. *University of Texas Quarterly* 30 (1961) 128–49.
—— 'The Discarding of Malbecco: Conspicuous Allusion and Cultural Exhaustion in the *Faerie Queene* III. ix–x'. *Studies in Philology* 66 (1969) 135–54.

Black, Max. *Models and Metaphors: Studies in Language and Philosophy*. Ithaca, NY: Cornell University Press, 1962.
Blake, William. *The Complete Poems of William Blake*. Ed. W.H. Stevenson. New York: Norton, 1971.
Blissett, William. 'Spenser's Mutabilitie'. In Millar MacLure and F.W. Watt (eds) *Essays in English Literature from the Renaissance to the Victorian Age: Presented to A.S.P. Woodhouse*. Toronto: Toronto University Press, 1964, pp. 26–42.
Brooks-Davies, Douglas. *Spenser's 'Faerie Queene': A Critical Commentary on Books I and II*. Manchester: Manchester University Press, 1977.
Carroll, Lewis. *The Complete Works of Lewis Carroll*. Ed. Alexander Woollcott. London: Nonesuch, 1939.
Cheney, Donald. *Spenser's Image of Nature: Wild Man and Shepherd in 'The Faerie Queene'*. New Haven, Conn.: Yale University Press, 1966.
—— 'Spenser's Hermaphrodite and the 1590 *Faerie Queene*'. *PMLA* 87 (1972) 192–200.
Christensen, C.C. *Art and Reformation in Germany*. Detroit, Mich.: Ohio and Wayne University Press, 1979.
Clarke, T.H. *The Rhinoceros from Dürer to Stubbs: 1515–1799*. London: Sotheby's Publications, 1986.
Colie, Rosalie L. *Paradoxia Epidemica: The Renaissance Tradition of Parodox*. Princeton, NJ: Princeton University Press, 1966.
Collinson, Patrick. *The Birth Pangs of Protestant England: Religious and Cultural Change in the Sixteenth and Seventeenth Centuries*. London: Macmillan, 1988.
Comito, Terry. *The Idea of the Garden in the Renaissance*. Hassocks: Harvester Press, 1979.
Curtius, E.R. *European Literature and the Latin Middle Ages*. Trans. Willard R. Trask. New York: Pantheon, 1953).
de Man, Paul. *Blindness and Insight: Essays in the Rhetoric of Contemporary Criticism*. London: Methuen, 1983.
DeNeef, A. Leigh. *Spenser and the Motives of Metaphor*. Durham, NC: Duke University Press, 1982.
Derrida, Jacques. 'White Mythology: Metaphor in the Text of Philosophy'. *New Literary History* 6 (1974) 5–74.
Durling, Robert M. 'The Bower of Bliss and Armida's Palace'. *Comparative Literature* 6 (1954) 335–47.
Elyot, Thomas. *Dictionary 1538*. Ed. R.C. Alston. Menston: Scolar Press, 1970.
Evans, Maurice. *Spenser's Anatomy of Heroism: A Commentary on the 'Faerie Queene'*. Cambridge: Cambridge University Press, 1970.
—— (ed.). *Elizabethan Sonnets*. London: Dent, 1977.
Ferry, Anne. *The Art of Naming*. Chicago: Chicago University Press, 1988.
Fletcher, Angus. *Allegory: The Theory of a Symbolic Mode*. Ithaca, NY: Cornell University Press, 1964.
Frazer, Ray. 'The Origin of the Term "Image"'. *English Literary History* 27 (1960) 149–61.
Frye, Northrop. *Anatomy of Criticism: Four Essays*. Princeton, NJ: Princeton University Press, 1957.

Giamatti, A. Bartlett. *The Earthly Paradise and the Renaissance Epic.* Princeton, NJ: Princeton University Press, 1966.
—— 'Spenser: From Magic to Miracle'. In Herschel Baker (ed.) *Four Essays on Romance.* Cambridge, Mass.: Harvard University Press, 1971, pp. 17–33.
Gilman, Ernest B. *Iconoclasm and Poetry in the English Reformation: 'Down Went Dagon'.* Chicago: Chicago University Press, 1986.
Going, W.T. 'The Term Sonnet Sequence'. *Modern Language Notes* 62 (1947) 400–2.
—— 'Gascoigne and the Term "Sonnet Sequence"'. *Notes and Queries* 199 (1954) 189–91.
Golding, Arthur. See Ovid.
Gombrich, E.H. *Art and Illusion: A Study in the Psychology of Pictorial Representation.* London: Pantheon, 1960.
Greenblatt, Stephen. *Renaissance Self-Fashioning: From More to Shakespeare.* Chicago: Chicago University Press, 1984.
Greenlaw, Edwin. 'Spenser and Lucretius'. *Studies in Philology* 17 (1920) 439–64.
—— 'Spenser's "Mutabilitie"'. *PMLA* 45 (1930) 684–703.
Gregerson, Linda. 'Protestant Erotics: Idolatry and Interpretation in Spenser's *Faerie Queene*'. *English Literary History* 85 (1991) 1–34.
Gross, Kenneth. *Spenserian Poetics: Idolatry, Iconoclasm, and Magic.* Ithaca, NY: Cornell University Press, 1985.
Guillory, John. *Poetic Authority: Spenser, Milton, and Literary History.* New York: Columbia University Press, 1983.
Halio, Jay L. 'The Metaphor of Conception and Elizabethan Theories of the Imagination'. *Neophilogus* 50 (1966) 454–61.
Hawkins, Sherman. 'Mutabilitie and the Cycle of the Months'. In William Nelson (ed.) *Form and Convention in the Poetry of Edmund Spenser.* New York: Columbia University Press, 1961, pp. 76–102.
Hollander, John. 'Spenser and the Mingled Measure'. *English Literary Renaissance* 1 (1971) 226–38.
Jewel, John. *The Works of John Jewel Bishop of Salisbury.* Ed. Rev. John Ayre. 4 Vols. Cambridge: Parker Society, 1847.
Kermode, Frank. *The Sense of an Ending: Studies in the Theory of Fiction.* New York: Oxford University Press, 1966.
Klibansky, Raymond, Panofsky, Erwin and Saxl, Fritz. *Saturn and Melancholy: Studies in the History of Natural Philosophy, Religion, and Art.* London: Nelson, 1964.
Knight, G. Wilson. 'The Spenserian Fluidity'. In Paul J. Alpers (ed.) *Edmund Spenser.* Harmondsworth: Penguin, 1969, pp. 222–32.
Lakoff, George and Johnson, Mark. *Metaphors We Live By.* Chicago: Chicago University Press, 1980.
Langland, William. *The Vision of Piers Plowman.* Ed. A.V.C. Schmidt. London: Dent, 1982.
Lewis, C.S. *The Allegory of Love: A Study in Medieval Tradition.* Oxford: Clarendon Press, 1936.
MacCaffrey, Isabel. *Spenser's Allegory: The Anatomy of Imagination.* Princeton, NJ: Princeton University Press, 1976.

Maiorino, Giancarlo. *The Portrait of Eccentricity: Arcimboldo and the Mannerist Grotesque*. London: Pennsylvania State University Press, 1991.
Marston, John. *The Selected Plays of John Marston*. Eds MacDonald P. Jackson and Michael Neill. Cambridge: Cambridge University Press, 1986.
Miller, George A. 'Images and Models, Similes and Metaphors'. In Andrew Ortony (ed.) *Metaphor and Thought*. Cambridge: Cambridge University Press, 1979, pp. 202–50.
Miller, Jacqueline I. 'The Courtly Figure: Spenser's Anatomy of Allegory'. *Studies in English Literature* 31 (1991) 51–68.
Miller, Milton. 'Nature in *The Faerie Queene*'. *English Literary History* 18 (1951) 191–200.
Montrose, Louis Adrian. 'Of Gentlemen and Shepherds: The Politics of Elizabethan Pastoral Form'. *English Literary History* 50 (1983) 415–59.
—— 'The Elizabethan Subject and the Spenserian Text'. In Patricia Parker and David Quint (eds) *Literary Theory/Renaissance Texts*. London: Johns Hopkins University Press, 1986, pp. 303–40.
Nelson, William. *Fact or Fiction: The Dilemma of the Renaissance Storyteller*. Cambridge, Mass.: Harvard University Press, 1973.
Nohrnberg, J. *The Analogy of 'The Faerie Queene'*. Princeton, NJ: Princeton University Press, 1976.
O'Connell, Michael. 'The Idolatrous Eye: Iconoclasm, Antitheatricalism, and the Image of the Elizabethan Theater'. *English Literary History* 52 (1985) 279–310.
Ong, Walter J. *Orality and Literacy: The Technologizing of the Word*. London: Methuen, 1982.
Ovid. *Shakespeare's Ovid: The Metamorphosis*. Trans. Arthur Golding. Ed. W.H. Rouse. London: Centaur Press, 1961.
Paglia, Camille. *Sexual Personae: Art and Decadence from Nefertiti to Emily Dickinson*. London: Yale University Press, 1990.
Parker, Patricia. *Inescapable Romance: Studies in the Poetics of a Mode*. Princeton, NJ: Princeton University Press, 1979.
—— 'The Metaphorical Plot'. In David S. Miall (ed.) *Metaphor: Problems and Perspectives*. Brighton: Harvester, 1982, pp. 133–57.
—— *Literary Fat Ladies: Rhetoric, Gender, Property*. London: Methuen, 1987.
Pelikan, Jaroslav. *The Christian Tradition: A History of the Development of Doctrine*. 5 Vols. Chicago: Chicago University Press, 1974.
Phillips, John. *The Reformation of Images: Destruction of Art in England, 1535–1660*. London: California University Press, 1973.
Plato. *Phaedrus*. Trans. C.J. Rowe. Warminster: Aris and Phillips, 1986.
Plotinus. *The Enneads*. Trans. Stephen MacKenna. Fourth edn revised by B.S. Page. London: Faber, 1969.
Puttenham, George. *The Arte of English Poesie*. In G. Gregory Smith (ed.) *Elizabethan Critical Essays*. 2 Vols. London: Oxford University Press, 1950.
Quilligan, Maureen. *The Language of Allegory: Defining the Genre*. Ithaca, NY: Cornell University Press, 1979.
Rajan, Balachandra. *The Form of the Unfinished: English Poetics from Spenser*

to Pound. Princeton, NJ: Princeton University Press, 1985.

Raleigh, Sir Walter. *The History of the World*. Ed. C.A. Patrides. London: Macmillan, 1971.

Ramsay, Judith C. 'The Garden of Adonis and the Garden of Forms'. *University of Texas Quarterly* 35 (1966) 188–206.

Richards, I.A. *The Philosophy of Rhetoric*. New York: Oxford University Press, 1950.

Ricoeur, Paul. *The Rule of Metaphor: Multi-disciplinary Studies of the Creation of Meaning in Language*. Trans. Robert Czerny. Toronto: Toronto University Press, 1977.

—— 'The Metaphorical Process as Cognition, Imagination, and Feeling'. In Mark Johnson (ed.) *Philosophical Perspectives on Metaphor*. Minneapolis: Minnesota University Press, 1981, pp. 228–47.

Roche, Thomas P. Jr. *The Kindly Flame: A Study of the Third and Fourth Books of Spenser's 'Faerie Queene'*. Princeton NJ: Princeton University Press, 1964.

Sasek, Lawrence A. 'Gascoigne and the Elizabethan Sonnet Sequences'. *Notes and Queries* 201 (1956) 143–4.

Shaheen, Naseeb. *Biblical References in 'The Faerie Queene'*. Memphis, Tenn.: Memphis State University Press, 1976.

Shakespeare, William. *Antony and Cleopatra*. Ed. M.R. Ridley. London: Methuen, 1978.

Sidney, Sir Philip. *An Apology for Poetry*. Ed. Geoffrey Shepherd. Manchester: Manchester University Press, 1989.

Sirluck, Ernest. 'A Note on the Rhetoric of Spenser's "Despair"'. *Modern Philology* 47 (1950) 8–11.

Smith, Hallet. *Elizabethan Poetry: A Study in Conventions, Meaning, and Expression*. Cambridge, Mass.: Harvard University Press, 1952.

Sparshott, F.E. '"As," or the Limits of Metaphor'. *New Literary History* 6 (1974) 75–94.

Spenser, Edmund. *The Works of Edmund Spenser: A Variorum Edition*. Ed. E.A. Greenlaw et al. 11 vols. Baltimore: Johns Hopkins University Press, 1932–57.

—— *The Mutabilitie Cantos*. Ed. S.P. Zitner. London: Nelson, 1968.

—— *Edmund Spenser: 'The Faerie Queene'*. Ed. A.C. Hamilton. London: Longman, 1977.

—— *Spenser's 'Faerie Queene'*. Ed. J.C. Smith. 2 Vols. Oxford: Clarendon Press, 1909, rpt. 1978.

Stampfer, Judah L. 'The Cantos of Mutabilitie: Spenser's Last Testament of Faith'. *University of Texas Quarterly* 21 (1951) 140–56.

Stevens, Wallace. *Collected Poems of Wallace Stevens*. London: Faber, 1984.

Stewart, Stanley. 'Sir Calidore and "Closure"'. *Studies in English Literature* 24 (1984) 69–86.

Stirling, Brents. 'The Philosophy of Spenser's "Garden of Adonis"'. *PMLA* 49 (1934) 501–38.

Stoker, Bram. *Dracula*. New York: Nelson Doubleday, 1987.

Thomas, Keith. *Religion and the Decline of Magic: Studies in Popular Beliefs in Sixteenth and Seventeenth Century England*. London: Weidenfeld & Nicolson, 1973.

Tilley, Morris Palmer. *A Dictionary of the Proverbs in England in the Sixteenth and Seventeenth Centuries*. Ann Arbor: Michigan University Press, 1950.

Todorov, Tzvetan. *The Poetics of Prose*. Trans. Richard Howard. Oxford: Blackwell, 1977.

Tonkin, Humphrey. *Spenser's Courteous Pastoral: Book VI of the 'Faerie Queene'*. Oxford: Clarendon Press, 1972.

Tournier, Michel. *The Erl-King*. Trans. Barbara Bray. London: Methuen, 1983.

Tuve, Rosemond. *Elizabethan and Metaphysical Imagery: Renaissance Poetic and Twentieth-Century Critics*. Chicago: Chicago University Press, 1968.

Warkentin, Germaine. '"Loves sweetest part, variety": Petrarch and the Curious Frame of the Renaissance Sonnet Sequence'. *Renaissance and Reformation* 11 (1975) 14–23.

Waters, D. Douglas. *Duessa as Theological Satire*. Columbia: Missouri University Press, 1970.

Watt, Tessa. *Cheap Print and Popular Piety 1550–1640*. Cambridge: Cambridge University Press, 1991.

Webster, John. *John Webster: Three Plays*. Ed. D.C. Gunby. Harmondsworth: Penguin, 1979.

Wells, Robin Headlam. *Spenser's 'Faerie Queene' and the Cult of Elizabeth*. London: Croom Helm, 1983.

Williamson, George. 'Mutability, Decay, and Seventeenth Century Melancholy'. *English Literary History* 2 (1935) 121–50.

Wind, Edgar. *Pagan Mysteries in the Renaissance*. Harmondsworth: Penguin, 1967.

Wofford, Susanne Lindgren. *The Choice of Achilles: The Ideology of Figure in the Epic*. Stanford, Calif.: Stanford University Press, 1992.

Yeats, W.B. 'Edmund Spenser'. Introduction to his edition of *Poems of Spenser* (1902). In Paul Alpers (ed.) *Edmund Spenser*. Harmondsworth: Penguin, 1969, pp. 172–8.

Index

Acrasia, 25, 136–9, 141, 143–4, 146–8, 150–3, 155–6, 168
Adam, 47–8, 211n19
Adonis, 106–7, 109, 110–11
Agdistes, 133–5
allegory: conception of, 94–6; and courtesy, 165; as figure of false semblant, 39, 132–4; and idolatry, 25–6, 129–31, 135–6, 141, 150–1, 155–6, 164, 169–70, 177, 180, 218–19n66; and morality, 140, 143; and riddle, 36–7; veil of, 38–9, 78–80, 128, 149, 153, 164, 176–7, 197–200; and vision, 172–3, 175–9
Alpers, Paul J., 64, 91, 207n12
Amaranthus, 109
Amoret, 94, 96, 100–2, 111–14, 121–3
Aquinas, St Thomas, 154
Archimago, 66–7, 76–7, 79–80, 129, 131
Arcimboldo, Giuseppe, 220n18
Ariosto, Lodovico, 37–8, 42–3; *Orlando Furioso*, 37–8, 41, 50
Aristotle, 1–2, 6, 9–10, 22, 89, 153, 219n8
Arlo Hill, 168, 189
art and nature, 144–7, 215–16n28
Artegall, 125
Arthur, 54–5, 100
Aston, Margaret, 215n24
Attridge, Derek, 144
Augustine of Hippo (St Augustine), 127–8, 137–8, 141–2, 167

Babb, Lawrence, 205n11
Bale, John, 129
Barthes, Roland, 59, 61–4, 220n18
Beardsley, Monroe, 210n7
beginnings, *see* origins
Bellamy, Elizabeth J., 218–19n66, 221n19
Belphoebe, 94, 96–8, 101–2, 160
Belt, Debra, 170
Bennett, Josephine Waters, 184, 190, 211–12n27
Berger, Harry Jr, 24, 99, 103–5, 146, 148, 216n30

Bible, 23, 67, 120, 127–8, 132, 136; Ezekiel, 56; Genesis, 74; Romans, 58; Song of Solomon 160, 162
Black, Max, 71
Blake, William, 89
Blandamour, 122
Blatant Beast, 165, 169–70, 180
blazon, 26, 159–62, 175, 217n46
blindness, 6, 46, 54, 70–2, 80, 200
Blissett, William, 219n10
Book of the World, 58–9, 62–3, 183
Bower of Bliss, 26, 83, 131–6, 138–9, 141–57, 162, 168–9, 214–15nn14,28
Braggadocchio, 121–22, 124–6
Britomart, 99, 112, 122
Brooks-Davies, Douglas, 56, 58, 206–9nn2,5,19,38
Busyrane, 100

Caelia, 65
Calepine, 26, 162–4
Calidore, 26, 157, 164–6, 169–74, 176, 180
Calvin, John, 64, 131
cannibals (in Book VI), 26, 158, 161, 164, 171, 173
carnality, 25–6, 136, 154, 156–62, 171, 173–5. *See also* concupiscence; cupidity
Carroll, Lewis, 35–6
Castle Ioyeous, 139
catalogue of trees, 28–30
Chaos, 190
Chaucer, Geoffrey, 200–1; dream visions of, 95
Cheney, Donald, 158, 212n34, 220n11
Christ, 47–9, 53, 55–6, 58, 157, 199, 201–2, 209–10nn38,2
Christensen, C.C., 217n41
Chrysogene, 94–6, 100, 102
Chrysostom, John, 131
Clarke, T.H., 205n6
cliché, *see* metaphor: conventional
closure, 23, 32, 72–5, 80, 113–14, 164, 176–7, 180, 188
clothing: metaphor of, 103–4, 121, 165

229

Index

Colie, Rosalie L., 194, 199, 206–7n4
Colin Clout, 157, 173–4, 176–9
Collinson, Patrick, 216n31
Comito, Terry, 214n11
conception, 94–8, 102, 110
concupiscence, 135–6, 141, 149–51, 153–5, 161, 164. *See also* carnality; cupidity
Contemplation, 64–5, 67–8, 70, 78; Mount of, 72, 79
copulation and metaphor, 111–13, 212n31
cultivation: metaphor of, 24, 98–9, 104–6
Cupid, 100–1
cupidity, 137–43, 153–4. *See also* carnality; concupiscence
Curtius, Ernst, 206n23
Cymocles, 136

Daniel, Samuel, 15, 212n36
dead metaphor, *see* metaphor: conventional
de Man, Paul, 70–2
DeNeef, 20, 66, 210n2
Derrida, Jacques, 199
Despair, 51–69, 78, 97, 131
Diana, 101, 171
dilation, 194–6, 202–3
Drayton, Michael, 11–18
Duessa, 39–41, 44–5, 49–50, 76–7, 79–80, 129, 131, 135, 195
Dürer, Albrecht, 8, 69
Durling, Robert M., 154

Elizabeth I, Queen, 160, 218n57, 220n19
Elyot, Thomas, 81
emblem, 83–4, 86–93, 115, 156
Encyclopaedia Britannica, cited, 4
endings, *see* closure
eroticism, 148–50, 154, 160. *See also* voyeurism
Errour, 29, 31–8, 78, 90, 180, 182
etymology, 31–2, 81, 85, 147, 169, 207n11
Evans, Maurice, 15–16, 208n26
Excesse, 143, 146

False Florimell, 24–5, 114–27, 129, 131, 182, 195, 214n17
Faunus, 171
Ferry Anne, 159, 214n16
Fidelia, 66–8

Fletcher, Angus, 93
Florimell, 99–100, 115, 117–26, 182
Fradubio, 37–41, 43–50
Fraelissa, 40, 44
Frazer, Ray, 216n37
Frye, Northrop, 219n4

Garden of Adonis, 24, 94, 99–111, 115, 206n22
Garden of Proserpina, 139
Gascoigne, George, 205n12
Gealousie, 82, 87, 92–3
generation, 24, 101, 103–6
Genius (in Bower of Bliss), 133–6, 214n14
Giamatti, A. Bartlett, 138, 174–5
Gilman, Ernest B., 215nn17,26
Gloriana, 142, 166, 178–9
Going, W.T., 205–6n12
Golding, Arthur, 82–3
Golding, William, 74
Gombrich, E.H., 8–9, 220n18
grace, 52, 54–8, 179
Graces, the, 26, 157, 170–9
Greenblatt, Stephen, 132, 143
Greenlaw, Edwin, 211n27, 219n6
Gregerson, Linda, 150, 213n8, 215n18
Griffin, B., 212n36
Grill, 83–4, 92, 156
Gross, Kenneth, 132, 213n8
Guillory, John, 176–7
Guyon, 25–6, 83–4, 100, 135–43, 148–51, 155–6, 162

Halio, Jay L., 94
Hamilton, A.C., 212n30, 215n23
Hawkins, Sherman, 220n11
Hellenore, 86
Hercules, choice of, 40
hermaphroditic figures, 112–13, 197
Hollander, John, 152
Hooper, John, 129–30
Horace, 1
Hoskins, John, 17
House of Holiness, 65–7

icon, 23, 88, 91, 93, 113, 122, 124, 126, 136, 216n37
iconoclasm, 26, 132, 155–7, 213–14n10
iconomach, 155; definition of, 215n24
Idle Lake, 136, 215n17
idleness, 57, 135–6, 143, 169
idolatry, 23, 25, 113, 122, 124, 126–32,

134–9, 141–8, 150–3, 155–8, 161–2, 164, 166–9, 171, 173–5, 177, 213n8; distinction between *dulia* and *latria*, 136–7; pun on idle, 135, 138, 143

Jealousy, *see* Gealousie
Jewel, John, 131, 137
Johnson, Mark, 11, 71
Jortin, John, 85, 210n9
Jove, 184, 186–7, 190, 192, 196

Kermode, Frank, 72–3
Klibansky, Raymond, 68–9
Knight, G. Wilson, 21–2

Lakoff, George, 11, 71
Langland, William, 47; *The Vision of Piers Plowman*, 47, 95
Lewis, C.S., 129–30, 214n14
locus amoenus, 24, 106, 132, 168, 207n5
Lownes, Matthew, 181
Luther, Martin, 156

MacCaffrey, Isabel, 169, 214n14
Maiorino, Giancarlo, 220n18
Malbecco, 24, 82, 84–93, 100, 111, 115, 131
Malecasta, 139
Mammon, 25–6, 137–41, 215n23
Mamoulian, Rouben, 93
Marinell, 100, 124–5
Marston, John, 210n12
metamorphosis, 24, 38, 42, 47, 81–93, 113
metaphor: abuse of, 52–3, 76–9, 113–21, 126, 129, 134, 143–6, 152–3, 155, 182–3; conventional, 8, 11, 13, 44, 83–4, 119–20; and the defence of poetry, 10–15, 50–1, 98, 127–8, 140, 144, 155, 158, 168–70, 188, 192; faith in, 23, 26–7, 52–6, 58, 61–4, 66–8, 70, 75, 89, 109, 126–7, 141–2, 144, 152, 164–5, 177–80, 183, 188, 199, 202–4; as an heuristic device, 1–3, 5–6, 9–10, 15, 19, 21, 23–4, 27, 71–2, 89, 114–15, 129, 155, 175–6, 179, 182–4, 188; literalization of, 3–6, 24, 26, 77, 86, 115, 117–20, 131, 159, 173–4, 182–3; and nomination, 77, 80, 84, 92–3, 111, 115, 119–22, 182–3, 188, 218–19n66; and predication, 77–8, 80–4, 92–3, 111, 114–15, 119, 142, 146, 155, 164, 172, 175, 179–80, 182–4, 188, 196, 218–19n66
metaphoric plots, 22–4, 76–7, 80–1, 114
metaphoric twist, 82, 89
Miller, George A., 207–8n13
Miller, Jacqueline T., 165
Miller, Milton, 212n29
mimesis, 1, 116, 126, 140, 146
Montrose, Louis Adrian, 160, 165
More, Sir Thomas, 217n44
Mount Acidale, 26, 157, 166, 168–70, 173–7, 218n66
Mutabilitie, 26–7, 114, 116, 184–96, 200, 202–3
Mutabilitie Cantos, 26, 114, 116, 168, 171, 181–4, 189–90, 196, 202–3
mutability, 108–11, 187–8, 196, 203–4

Nature (Goddess of), 113, 116, 168, 184, 186, 189, 192–203
Nelson, William, 48, 208n25
Neoplatonism, 68, 105, 184, 194–5
New Jerusalem, 35, 65
Nohrnberg, James, 36, 47–8, 207n11, 213n8, 215n18, 217–18nn40,43,52

O'Connell, Michael, 148
Odysseus, 142
OED, cited, 4, 46, 86, 212n32
Ong, Walter J., 216n31
Order, 168, 192–3
Orgoglio, 56, 135
origins, 72–5, 164–5, 176–7. *See also* conception; generation
Ovid, 82

Paglia, Camille, 149
Palmer, the, 83–4, 148, 150, 156
paradox, 70, 77, 109–10, 198–204, 206–7n4, 220n18
Paridell, 91
Parker, Patricia, 76–7, 211–12nn22, 31, 217–18nn39,52,56, 220n19
pastoral, 35, 89, 157, 165
Pastorella, 157, 165, 171
Peacham, Henry, 214n16
Pelikan, Jaroslav, 215n20
personification, 87–8, 90, 92, 154, 165
Petrarch, 16
Phaedria, 136, 215n17
Phillips, John, 216n31, 217n44
Philotime, 139
pictorialism, 41, 84–6, 88, 153, 171–2,

Index

pictorialism – *continued*
  174, 216n37. See also emblem; icon; speaking picture
Pilate, 140
Plato, 24, 51, 106, 132; Platonic Ideas, 184, 194
Plotinus, 105, 194–5
psychomachia, 53
pun, 31–2
Puttenham, George, 132, 134, 144, 165, 214–15nn16,28

Quilligan, Maureen, 31, 212n28

Rajan, Balachandra, 207n10
Raleigh, Sir Walter, 74; Spenser's Letter to, 51, 75, 219n9
Ramsay, Judith C., 105–6, 211n20
Reader: education of, 22, 29–31, 66–7, 127, 148, 170, 178; experience of, 29, 44–5, 49–50, 65, 67, 72, 77, 88, 119, 133, 188–9; and misinterpretation, 31, 36–7, 72, 86, 145, 173–6; role of, 59–64, 76–8; temptation of, 25–6, 45, 140, 143–4, 148–53, 169–70
Redcrosse, 28–35, 37–9, 41–60, 64–9, 72, 76–9, 135–6, 180, 182–3
Richards, I.A., 207n6
Ricoeur, Paul, 81, 89, 219n3
riddle, 36–7
Ridley, Nicholas, 217n43
Roche, Thomas P. Jr, 113
rose song, the, 153–4

salvation, 35, 43, 78, 109–10, 202
Sasek, Lawrence A., 205–6n12
Satan, 56, 62, 120, 210n2
Saturn, 190
Scudamour, 111–14, 121–2
Serena, 26, 157–64, 217n46
Shaheen, Naseeb, 217n49
Shakespeare, William, 16; *Antony and Cleopatra*, 2–6, 57; *King Lear*, 89; *Macbeth*, 65; *Othello*, 91; *Sonnets*, 15
Sidney, Sir Philip, 1, 6–10, 15–16, 51, 94–5, 104, 109, 161, 211–12nn19, 35–6;
simile, 4, 9, 20, 35, 88, 112, 117–18, 123, 126, 147, 151–2, 172, 190–2, 198, 200
Simonides, 1
Sirluck, Ernest, 208–9nn23,28
Smith, Hallet, 40

sonnets: collective terms for, 15–16, 205–6n12; structuring principles of, 16–19; traditional images in, 212nn35–6. See also Daniel; Drayton; Shakespeare; Sidney; Spenser
Sparshott, F.E., 54, 80
speaking picture: of poetry, 1, 7, 67
Spender, Stephen, 54
Spenser, Edmund: *Amoretti*, 15, 19–21, 212nn35–6; *The Faerie Queene*, see listings under separate characters and places; Letter to Raleigh, 51, 75, 219n9
Stampfer, Judah L., 219n1
Stevens, Wallace, 80
Stewart, Stanley, 217–18n51
Stirling, Brents, 211n27
Stoker, Bram, 219n67

Tantalus, 140
Tenniel, Sir John, 36
Terwin, Sir, 50, 52
Thomas, Keith, 213n3
Tilley, Morris Palmer, 206n1, 209n29
Timias, 100
Titan, 190
Todorov, Tzvetan, 142, 209–10nn42, 47
Tonkin, Humphrey, 217n50
Tournier, Michel, 73
Teruisan, Sir, 51–3, 55
Tuve, Rosemond, 16–17, 205n3
Tyndale, William, 217n44

Una, 28–30, 35, 38–40, 52, 56, 61, 66, 69, 76–9, 197

veil, see allegory: veil of
Venus, 100–1, 109–11, 113, 151, 168, 174, 184, 197; Mount of, 109, 169
Verdant, 136, 151, 155, 217n39
visions and the visionary, 26, 35, 144, 157, 166–80, 199–204
voyeurism, 149, 160, 162, 171, 174–5. See also eroticism

Wandering Wood, the, 29, 31, 60
Warkentin, Germaine, 16
Warton, Thomas, 85
Waters, D. Douglas, 213n4
Watt, Tessa, 216n31
Webster, John, 209n29
Wells, Robin Headlam, 218n57

Williamson, George, 185
Wind, Edgar, 213n2
Witch (creator of False Florimell), 115–21, 129
Wofford, Susanne Lindgren, 157

Yeats, W.B., 213n9

Zepheria (anonymous), 212n36
Zitner, S.P., 219n2
Zwingli, Ulrich, 217n43

WITHDRAWN